DISMISSAL
LAW

Dedicated to Helena

DISMISSAL LAW

A PRACTICAL GUIDE
FOR MANAGEMENT

SECOND EDITION

Martin Edwards

KOGAN
PAGE

First published in 1984
by Waterlow Publishers Limited
Second edition published in 1991
by Kogan Page Limited

Kogan Page Limited
120 Pentonville Road
London N1 9JN
© Martin Edwards 1991

British Library Cataloguing in Publication Data

A CIP record for this book is available from the British Library.

ISBN 0 7494 0287 3

Typeset by CG Graphics, Aylesbury, Bucks
Printed and bound in Great Britain by Richard Clay Ltd, The Chaucer Press,
Bungay, Suffolk

Contents

Contents

Contents

Preface

'These statutory provisions are of inordinate complexity exceeding the worst excesses of a taxing statute; we find that especially regrettable bearing in mind that they are regulating the every-day rights of ordinary employers and employees. We feel no confidence that even with the assistance of detailed arguments from skilled advocates, we have now correctly understood them: it is difficult to see how an ordinary employer or employee is expected to do so.'

The Employment Appeal Tribunal: *Lavery v. Plessey Telecommunications Limited (1982)*

Dismissal law is controversial. It is also one of the most fascinating, important and, at times, baffling of all legal subjects. The above quotation is taken from a case dealing with the inter-relationship between unfair dismissal and maternity leave rights. Equally scathing criticism can be – and has been – made of the operation of dismissal law in many other areas.

Nevertheless, it is essential to grasp in outline at least how the legal rules work in practice. Employers need to be able to know when, and how, it is proper to dismiss, just as employees need to be able to identify when they have been treated unlawfully. The cost of ignorance can be very high – not just in the financial sense, but also in terms of lost management time and soured industrial relations.

This book is intended as a practical guide through the minefield. My primary aim is to assist employers, company secretaries, personnel officers and managers in the handling of problems which may give rise to, or result from, the dismissal of an employee. I hope too that employees, trade union officials, advice centres and non-specialist professional advisers will find something here of interest. The scope and approach of this text is outlined more fully in the section 'How to use this book' (p13).

My most difficult task in preparing this book has been to decide what to leave out in order to keep the text readable. In seeking a rounded view, rather than one that is narrowly legalistic, I have discussed many of the key issues with employers, employees, and those professionally involved in the boom industry of employment law. Their opinions have been most enlightening, but the responsibility for the views expressed here is mine alone. I would like to thank all those who have assisted and encouraged me, including in particular my wife, Helena, my colleagues at Mace & Jones and all those at Kogan Page who have worked on this book.

Martin Edwards
Liverpool, 1991

How to use this book

Understanding dismissal law entails understanding both contractual rights under the common law and the implications of modern job security legislation. The dynamic growth of the law in this area during the 1970s and 80s has been quite remarkable. There is now an elaborate framework of statutory rules, supplemented by a wealth of reported cases.

This book combines a summary of the main statutory provisions with suggestions on the handling of particular dismissal problems. The aim is to simplify complex legal points without undue distortion. This is far from easy but, to give readers a 'feel' for the subject, the emphasis here is on areas that give rise to the most usual questions, and decided cases – most of them quite recent – which illustrate key points or lay down important principles.

Of course, guidelines should not be elevated into hard and fast rules. Courts and tribunals must direct themselves in accordance with the legislation passed by Parliament, even where that legislation is vague or obscure, or both. All too often there is no definitive 'right' or 'wrong' answer to a question arising from dismissal law, but that does not diminish the value of guidelines, as long as they are properly interpreted. With this in mind, I have tried to convey the spirit of the law in a positive manner wherever possible.

This book, which includes references up to 31 August 1990 (and which, for the sake of convenience, generally refers to employers and employees in the masculine gender), concentrates on the legal position in England and Wales, although there are many points of similarity with employment law within Scotland and Northern Ireland. You should bear in mind that the law continues to evolve and that, inevitably, a book of this kind must be selective rather than exhaustive. Every effort has been made to ensure that the book correctly states the law, although neither the publishers nor the author can accept liability for any errors or omissions. There is no substitute at the end of the day for expert professional advice based upon a precise study of the legislation in the light of particular circumstances. Nevertheless, if this book contributes towards the wider understanding of dismissal law, it will have served its purpose.

1
Overview

1.1 Introduction

The complexity of dismissal law troubles not only employers and employees, but also the legal profession. In 1978, for example, Lord Justice Lawton expressed his dismay that, in industrial tribunals, '. . . legalism has started to take over. It must be driven back if possible.'

Ten times as many cases are reported annually in connection with employment law, it has been estimated, than in relation to any other legal topic. Lord Denning was once moved to say:

'If we are not careful, we shall find the industrial tribunals bent down under the weight of the law books or, what is worse, asleep under them.'

Unfortunately, in the years since those comments were made, it has become clear that much of the law is so intricate and, in some instances, so unhappily drafted, that continuing litigation and debate are inevitable.

Industrial tribunals are supposed to provide a quick and cheap remedy for injustices in the employment sphere, but they have to interpret the law in order to do so. Managers who wish to understand dismissal law and operate effective industrial relations policies must to some extent try to predict the unpredictable. It is easier said than done. Managers are sometimes under the impression that to every 'rule' there may be an unexpected exception. However, it is possible to understand the subject without becoming submerged in the minutiae and, furthermore, to understand it well enough to avoid problems in most cases.

1.2 Myths of dismissal law

Myths abound in dismissal law. Unfair dismissal, in particular, is the source of many misconceptions. In part, this may be due to selective, distorted reporting of outlandish cases in the media. Misunderstanding is widespread and is not confined to idle gossip; sometimes it extends to the utterances of politicians, employers' organisations and trade union leaders.

This is not to deny that, at the core of some of the sweeping generalisations often made (four of which are considered in this section), there is a grain of truth. What is important is to keep matters in perspective. Dismissal law, like industrial relations generally, should not be regarded as a subject of extremes.

Is dismissal difficult?

The most firmly established dismissal law myth is summed up by the assertion in the *Oxford Companion to Law* that it is now

'extremely difficult for an employer, without incurring liability for compensation, to get rid of the incompetent, the lazy and the troublemaker'.

As this book attempts to show, that is an exaggeration. It is true that around 30,000 complaints are made to industrial tribunals each year, of which the vast majority concern unfair dismissal. However, only a very small percentage of all employment terminations result in tribunal claims. Furthermore, roughly two-thirds of all complaints made are resolved without the necessity for a hearing. According to current figures, of the cases that do proceed, in less than one half does the applicant succeed.

Industrial tribunals and the appellate body, the Employment Appeal Tribunal (EAT), comprise two lay members, one from each side of industry, as well as a lawyer chairman. The approach of tribunal members is not partisan. Interestingly, the vast majority of decisions are unanimous. Similarly, the Advisory, Conciliation and Arbitration Service (ACAS) performs its conciliatory functions in an impartial manner which helps to encourage the early resolution of complaints. Neither employees nor employers should believe that the system, whatever its specific weaknesses, is inherently biased against them.

Is recruitment discouraged?

It is often said that dismissal law discourages employers from taking on fresh labour, but there is little hard evidence to substantiate this. It may be true that employers have become more careful about checking the quality of new recruits, but that is no bad thing.

The requirements of the business at any particular time generally represent a far more important criterion for employers when deciding whether or not to expand the workforce. In any event, the need for an employee to serve a qualifying period of 'continuous employment' to become entitled to the vast majority of dismissal rights means that there is in effect a lengthy probationary period during which employers are relatively free to weed out unsatisfactory workers at minimal cost. The normal qualifying period for the right not to be unfairly dismissed, for example, has increased since the Conservative Government first came to office from six months to two years.

Is dismissal expensive?

The maximum compensation theoretically available under statute to a dismissed employee has steadily increased over the years. Since the Employment Act 1982 came into force, there has been no upper limit to the amount that can, in certain uncommon circumstances, be awarded to a successful applicant.

Away from the realms of theory, the median award of compensation made by tribunals in unfair dismissal cases, despite having risen over the years, remains surprisingly low. In 1988–89, the last year for which figures were available at the time of writing, it was still less than £2,000. The median amount paid under conciliated settlements is even lower. For a highly paid executive, the cash value of an unfair dismissal complaint – even if he wins his case – may seem derisory.

However, it must be said that there are hidden costs. Legal proceedings can make expensive demands upon management time, and the cost of legal representation, if it is sought, may in some cases be disproportionate to the amount of compensation actually at stake. The very restricted rules on costs (see section 25.10 Costs p256) mean that even a wholly justified dismissal may leave an employer very much out of pocket. Even in its unsatisfactory features, however, the system is not one-sided. Legal aid for representation at a tribunal hearing is not available to employees. For an unemployed person who cannot afford substantial legal fees, the disadvantages in a complex case can be very great.

Is professional advice unnecessary?

Dismissal law was not intended to profit the legal profession. Litigants may represent themselves before an industrial tribunal or be represented by anyone they choose, whether or not the representative has legal qualifications.

Nevertheless, the past decade has seen a significant and increasing tendency for parties to be legally represented at tribunal hearings. There are lies, damned lies and statistics, but figures published by the Department of Employment do suggest that, for whatever reason, a party who is legally represented is more likely to succeed than one who is not.

Employers and employees have to consider whether they need to take expert advice. Nowadays, many employers consult professional advisers at an early stage, when they first begin to think about taking action which may lead at a later stage to a complaint being made to a tribunal.

The decision is very much a personal one for each employer and employee. There is no 'right' or 'wrong' answer, but it may be useful to outline the considerations which most frequently arise. Some of those considerations favour the instruction of professional advisers; some do not.

It is usually unwise for a person who is also a key witness to conduct the case. Separating the two functions is far more difficult in practice than it may seem in theory. Giving evidence requires a witness's undivided attention: it is all too easy for even the most honest and intelligent individuals to become confused. Furthermore, there will often be cases involving complex facts or points of law where specific professional skills are particularly relevant. For example, special knowledge may be needed in preparing the case for hearing, in analysing the legal issues and in employing effective techniques in cross-examining witnesses.

On the other hand, the legal costs – which may be substantial and irrecoverable for anyone who does not have comprehensive legal expenses insurance cover – have to be borne in mind. Sometimes, an experienced personnel manager may be better able to grasp key issues than a non-specialist lawyer. Tribunals will be sympathetic to unrepresented parties, and they will not expect legal expertise from laymen. However, there is no reason to believe that they will sympathise with an unrepresented applicant to the extent that it will actually disadvantage a professionally represented employer.

In *Lee v. IPC Business Press Ltd* (1984), for example, the EAT pointed out the value of representation in difficult cases:

> '... it is possible that this matter went wrong, as it obviously did, because the tribunal did not get the sort of assistance in disentangling the complicated issues ... which they would have got, if the chairman had had lawyers helping him to sort it out.'

If professional advice is to be sought, this should be done at the outset. It seldom makes sense to delay instructing advisers until the last minute. The saving in costs (if any) may be marginal, and the way in which the matter has been handled in the meantime may curtail the freedom of the expert to conduct his client's case to the best advantage.

Finally, it should be noted that expertise in dismissal law is not confined to lawyers. Employers' organisations, personnel consultants, trade unions and advice centres are among those who may also be able to assist. Whether or not they possess the requisite skills is the crucial question, and a recommendation from an unbiased and satisfied former client may provide the answer.

1.3 Consistency versus flexibility

Every case, in the end, depends upon its own facts. Tribunals have to be flexible in the way they examine and adjudicate upon those facts, so as to ensure that justice is done in each case.

On the other hand, it is equally important that laws should be clear and that their operation should be predictable. Employers and employees need to know what the consequences of their actions will be before they take those actions. It is vital in dismissal law, as in other areas of the law, to strike a balance between flexibility and certainty.

A former President of the EAT has convincingly argued that the EAT has an important role to play

'in declaring uniform principles of good industrial relations practice by reference to which employers and employees can regulate their conduct'.

The EAT is well equipped in its lay members to declare for the time being what these principles are.

In this role, the EAT has from time to time, set out guidelines for good industrial practice, such as the general test for suspected misconduct (see The legal test p153), and the approach to be followed where redundancies are to be declared in a unionised workforce (see Observing current industrial practice p140).

The EAT has often stressed that, in suggesting such guidelines, it is not laying down strict law. However, there has been a tendency in some cases for the guidelines to be regarded as firm rules, and this has in turn led to condemnation of those who misinterpret the guidelines. As long ago as 1978, the Court of Appeal went so far in one case as to suggest that it was unwise to set out guidelines at all. In doing this, the Court of Appeal was emphasising (as it has done on many subsequent occasions) that, just because there is a failure in a particular case to follow a procedure that is normally accepted as fair, that does not *necessarily* mean that in those circumstances dismissal will be unfair. A tribunal is entitled to conclude in any case that the facts are exceptional. Its unwillingness to apply non-statutory guidelines rigidly in such a case should not entitle the losing party to appeal successfully on the ground that the tribunal has erred in law.

Similarly, the contents of industrial relations codes of practice – which tribunals should take into account when reaching a decision – should not be considered holy writ. Moreover, the recommendations in the ACAS advisory handbook *Discipline At Work*, which supplements the codes, are just that – recommendations, and no more. There may be cases where an employer is entirely justified in treating a problem in a different way.

However, informal guidelines, whether offered by the EAT, by ACAS or here, can be useful. There is often a great deal at stake in employment cases. If consistency is always sacrificed for the sake of flexibility, the result will be chaos. There are no simple and universal cure-alls for every ill in industrial relations.

Employers who regard recommendations for the handling of dismissal problems as a practical and worthwhile source of help, rather than as a means of papering over the cracks of bad man management, will find that many of those problems can be solved, and less painfully than they may have feared.

2
Qualifying for Statutory Rights

2.1 Introduction

Not every individual who works for another is entitled to all or any of the dismissal law rights which are discussed here. Broadly speaking, a person may fail to qualify for those rights if:

1. he is not an employee;

2. his contract of employment is unenforceable;

3. he falls within a category of worker which is specifically excluded from protection;

4. he is excluded from protection because he does not comply with a specific statutory qualifying condition.

Furthermore, the law imposes various time limits for instituting claims. An employee who 'sleeps on his rights' runs a serious risk of being debarred from proceeding. Relevant time limits are referred to in appropriate parts of this book and the rules relating to late claims are dealt with in section 25.3 Presenting a claim in time, p 247.

An employee can contract out of his statutory rights only in the limited circumstances examined in Chapter 23.

2.2 Who is an employee?

Often it is obvious whether an individual is or is not an employee, yet there are many cases where the distinction between employees and other workers (such as self-employed independent contractors) is blurred. This existence of grey areas is unfortunate, because so

22

much depends upon the distinction. For example, the many rights conferred by the 1978 Act are available only to employees.

The 1978 Act defines an employee as an individual who has entered into or works under or worked under a contract of service or apprenticeship. The contract may be express (ie stated specifically), or implied. If it is express, it may be oral or in writing.

Varying definitions appear in other enactments. The sex and race discrimination legislation, for example, protects 'a person employed'. Generally, however, the key factor is the existence of a contract of service, ie of employment. In order to ascertain whether a contract of employment exists, it is necessary to investigate the precise nature of the agreement between the parties.

Traditionally, the doctrine of freedom of contract implied that the parties were free to contract upon whatever terms they wished. If they wanted, they could provide that their relationship was *not* one of employer and employee. This appeals to many employers who do not wish to be constrained by dismissal law; equally, a worker may prefer for tax reasons not to be regarded as an employee.

It is now clear, however, that there are extremely important limitations upon the ability of the parties to arrange their affairs so that they are not tied by inconvenient legislative provisions.

The legal test

The courts have struggled for many years to devise a satisfactory test for differentiating between a contract of service, ie of employment, and a contract for services, ie of self-employment. They have met with only limited success.

Originally, it was thought to be enough to ask whether the man concerned worked under the control of another, not only in what he had to do but also in how and when he had to do it. *Control* clearly remains an important element in many contracts of employment. However, the increasing sophistication of certain types of employment led to the recognition that 'control' alone was sometimes an inadequate criterion.

The search for a concise alternative test has proved fruitless. For a time it was suggested that an enquiry could be made as to whether the work done was performed as an integral part of the business or merely as accessory to it, but this raised as many questions as it answered. As the Privy Council said in *Lee v. Chung*

(1990), the key question is whether a person engaged to perform services is performing them as a person in business on his own account.

Perhaps the most practical approach is to ask the following three questions:

1. Did the worker agree to provide his own work and skill in return for remuneration?

2. Was there a sufficient degree of control to enable the worker fairly to be called an employee?

3. Were there any other factors inconsistent with the existence of a contract of employment?

Relevant factors

In deciding whether a contract of employment exists or not, a tribunal may consider any or all of the following points. It can look at whether the worker is:

1. paid wages or salary (although piece-workers may be employees);

2. paid during sickness absence;

3. paid during holidays;

4. a member of a company pension scheme;

5. subject to the employer's disciplinary rules and procedures;

6. prohibited from working for other employers;

7. entitled to decide whether he will turn up for work or decline to work;

8. taxed as an employee;

9. regarded and described by the parties as an employee;

10. responsible for providing his own equipment;

11. responsible for having his own assistants;

12. responsible for some or all of the financial or business risk of the enterprise;

13. able to profit directly from sound management in the performance of his task.

Inevitably, the answer will not always be clear cut. There may in the same relationship be factors apparently inconsistent with a contract of employment, as well as different factors which seem to be inconsistent with a self-employment contract.

Each case will turn upon its own facts. Perhaps strangely, the answer to the question of whether or not there is a contract of service may depend upon the reason for asking the question. A man who is taxable on a self-employed basis may still have the right of an employee to claim unfair dismissal. Different tribunals may interpret the same facts in different ways. Indeed, the same court may regard a man as an employee for some purposes but not for others.

Practical problems

A contract may be a contract of employment even if the parties assert categorically that their relationship is not that of employer and employee. The courts may say that the parties put the wrong label on the arrangement.

The intention of the parties is often relevant. In *Massey v. Crown Life Insurance* (1978), the Court of Appeal had to consider a written agreement by which the parties had deliberately sought to contrive a contract for services. From 1971 to 1973 the company treated the applicant as an employee. In 1973 he entered into a new agreement with the company in order to reduce his liability to income tax. There were few important changes to his terms of employment, but the Inland Revenue seems to have accepted the change without query. In 1975 the company terminated the agreement.

The applicant's unfair dismissal claim failed. The 1973 agreement was held to be effective in establishing him as self-employed. While a mere 'label' was inconclusive, it was open to the parties to choose how to resolve the ambiguity of their relationship.

In the extremely significant case of *Young and Woods Ltd v. West* (1980), the Court of Appeal considered that there was no such ambiguity. When the applicant joined the company he was offered alternative methods of payment, either as an employee or on a self-employed basis. He chose the latter. Income tax was therefore not deducted from his pay, he was responsible for his own national insurance contributions and he received no holiday pay or sickness pay. Again, the Inland Revenue did not object to the arrangement.

Despite all that, the Court of Appeal held that the applicant was an employee. He therefore had the right not to be unfairly dismissed. It had been suggested that it would be contrary to public policy to allow an individual to 'have his cake and eat it' in this way. The judicial response was to suggest that the Inland Revenue might look again at the applicant's tax position. His victory might, as a result, prove hollow and indeed expensive.

The Court of Appeal clearly saw the importance of ensuring, as a matter of policy, that an employer should not be able to avoid his statutory responsibilities by inducing those who are really employees to enter purported self-employment contracts. To do otherwise would enable employees to contract out of their statutory rights by the back door. The circumstances in which the law allows contracting out are strictly limited.

The company might easily have thought that it had done enough to ensure that the applicant was not an employee. Unfortunately, by misinterpreting the legal position, an employer may suffer the worst of all possible worlds. For example, disciplinary and other procedures relevant to employees will not be followed. The employer will be extremely vulnerable to a finding of unfair dismissal following the termination of the relationship.

The factual reality is the key and highly artificial arrangements should be avoided. It is preferable to cope with statutory impositions from the outset and from day to day, rather than to find them applied in the courtroom years later with retrospective effect.

2.3 Specific types of employee

A number of types of work give rise to particular difficulties. Again, each case turns upon its own facts, but a number of general conclusions may be drawn.

Homeworkers

People who work at home rather than on the employer's premises are quite capable of being employees in the legal sense. Having regular work is an important factor, and even workers who have the right to refuse work may sometimes be regarded as employees. In *Nethermere (St Neots) v. Gardiner and Taverna* (1983), where trouser machinists could decide how much work they did (subject to it being worthwhile for the firm's van driver to call), the lay members of the EAT held that they were employees. The 'economic reality' was that in practice the workers would not refuse work and they could not be described as being in business on their own account.

Casual workers

Casual workers are only likely to be regarded as employees if they are *obliged* to work when called upon to do so. People such as fruit pickers, who are paid on a 'piece-work' basis at the end of each day, and who are at liberty not to turn up the day after, will seldom be entitled to dismissal rights. In *O'Kelly v. Trusthouse Forte* (1983), the Court of Appeal upheld a tribunal's finding that 'regular casuals' in the hotel banqueting business, who could decide whether or not to accept rostered work, were not employees. In line with recognised custom and practice, they worked under successive contracts for services.

Company directors

A company director is not necessarily an employee. Non-executive directors who simply attend board meetings from time to time are seldom employees. There are, however, many working directors who are employed under contracts of service. The Companies Act 1985 requires that a copy of such a contract (or a memorandum of its terms, if not in writing) should be kept by the company.

No such record was kept by the company in the case of *Albert J Parson & Sons Ltd v. Parsons* (1979). The Court of Appeal held that a full-time working director who was paid directors' fees rather than a salary, and had not been treated as an employee for national insurance purposes, was not an employee.

In *Eaton v. Robert Eaton Ltd* (1988), the EAT said that the starting point was that generally a company director is the holder of an office and not in employment. Evidence is required to show that he is an employee. Among the matters which may be relevant (although none of them is in itself conclusive) are whether:

1. his terms of employment were recorded in a board minute;

2. his remuneration is fixed in advance or agreed on an *ad hoc* basis;

3. his remuneration was gratuitous or an entitlement;

4. he merely acted in a directorial capacity or was under the board's control;

5. he was described as a managing or working director.

Bearing in mind that a company is a separate legal entity from its shareholders, it seems possible in theory (although there has been one decision which suggests the contrary) for a director who holds a majority of the issued share capital, and who therefore has control of the running of the company, nevertheless to be an employee.

A company director who is not an employee by virtue of that office may nevertheless be regarded as an employee, in appropriate circumstances, if he is also the company secretary.

Miscellaneous

The following specific employments are among those which have been considered by industrial tribunals:

• barristers' clerks;

• clergymen;

• sub-postmasters;

• members of an orchestra;

• social club secretaries;

• employment agencies' 'temps';

• workers in co-operatives.

There is no legal reason why persons falling into any of the above categories should never be regarded as employees. It is unwise to generalise, since everything depends upon the circumstances of each case.

2.4   Illegal contracts of employment

An employee may sometimes find that he is unable to enforce his contractual or statutory rights against his employer because his contract of employment is tainted by illegality.

The general law relating to the unenforceability of certain

contracts is far from straightforward. The judicial attitude tends to be robust. AP Herbert once picturesquely summarised it as: 'the dirty dog gets no dinner here'.

There has never been any real doubt that the common law principles of illegality apply to contracts of employment. Equally, it did not take long to establish that those principles also affect contemporary statute-based labour law.

Courts and tribunals have sometimes found it necessary to consider the knowledge of the parties that the act to be performed, or its proposed mode of performance, was illegal. However, in *Corby v. Morrison t/a The Card Shop* (1980), a case involving tax evasion, the EAT held that knowledge of illegality was irrelevant. Ignorance of the law is no excuse. Alternatively, (or where the contract appears to be legal and therefore knowledge becomes relevant), the test is not whether a reasonable person would have known that the contract was illegal, but whether the claimant was so aware.

The question of illegality usually arises in tax fraud cases. Exceptionally, *Coral Leisure Group Ltd v. Barnett* (1981), concerned a contract of service under which the employee alleged he was required to procure prostitutes for the employer's clients.

The EAT drew a distinction between:

1. cases in which there is a contractual obligation to do an act which is unlawful; and

2. cases where the contractual obligations are capable of being performed lawfully and were initially intended so to be performed, but which have in fact been performed by unlawful means.

In the former case the EAT said that enforceability by a person who knew of the illegality depends upon the rules of severance, in other words, how far it is possible to separate the tainted contractual obligations from the untainted. In practice, the courts rarely permit severance.

In the latter case, the question is whether someone's unlawful act precludes his further enforcement of the contract. Here the courts have rather more discretion as to whether or not to allow the contract to be enforced. To take a simple example, a company driver who breaks the speed limit will not lose his employment protection rights by doing so.

Even an illegal practice of a short-term nature can prove highly significant if it breaks the employee's period of continuous employment. The result of this can be that, if he is later dismissed, he has not been employed legitimately for long enough to qualify for key statutory rights.

When the employer's defence to a claim includes the assertion that the contract was tainted by illegality, the employee may possibly argue that:

1. he was less blameworthy than the employer; or

2. service prior to a period of illegality should be deemed to be continuous with service subsequent to that period; or

3. the illegality was trivial (for example, the amount of tax evaded was paltry).

On the whole, such attempts to circumvent the serious consequences to employees of illegality have in the past been given short shrift. It is not too far-fetched to suggest that an unscrupulous employer may encourage employees to agree to illegal arrangements so that they are deprived of their employment protection rights. The EAT has therefore indicated that, in tax fraud cases, the appropriate papers may be passed to the Inland Revenue.

It is also possible that in appropriate cases a tribunal will rule that the public policy of employment protection outweighs the public policy of deterring illegal activities, especially where the employer is the prime mover in those activities.

2.5 Specific statutory exclusions

Where statutory rights are considered in this book, a brief summary of excluded employees is included.

Specific exclusions from statutory rights fall into two broad categories. First, a number of classes of employment are excluded. Those classes vary, depending upon the right concerned. For example, Crown servants have no right to a redundancy payment but most have the right not to be unfairly dismissed. Conversely, police service employees have the right to a redundancy payment, but have no right to be unfairly dismissed. Employees of foreign governments may be protected, but not foreign diplomatic staff who are on a temporary posting to the UK.

Secondly, there are a number of circumstances in which an

employee who would otherwise qualify for rights will be excluded. Thus, an employee may be excluded where (speaking in general terms) he:

1. has not been employed for the requisite period of continuous employment; or

2. works overseas; or

3. is above the relevant age limit (if any).

The detailed rules are complex. Again, it has to be stressed that the qualifying rules may differ substantially from one area of the law to another. Most of the problems in practice have arisen in relation to the right to complain of unfair dismissal (see Chapter 10).

The rules for calculating a period of continuous employment are set out in Chapter 22. It is important to note that, because of the technical definition of continuous employment, many part-time employees will in practice be excluded from the statutory rights.

3
Is There a Dismissal?

3.1 Introduction

Almost all the rights of employees discussed in this book depend upon there having been a dismissal. It is therefore essential to be able to differentiate between an employee who has left work voluntarily and one who has been dismissed. In theory, the dividing line can easily be drawn. In practice, complex legal questions sometimes arise.

For unfair dismissal and redundancy payments purposes, dismissal has a statutory meaning. The definitions, contained in sections 55(2) and 83 respectively of the 1978 Act, are similar, but not identical. Three situations are covered:

1. where the employer terminates the employment contract with or without notice;

2. where the employee is employed under a fixed term contract and that contract expires without being renewed;

3. where the employer's conduct entitles the employee to terminate the employment contract with or without notice, ie 'constructive dismissal' (see Chapter 4). This does not cover, for redundancy payments purposes, termination by reason of a lock-out.

The general rule is that if an employer gives the employee notice of termination, he cannot retract that notice without the employee's consent. Equally, an employee cannot unilaterally retract a resignation.

One case, *Martin v. Yeomen Aggregates Ltd* (1983), indicates that dismissal or resignation in the heat of the moment may be withdrawn if the withdrawal is not long delayed. Possibly this reflects sensible industrial relations practice. It is difficult, however, to reconcile the decision with settled principles of contract law, which do not provide for 'cooling-off' periods before the termination of a contract becomes effective. The case should be viewed with caution, but it provides a useful reminder that important employment decisions should neither be taken nor acted upon 'off the cuff'.

The complexities of contract law gives rise to many conceptual difficulties. Courts, tribunals and academic commentators have wrestled for years with nice legal points about whether or not unlawful repudiation of the contract (without notice) by either employer or employee *automatically* terminates the contract, or whether that repudiation must be 'accepted' by the innocent party. The case law is so messy as to make a brief, definitive statement of the law impossible. The area which most frequently gives rise to practical problems is that where the employer argues that the employee has 'dismissed himself'; see section 3.4 Self-dismissal p36.

A dismissal without notice may give rise to a wrongful dismissal claim; see Chapter 6. Furthermore, although the common law does not impose any requirements as regards the giving and timing of notice, the contract itself may impose certain formalities, such as an insistence that notice must be given in writing.

It is possible for notice to be given or received by one person on behalf of others. One example is where a union official is given notice on behalf of his members in response to industrial action or prior to a lock-out. Such a person must be authorised to give or receive notice as an agent for others. The prudent employer will give notice directly to all the individuals concerned. Similarly, if a third party (whether union representative, relative or friend) purports to give notice on behalf of an employee, it is wise to check with the employee himself before relying on that notice.

3.2 Words of dismissal

Sometimes it is open to doubt whether the language used by the employer, taken in context, amounts to a dismissal. Ambiguous words spoken in anger, or intended merely as a reprimand, may (even if not amounting to constructive dismissal) be interpreted by the employee as words of dismissal.

The other side of the coin is where an employee uses ambiguous words which the employer treats as a resignation which, subsequently, he will not allow the employee to retract.

The cases do not display a wholly consistent approach to the thorny problem of ambiguity, but three propositions relevant to ambiguous 'resignations' and 'dismissals' may be gleaned from the judgment of the EAT in *BG Gale Ltd v. Gilbert* (1978):

1. certain words or acts can, as a matter of law, be interpreted only as amounting to a dismissal or resignation;

2. some words or acts are ambiguous and may or may not constitute a dismissal or resignation. Here the question is subjective: did the person hearing the words in fact interpret them as a dismissal or resignation? If he did, there is a dismissal or resignation;

3. if it is not clear how the words were in fact understood, the question is how a reasonable listener would have interpreted them in the particular circumstances. In the *Gilbert* case, during an argument, the employee said to his manager, 'I am leaving, I want my cards.' These words were capable of constituting a resignation and the manager reasonably interpreted them as such.

Nevertheless, all the facts of each case must be considered. In *Barclay v. City of Glasgow District Council* (1983), the EAT held that clear words of resignation uttered by a mentally impaired employee did not necessarily amount to a resignation. There was a duty upon the employer to have regard to the special circumstances of the employee. Before treating him as having resigned, the employer should have sought some form of confirmation that his act of resignation was in fact genuine and fully understood.

Conversely, in *Sothern v. Franks Charlesly & Co* (1981), the applicant used the words, 'I am resigning.' The Court of Appeal held that the words were unambiguous. The employee was not immature, speaking in the heat of the moment or acting under duress. There was therefore no reason why her resignation should not have the normal legal consequences.

In *Sovereign House Security Services Ltd v. Savage* (1989), however, the Court of Appeal ruled that words, apparently of resignation, but uttered in the heat of the moment by an employee who had by implication been accused of theft, should not have been taken at face value.

For safety's sake, therefore, an employee should usually be asked to confirm an oral resignation in writing.

3.3   Ultimatums and warnings

An employee's departure under duress is not a resignation. This means that if an employer says 'resign or be sacked', that amounts to a dismissal.

The precise interpretation of an ultimatum may be open to debate. It is a question of fact for the tribunal whether, in the circumstances, the employer's conduct forced the employee to resign. In some cases, a threat of dismissal may be regarded as constructive, rather than express, dismissal. *Compulsory* 'early retirement' will also amount to a dismissal. In *Caledonian Mining Co. Ltd v. Bassett and Steel* (1987), a company which inveigled employees into resigning in order to deprive them of their right to redundancy payments was held by the EAT to have dismissed them.

Different principles apply where the employer suggests that the employee should resign and seek alternative employment because the employer intends to dismiss him at some future date.

Typical at a time of economic recession are the facts of *International Computers Ltd v. Kennedy* (1981). In October 1979, the applicant's employers announced that the factory at which she worked was to be closed down by the end of September 1980. Employees were advised to make every effort to find other jobs as quickly as possible.

Negotiations had yet to be concluded with the trade unions as to the timings of the redundancies, but the applicant quickly found another job. She left the company and claimed a redundancy payment. Her claim failed. No date had been ascertained for the termination of her contract.

It may be argued that this means that if an employer knows a factory is going to close down and redundancy payments are in prospect, he will be tempted to give a vague oral warning to employees in the hope that they will leave before the moment of their dismissal arises.

Whatever the merits of the argument, it seems clear that an employee who heeds such a warning and leaves will be held to have resigned and will lose his dismissal law rights.

3.4 Self-dismissal?

Vexed questions arise where the employee is guilty of a fundamental breach of the employment contract. If, by his own act, he can be said to have terminated the agreement, there is no dismissal. If, however, the correct view is that the contract is only terminated when the employer elects to accept the employee's repudiation, there is a dismissal.

Such legalistic considerations have tempted courts and tribunals to toy with the elusive concepts of 'self-dismissal' or 'constructive resignation', in other words, where the employee behaves in such a way that a reasonable employer might believe that he has resigned. The results are unsatisfactory in the extreme.

A prime example is the case of *London Transport Executive v. Clarke* (1981). The employee absented himself from work for seven weeks without permission in order to visit Jamaica. His employers had previously warned him that his absence could result in his name being removed from the books. They wrote to him stating that unless he returned it would be assumed that he did not wish to remain in employment. They subsequently informed him that his name had been permanently removed from the books. When he returned home from Jamaica, he was refused employment.

Regrettably, the three members of the Court of Appeal travelled on different routes towards allowing the appeal against a finding of unfair dismissal. Lord Denning alone held that this was a case where the employee had dismissed himself. The generalised concept of self-dismissal was, however, rejected by the majority of the Court of Appeal.

Support for the idea of 'self-dismissal' seems to derive mainly from a wish to do justice in hard cases when it appears that the logic of strict contractual principles operates unfairly in particular cases. It should be remembered however, that, even where there is a dismissal, that dismissal will by no means necessarily be unfair. Employers will be wise not to rely on the argument that an employee has 'dismissed himself'.

3.5 Mutual consent

An employment contract may be brought to an end by the mutual consent of the parties. If so, there will be no dismissal. There is no genuine mutual consent, however, if the termination has in reality been initiated by duress or by the threat of dismissal.

In *Staffordshire County Council v. Donovan* (1981), the employers indicated during the course of disciplinary proceedings that they would be prepared to allow the employee, if she chose, to terminate her employment on the last day of the year. Terms were offered as to suspension on pay and the provision of a reference. The employee eventually gave notice on this basis but subsequently claimed unfair dismissal.

The EAT held that this was a case of mutual consent. Where parties are seeking to negotiate in the course of disciplinary proceedings and an agreed formula is worked out, it would be 'most unfortunate' if the mere fact that agreement was reached during disciplinary proceedings entitled the employee to say later that there was a dismissal.

Similarly, in *Logan Salton v. Durham County Council* (1989), an employee facing summary dismissal decided to resign. Acting on his instructions, his union negotiated a final settlement on the basis of 'termination by mutual agreement'. An industrial tribunal held that he had, on the evidence, entered into the agreement freely and not under duress. His appeal to the EAT failed.

Tribunals must, however, be vigilant to ensure the reality of alleged mutual consent. For example, where an employer has decided to make some volunteers redundant, and volunteers come forward to accept redundancy, there is clearly a dismissal.

Cases concerning employees whose employment comes to an end after they fail to return from an overseas visit on the due date have given rise to recurrent difficulties. The key decision is that of the Court of Appeal in *Igbo v. Johnson Matthey Chemicals Ltd* (1986). An employee agreed that if she did not resume work by a specified date her contract would 'automatically terminate on that date'. The Court of Appeal ruled that this was, in effect, an attempt to contract out of the 1978 Act which was void; see section 23.1 Contracting out and conciliation p228.

This outcome contrasts with that in *Birch and Humber v.*

University of Liverpool (1985), where the Court of Appeal held that employees who volunteered for early retirement had not been dismissed. They had agreed to the actual act of termination itself, whereas Ms Igbo simply accepted the risk that her contract would end if she did not meet the deadline for resuming work. The distinction between the two cases is a fine one and will not always be easy to apply in practice.

3.6 Frustration of the contract

A contract is frustrated where some unforeseen event makes performance of the contract either totally impossible, or something radically different from what the parties originally agreed.

Depending upon the terms, express or implied, of the contract, frustration may arise because of death, a change in the law or war.

In the employment context, the doctrine of frustration may be encountered as a result of the prolonged sickness or imprisonment of the employee.

Prolonged sickness

In this area, useful guidelines were set out in the case of *Marshall v. Harland & Wolff Ltd* (1972). In determining whether the contract has been frustrated by the long-term absence due to illness of the employee, account should be taken of:

1. the terms of the contract, including the provisions as to sick pay. There can be no frustration if the employee is likely to return within the period during which sick pay is payable. But frustration will not necessarily occur as soon as the right to sick pay comes to an end;

2. how long the employment was likely to last in the absence of sickness. A short-term contract is more likely to be frustrated than a long-term job;

3. the nature of the employment. If the employee occupies a key position, frustration is more likely;

4. the nature of the illness or injury and how long it has already continued and the prospects of recovery;

5. the employee's length of service.

Later cases have indicated that the employer's actions, and in particular whether he has taken steps to end the employment (because it has been frustrated), is also a relevant factor.

Courts and tribunals are usually reluctant to hold that the doctrine of frustration applies in sickness cases, and the ACAS handbook *Discipline At Work* says that it is 'better for the employer to take dismissal action'. It is therefore clear that employers should not be quick to regard it as a convenient escape route from the impositions of dismissal law. Most long-term sickness cases will have to be dealt with on the basis that the principles discussed in Chapter 16 apply.

Imprisonment

An employee's imprisonment can frustrate his employment contract. After years of uncertainty, this point was confirmed by the Court of Appeal in *FC Shepherd & Co. Ltd v. Jerrom* (1986). What is much less clear is how long a jail term must be in order for frustration to occur.

In *Jerrom*, a borstal period of at least six months (expected to be 39 weeks in practice) frustrated an apprentice's contract which had over two years to run. In another case, a 12-month sentence frustrated the contract, even though the employers knew that an appeal was planned (which in the event led to an acquittal).

In *Chakki v. United Yeast Co. Ltd* (1982), the EAT suggested the following test:

1. From a practical commercial point of view, when was it necessary to decide on the employee's future?

2. When the decision had to be taken, what would a reasonable employer have considered to be the likely length of the employee's continuing absence?

3. If it was necessary to replace him, was it reasonable to engage a permanent replacement rather than a temporary one?

As with cases of long-term sickness, in practice an employer in such circumstances will be wise to proceed on the basis that the fairness of the dismissal may ultimately be tested before a tribunal. The principles discussed in Chapter 12 are therefore highly relevant.

3.7 Expiry of a contract for a fixed term or a specified purpose

An employer's failure to renew a fixed-term contract is deemed to constitute a dismissal. Unfortunately, the legislation does not define what is meant by a 'fixed-term contract'.

The Court of Appeal held in *British Broadcasting Corporation v. Dixon and Constanti* (1979), that a fixed-term contract is a contract for a specific stated term, even though it may be determinable by notice within that term. This decision closed a loophole which enabled employees to evade dismissal law by entering into fixed-term contracts which were then terminated by notice and not renewed.

In certain circumstances, however, the legislation does allow 'contracting out' by means of a fixed-term contract; see section 23.2 Fixed-term contracts p229.

Where a contract for a specific purpose comes to an end, as with the contract of a seaman for a voyage, it is discharged by performance and not by expiration. There is therefore no dismissal.

In *Brown v. Knowsley Borough Council* (1986), a teacher was employed 'only so long as sufficient funds [were] provided' by an outside body. Funding ceased, her job ended, and she claimed a redundancy payment. Surprisingly, the EAT ruled that she had not been dismissed, as the contract had come to an end automatically when the money ran out. The logic of this decision cannot be pressed too far; otherwise, contrary to public policy, it would enable employers easily to circumvent dismissal law.

In practice, it is often difficult to distinguish a contract of this kind from one of fixed duration. The Court of Appeal considered the position in *Wiltshire County Council v. NATFHE and Guy* (1980). The employee was employed as a part-time teacher from 1969 to 1977. She entered into a fresh contract each academic year, but her appointment was not renewed in 1977/78.

The Court of Appeal held that there had been a dismissal. The employee worked under a contract for a fixed, specified period from the start of the autumn term to the last day of the summer term. The argument that she was employed for the specific purpose of teaching students, and therefore not eligible for dismissal law rights, was rejected.

3.8 Miscellaneous cases

Change in partners

Theoretically, a change in the members of an employing partnership will end the contracts of the employees at common law. This seldom arises in practice unless there is a dissolution of the business or other major change. In most cases, the mere coming or going of a partner, which has no material effect upon the employee, will not be considered as terminating the contract. In any event, the Transfer of Undertakings (Protection of Employment) Regulations 1981 will now frequently apply; see Chapter 20.

Receivership

The appointment of a receiver of the business will probably terminate the contracts of employees if made by the court, or if the receiver is to be an agent for creditors of the business.

In practice, however, receivers are frequently appointed by debenture holders pursuant to a trust deed providing that the receiver shall act as agent for the company. Such an appointment will usually not be inconsistent with continuing the employment of some or all of the employees.

Winding-up order

A compulsory winding-up order terminates the contracts of employment, or at least operates as formal notice of dismissal.

Whether or not a resolution for voluntary winding up operates in this way is less clear. The answer may depend upon whether the business is to be discontinued or merely reorganised. In the latter case, the resolution may not terminate the contracts of employees other than those whose continued employment is inconsistent with the reorganisation.

Death

The death of an employee or sole employer will normally terminate the contract automatically. However, a deceased employer's personal representative or trustees may continue the employment, in which case the principles of continuity referred to in Chapter 22 will apply.

Transfer of undertakings

Where the Transfer of Undertakings (Protection of Employment) Regulations 1981 apply, there is generally no dismissal upon the transfer of employees in an undertaking from one employer to another. The relevant principles are summarised in Chapter 20.

4
Constructive Dismissal

4.1 Introduction

Constructive dismissal is much misunderstood. Put simply, it arises where an employee becomes entitled to dismissal law rights despite not having been explicitly 'fired' by his employer.

In the past, the varying interpretations of the concept by courts and tribunals caused considerable concern amongst employers. At one time it was suggested that, for some sensitive employees, claiming constructive dismissal was the next best thing to winning the pools. Since then a series of cases has made it clear that the impact of constructive dismissal is not as damaging as had been feared.

Briefly, an employee who claims that he has been constructively dismissed must show that:

1. the employer has breached the contract of service; and that

2. the breach was so fundamental as to justify the employee terminating the contract (or that it was 'the last straw'); and that

3. he terminated the contract as a direct result of the breach; and that

4. he did not delay too long in terminating the contract.

4.2 Breach of contract

The legal test

Difficulties used to arise because of confusion surrounding the

43

proper legal test for constructive dismissal. In the mid-1970s, tribunals asked themselves whether the employee was forced to resign by the unreasonable behaviour of the employer. This loose approach made it hard for employers to gauge whether their actions would retrospectively be considered so unreasonable as to entitle employees to leave.

The Court of Appeal made it clear in *Western Excavating (ECC) Ltd v. Sharp* (1978), that the proper test is whether the employer was guilty of a fundamental breach of the employment contract, showing he no longer intended to be bound by one or more of its essential terms.

The decision in the *Sharp* case was a turning point, not only in theory, but also in practice. An employee claiming constructive dismissal has to surmount a number of hurdles; the first is to identify the contract term that has been breached.

Express terms

The breach of an express term of the contract can in most cases be shown quite easily. Typical examples of unilateral action by an employer are pay cuts and changes in job duties. Lay-offs and business reorganisations are apt to give rise to such breaches.

Of course, if the employer acts within the terms of the employment contract, there will not be a breach. A 'mobility' clause, for example, may entitle him to move the employee to another site. A 'flexibility' clause may enable him to ask the employee to undertake new duties. Disciplinary suspension or lay-off without pay, which might otherwise amount to constructive dismissal, may be perfectly legitimate if provided for in the agreement between the parties.

It is sometimes thought that a written statement of particulars of terms of the contract, required by section 1 of the 1978 Act to be given to employees, is a statement of express contractual terms. However, in *Robertson v. British Gas Corporation* (1983), the Court of Appeal confirmed that the statutory statement is neither the contract itself nor conclusive evidence of it. It is therefore quite possible for the courts to imply into the contract terms which conflict with the written statement.

Furthermore, it is becoming apparent that in some cases there are limits on the effectiveness even of widely and skilfully drafted terms of the contract itself. Recent cases suggest a willingness on the part of tribunals and courts to imply terms which restrict an employer's freedom to act in accordance with express terms.

United Bank Ltd v. Akhtar (1989) illustrates the point. An express mobility clause empowered a bank to transfer the employee, either temporarily or permanently, to any of its places of business within the UK. Controversially, the EAT agreed with the industrial tribunal that this right was subject to the following implied constraints:

1. that the employer must give reasonable prior notice of the transfer; and

2. that instructions to transfer should be such that compliance with them was feasible.

Customary practice

Implied terms

Terms of an employment contract are often not expressly stated. Terms may be imposed by statute or incorporated from collective agreements. Even more importantly in practice, terms may be implied into the contract by the common law.

Intriguingly, the courts have occasionally implied a term to the effect that specific terms (for example, as to duties or place of work) can be varied unilaterally in certain circumstances. In *Millbrook Furnishing Industries Ltd v. McIntosh* (1981), the EAT considered that an employer could in certain circumstances, and without having the express right to do so, transfer an employee temporarily without being in breach of contract. It would, however, be unwise to expect this approach to be stretched too far.

When will terms be implied? Custom and practice is one well-established source of implied terms. And it has long been established that a term will be implied when business efficiency so requires, or where the parties have clearly failed to state the terms in full and there is no doubt that they would have agreed to the additional term.

In recent years, courts and tribunals have adopted a more liberal approach. They have in some cases been prepared to imply terms when it seems reasonable to do so in the circumstances. In *Mears v. Safecar Security Ltd* (1982), for example, the Court of Appeal accepted that, where there were no indications to the contrary, it would be normal to imply a term that wages would be paid to an employee absent because of sickness.

There is no general implied 'right to work' in the contract of employment; nor is there a general right to job satisfaction. Yet specific cases can arise where an employee denied work to do or job satisfaction may, on the facts, be entitled to claim to have been constructively dismissed. This is most likely to arise in the case of certain senior employees, employees in the leisure and entertainment industries whose career development requires exposure to the public eye and employees whose pay is closely linked to performance. This is a potentially dynamic area of the law; its possibilities have yet to be fully explored.

Sometimes judicial flexibility works in favour of the employer. *Courtaulds Northern Spinning Ltd v. Sibson & TGWU* (1988) is a case in point. In the absence of an express mobility clause, the Court of Appeal was willing to imply a term on the basis that, had they directed their minds to it, the parties would have agreed that the employer had the right to direct the employee to work anywhere within reasonable daily reach of his home. The request itself need not be 'reasonable' nor for 'genuine operational reasons'.

The *Akhtar* case mentioned in the section Express terms p44 is perhaps more typical in that the outcome of judicial creativity in this field was to the benefit of the employee. The same was true in *Prestwick Circuits Ltd v. McAndrew* (1990), where the Scottish Court of Session considered it was necessary (not merely 'reasonable') to qualify an employer's right of transfer so as to protect an employee from being asked to move at a moment's notice, even if the proposed transfer was to somewhere within a reasonable distance. Whether the notice given in a particular case is 'reasonable' is a question of fact and degree for the industrial tribunal to determine.

Such decisions are not inconsistent with *Sharp*. The courts are not prepared to impose on employers a general implied duty to act reasonably, but the creative use of implied terms enables courts and tribunals to do justice – as they see it – in hard cases. The trouble is that this means that uncertainty is creeping back into the law on constructive dismissal. If the exact scope and effect of implied terms is difficult to predict, neither employers nor employees can be quite sure where they stand. This problem arises most acutely in the context of the implied duty of mutual trust and confidence.

Mutual trust and confidence

There is in every contract of employment an implied term that

> 'the employers would not, without reasonable and proper cause, conduct themselves in a manner calculated or likely to destroy or seriously damage the relationship of confidence and trust between the parties'.

Woods v. WM Car Services (Peterborough) Ltd (1981).

The existence of such a term casts a reciprocal duty of trust and confidence upon the employee.

Examples of employer conduct which may, depending upon the circumstances, breach the obligation of mutual trust and confidence are innumerable, but include:

- sexual harassment;

- language which is offensive in the circumstances;

- unreasonable accusations of dishonesty;

- humiliating an employee in the presence of his colleagues;

- turning a blind eye to harassment of an employee by colleagues;

- persistent attempts to vary unilaterally terms of the employment contract;

- failure to provide proper working conditions;

- failure to provide an overworked employee with reasonable support;

- penalising minor breaches of discipline with disproportionate severity;

- reducing an employee's status, for example by changing the emphasis of his duties.

Failure to give a pay rise

Does failure to give a pay rise amount to constructive dismissal? At a time of economic recession the answer might be thought to be 'no', but the position is not so simple. In *FC Gardner Ltd v. Beresford* (1978), the employee was given no pay increase for two years. Others did receive rises during that time. The EAT thought that in most circumstances it would be reasonable to infer a term along the lines that an employer will not treat his employees arbitrarily, capriciously or inequitably in matters of remuneration. Failure to grant a pay rise could amount to constructive dismissal if it reflected victimisation.

Some commentators suggested that the *Beresford* case paved the way for a wide-ranging non-discrimination or 'equality' clause to be implied into employment contracts. So far, however, tribunals have proceeded with caution in this area and in *Murco Petroleum Ltd v. Forge* (1987), the EAT stressed that there is no implied term that an employee is entitled to an annual pay rise.

4.3 Fundamental breach

Sometimes the incident which directly leads to an employee's departure, while minor, may be regarded as the 'last straw'. If there has been a history of such incidents the tribunal may say that an employee is entitled eventually to say 'enough is enough' and leave.

The general rule, however, is that the breach of contract complained of must in itself be so serious as to justify the employee in terminating the relationship. In other words, a single trivial occurrence does not entitle an individual to claim that he has been constructively dismissed.

An interesting example of a minor breach that did not warrant the employee's departure is provided by *Gillies v. Richard Daniels & Company Ltd* (1979). The employee had received an extra payment of £1.50 per week for doing a particular job. The employer thought it would be fairer for him to share this with other employees who assisted him. The resulting small pay cut was held not to constitute a serious breach of contract. However, employers should treat this decision with caution; it does not give them *carte blanche* to chip away at employees' earnings.

In another case, an employer's failure to pay salaries on time was held not to constitute constructive dismissal, even though such a failure had occurred before. Whether or not a breach of contract of this kind will be so serious as to justify resignation will always depend on the full facts of the case: *Adams v. Charles Zub Associates Ltd* (1978). Again, employers should be wary of relying on such a decision as a precedent for their own behaviour.

What is the position if the employer misunderstands the terms of the contract? In the controversial case of *Frank Wright & Co (Holdings) Ltd v. Punch* (1980), the EAT indicated that if there is a genuine dispute about the terms of the agreement, the employer is not constructively dismissing an employee by requiring him to carry out the contract in accordance with his (the employer's) own interpretation of its terms. This is so even if his interpretation is incorrect.

The decision was based upon established general principles of contract law. In theory it could prove significant in restricting the scope of constructive dismissal. Employers faced with a constructive dismissal claim may tend to argue that they were merely adhering to a (possibly mistaken) view of the terms of the contract, rather than committing a fundamental breach of those terms.

In practice, it seems from most of the subsequent case law that the *Punch* decision is likely to be narrowly interpreted. The law remains uncertain; in this area the conflict between contract principles and good industrial relations practice is again evident.

4.4 The employee's response

A serious breach of contract by the employer does not itself end the contract. It only gives the employee the right to choose to do so. In order to claim that he has been constructively dismissed, the employee must terminate the employment in response to the employer's breach: *Walker v. Josiah Wedgwood & Sons Ltd* (1978).

Merely going on strike does not amount to such a termination; neither does the act of lodging an unfair dismissal application if the employee continues to report for work.

The employee need not give formal written notice of termination, but he should not say or do anything which is inconsistent with termination. He must make it clear by words or conduct that he is exercising his entitlement to treat himself as having been constructively dismissed. This does not amount to a requirement that he must explain his action to his employer. A sophisticated appreciation of constructive dismissal law is not necessary. In cases where the employee uses ambiguous words, tribunals should approach the facts with common sense.

An employee is not obliged to pursue a complaint in accordance with the employer's grievance procedure before claiming constructive dismissal. Nor is it necessarily fatal to the claim if he gives notice of termination rather than walking out on the spot, in other words, terminating the contract summarily.

Jumping the gun

Sometimes employees 'jump the gun'. For there to be a constructive dismissal there must either have been a serious breach of contract by the employer in fact, or an 'anticipatory breach', where the employer has made it clear that he will break the contract. For example, if an employer says that he is thinking of implementing a pay cut, but indicates that his mind is not closed and that he is prepared to discuss the matter further, that will not in itself amount to constructive dismissal. Again, in *Haseltine, Lake & Company v. Dowler* (1981), it was not an anticipatory breach of contract to tell an employee that if he did not find a job elsewhere, his employment would eventually be terminated. There was nothing to suggest that the employers intended ultimately not to give proper notice.

Even if there is an anticipatory breach, that breach must be continuing to found a constructive dismissal. If the threat is withdrawn before the employee responds to it, his subsequent resignation will not be regarded in law as a constructive dismissal – as in *Harrison v. Norwest Holst Group Administration Ltd* (1985), where a company retracted its threat to deprive the employee of his directorship at a specified future date.

Delaying too long

When an employer is guilty of a serious breach of contract, the employee must not delay too long in his response. If he continues to work without leaving, he will ultimately lose his right to claim constructive dismissal.

A good example of how this principle operates is provided by the case of *WE Cox Toner (International) Ltd v. Crook* (1981).

An employee who was reprimanded at the end of July 1980 subsequently demanded, through his solicitors, that the letter of reprimand be withdrawn. On 6 February 1981 he was told that the letter would not be withdrawn. On 3 March 1981 he left. His claim that he had been constructively dismissed failed because of the lapse of time after 6 February 1981 before he took action. However, his failure to leave *prior* to 6 February 1981 did not necessarily mean that he had 'waived' the alleged breach of contract and affirmed the contract subsequent to the breach.

It seems that an employee will be allowed a reasonable period of time to decide whether or not to leave the employment. In each case, the difficulty will be in determining what is a 'reasonable period'. Much will probably depend upon whether the breach is a single, unequivocal act (such as suspension in breach of contract), or involves more far-reaching considerations (such as a change in job duties or status).

In the latter case, the tribunals may well be prepared to allow a 'trial period' during which the employee is entitled to assess the effect of the altered terms, without losing his right to claim that he had been constructively dismissed. However, there is no statutory equivalent as regards non-redundancy constructive dismissals to the 'trial period' provided by statute in redundancy cases; Acceptance of offer on different terms p90. How long he may wait is therefore dependent on all the circumstances, including the length of his previous service.

An employee who works under protest for a limited period of time will not be penalised for attempting to resolve the dispute through negotiation or by following the grievance procedure. He should, however, make clear at all times his rejection of his employer's conduct.

It has sometimes been suggested that employers should 'inquire how things are coming along and what the employee is going to do' in cases where a constructive dismissal claim is feared. Whether or not this will always be practicable or sensible is doubtful.

4.5 Fair constructive dismissal

The vast majority of constructive dismissal cases involve an unfair dismissal claim. It is vital to grasp, however, that an employee who is constructively dismissed may nevertheless have been fairly dismissed.

If the employer denies having dismissed the employee, the onus will first be on the employee to convince the tribunal, on the balance of probabilities, that he was dismissed. If he succeeds, the normal questions in an unfair dismissal case have to be asked, as follows.

1. Has the employer shown that the employee was dismissed for a potentially fair reason? And if so,

2. did he act fairly in all the circumstances in dismissing the employee for that reason?

If dismissal is admitted, these questions will again be asked. The principles of unfair dismissal are discussed in detail in later chapters.

An employer who wishes to contest dismissal will be well advised to do so from the outset. Equally, if he wishes to fall back on the argument that, even if there was a dismissal, it was nevertheless fair, he should advance that argument in his notice of appearance; see section 25.4 The notice of appearance p249. This is called 'pleading in the alternative'. Although the concept is familiar to lawyers, many employers might be wary of saying both that there was no dismissal and that, if there was, it was fair. Yet to raise the latter argument only at a late stage will, even if permitted, seriously diminish the employer's credibility.

Fair constructive dismissals can occur for a variety of reasons. The most normal context is that of a business reorganisation where the reorganisation is *bona fide* and undertaken for the good of the enterprise. The refusal of an employee to co-operate may justify the employer in either expressly dismissing him (see Dismissal for refusal to agree to a change p208), or implementing the change in breach of contract. The employer has to show a sound business reason for the reorganisation and, crucially, that he observed the principles of good industrial relations practice (including full consultation and consideration of alternative courses) before taking action.

4.6 Business transfers

Special provisions about constructive dismissal are contained in the Transfer of Undertakings (Protection of Employment) Regulations

1981. The Regulations are discussed in Chapter 20. Briefly, where the Regulations apply, an employee is transferred from one employer to another. The mere fact that the identity of his employer has changed will not found a constructive dismissal claim.

However, there can be such a claim where:

1. the transferee makes a substantial change in his working conditions to his 'detriment'; or where

2. the employee shows that the change of identity of the employer is a significant change and is to his detriment.

'Detriment' is not defined, but presumably it must arise from some breach of contract by the transferee.

4.7 'Squeezing out' employees

There is no doubt that the *Sharp* decision is good law. Yet in practice, the need to show a breach of contract has made it rather more difficult to establish constructive dismissal.

The EAT acknowledged in the *Woods* case (see Mutual trust and confidence p47) that the *Sharp* test had in some cases enabled unscrupulous employers to 'squeeze out' unwanted employees by conduct falling short of a clear breach of contract.

The solution is simple. Such conduct may be regarded as a fundamental breach of the implied duty of mutual trust and confidence. The 'last straw' principle may also be relevant.

Nevertheless, an employee who claims that he has been constructively dismissed may have to surmount a number of tricky legal hurdles. In practice, he will have to be reasonably sure of his ground before committing himself to the uncertainties of litigation – and possible long-term unemployment – in a wintry economic climate. The sensible handling of industrial relations ought in most cases to reduce to a minimum the risk of successful constructive dismissal claims by disgruntled and over-sensitive employees.

5
The Significance of Dismissal

5.1 Introduction

Dismissal may give rise to a variety of legal rights, some of which are discussed in this chapter. An employee is, for example, entitled to notice of termination of the contract – unless he has been guilty of conduct justifying summary dismissal.

Modern employment protection legislation provides for minimum notice periods, which are discussed in section 5.3 Statutory minimum notice period p60. An employee's contract may entitle him to a longer period of notice than the statutory minimum. If insufficient notice is given, or none at all, he may claim he has been wrongfully dismissed; see Chapter 6.

For a variety of reasons, an employer may prefer the employee not to work out his notice period. Pay in lieu of notice may therefore be given. There has been considerable debate about whether pay in lieu of notice is taxable. If (as is often the case) there is no contractual entitlement to pay in lieu of notice, it is probably – but not certainly – correct to say that such pay is a payment of compensation for the employer's breach of contract in not giving due notice. If so, the payment would not be taxable under the general principles of Schedule E income tax. It can also be argued that, as the employee has only lost the amount of his net wages, that is all that need be paid. In practice, many employers pay the gross amount – perhaps in order to maintain good industrial relations.

5.2 Ascertaining the date of termination

It may be necessary to ascertain the date of termination of employment in accordance with the statutory rules in order to establish:

1. whether the employee has the relevant period of continuous employment to qualify for various dismissal law rights;

2. the amount of any redundancy payment or unfair dismissal 'basic award' to which he may be entitled;

3. from when his time begins to run for presenting any complaint to an industrial tribunal;

4. whether at the date of termination he exceeded any age limit for qualifying for rights.

The basic rules

The statutory date of termination is called 'the effective date of termination' in the unfair dismissal context and 'the relevant date' in relation to redundancy pay entitlement. The basic rules are that the termination date is:

1. where the contract is terminated by notice, whether given by the employer or the employee, the date on which that notice expires;

2. where the contract is not terminated by notice, the date on which the termination takes effect;

3. where there is a fixed-term contract, the date on which that term expires.

Where a failure to allow an employee to return to work after maternity leave is treated as a dismissal (see section 17.3 The right to return to work p181), the termination date is the date notified by her as the date of her return.

A number of exceptions to the above rules are dealt with below.

Dismissal with notice

Conceptual difficulties arise where a 'payment in lieu' is made to the employee, who does not work out his notice. The termination date will often be the date when the notice expires, but that will not invariably be the case. The date when the employee receives his P45 is not, however, relevant in ascertaining the date: *Newham London Borough v. Ward* (1985).

Some specific cases are dealt with in the remainder of this section.

Ambiguous dismissal letters

Interpreting the facts correctly is often made even trickier by the ambiguous way in which many dismissals are implemented. A classic example occurred in *Adams v. GKN Sankey Ltd* (1980). A letter written in November 1979 said: 'You are given 12 weeks' notice of dismissal from this company with effect from 5.11.79. You will not be expected to work out your notice but will receive money in lieu of notice . . .' The payment was made with deduction of tax and pension rights were treated as ending on 5 November 1979.

Nevertheless, the EAT held that the termination date occurred only upon expiry of the 12-week notice period. This was a case of an employee being sent home on paid leave during his notice. The right to require his actual service was waived.

A similar result was achieved in *Chapman v. Letheby and Christopher* (1981). The EAT made it clear that whether a letter indicates an intention on the employer's part to terminate at once or not depends upon the construction of the letter. In construing the letter the tribunal should be guided by:

1. the way in which an ordinary, reasonable employee would understand the words used;

2. the facts known to the employee at the date he received the letter;

3. the principle of interpreting ambiguous phraseology against the person who used it (so as not to encourage employers to mislead employees by deliberate ambiguity).

This means that an employer who wishes the dismissal to take effect immediately rather than at the end of the notice period should:

1. state unambiguously the intended date of termination;

2. make it clear that any payment made is, in effect, made by way of damages for breach of contract;

Still, given the complexities which shroud the area, it seems unlikely that the last judicial word on this subject has yet been uttered.

Shortening the notice period

An employer who has given an employee notice may sometimes seek at a later stage to terminate the contract on a date earlier than that originally specified. To do so will not always bring the termination date forward. Tribunals will construe any ambiguity in favour of an employee who might be disadvantaged by what the employer purports to have done.

But there are limits to the extent to which tribunals can lean in favour of an employee in these circumstances. In *Stapp v. Shaftesbury Society* (1982), the employer brought the employment to a premature end before the expiry of the one-month notice period originally specified. The effect was to bar the employee from entitlement to claim unfair dismissal, even though he would have had sufficient continuous employment to found a claim, had the original termination date stood.

The Court of Appeal did not take the view that the second notice was invalid because it amounted to a means of depriving the employee of his statutory rights. However, the second notice was clearly given in breach of contract. It was indicated that, in any subsequent wrongful dismissal action, damages might include the loss of the right to claim unfair dismissal; the employee would have been entitled to this if the contract had been honoured.

The *Stapp* case was not referred to in *TBA Industrial Products Ltd v. Morland* (1982). The Court of Appeal, in a majority decision, indicated that, in effect, the statutory termination date is fixed at the time of dismissal and cannot be brought forward by agreement. However, this interpretation of the law is perhaps open to doubt.

Finally, if an employee, having been given notice by his employer, gives a counter-notice to terminate the contract at an earlier date, the termination date is the date of expiry of the counter-notice.

Dismissal without notice

If no notice is given, the termination date is the date on which the termination takes effect. This has generally been assumed to be the actual date of dismissal, subject to the provisions which apply in the exceptional circumstances discussed in Statutory postponement of the termination date, below.

Some doubts have now arisen on this point due to increasing awareness of the complexities which contract law principles create (outlined in Chapter 3). It is to be hoped that the tribunals will manage to steer clear of the legalistic booby-traps that exist in this area. If not, the effect will be that the ordinary employer and employee will be unable to understand the position.

If a letter of summary dismissal is sent to an employee, is the termination date the date when it is sent, received or actually read? It has been suggested that the dismissal only becomes effective once the employee reads the letter, but this raises in turn a problem. What happens if the employee deliberately avoids opening or reading the letter, or has failed to advise his employers of a change of address? This question has not yet been finally answered by the courts, but in such cases it might be argued that the termination date was when the employee had a reasonable opportunity of reading the letter.

Statutory postponement of the termination date

Where an employer has to give contractual notice to the employee and gives insufficient notice, section 55(5) of the 1978 Act as substituted provides that the termination date for qualifying for certain rights will be when either:

1. the actual notice given expires; or

2. when the minimum *statutory* notice period (see section 5.3 Statutory minimum notice period p60) would have expired,

whichever is the later.

It has to be stressed that the *contractual* notice period is not added to his period of service. This disadvantages employees who do not have sufficient continuous service to qualify for rights if the statutory notice period is added, although they would have had sufficient continuous service if the longer notice period to which they were contractually entitled had been added.

An employee who has validly been dismissed for gross misconduct cannot add the statutory minimum notice period to his period of service. The statutory postponement does not apply either for purposes of ascertaining whether the employee has made a complaint to an industrial tribunal within the requisite time limit.

The postponement does, however, apply for calculating:

1. the qualifying period for the right to a written statement of reasons for dismissal – see section 11.2 Written statement of reasons for dismissal p115;

2. the qualifying period for the right to claim unfair dismissal – see section 10.3 Qualifying service p111;

3. the qualifying period for quantifying an unfair dismissal basic award – see section 24.3 The basic award p237.

The postponement also applies for these purposes to constructive dismissal cases.

In the redundancy payments context, there are a number of exceptional provisions, notably:

1. where there has been a statutory trial period (see Acceptance of offer on different terms p90), the six-month time limit for claiming a redundancy payment runs from the end of the trial period, but for all other purposes, the trial period is ignored;

2. for the purposes only of calculating the two-year qualifying period, length of service and the amount of 'a week's pay' (see section 22.5 A week's pay p226), then where the statutory minimum notice (see section 5.3 Statutory minimum notice period p60) should have been given, but was not, the 'relevant date' is the date when that notice would have expired, if later than the date ascertained under the normal rules.

Internal Appeals

When an employee appeals against his dismissal and that appeal is rejected, what is the statutory date of termination – the date of dismissal or the date of final rejection?

The answer will depend upon how the appeals procedure is framed. There is little purpose in examining in detail supposed precedents in this field. Where payment of wages continues until the date of final rejection, that date is likely to be the termination date, but in most cases, the original date of dismissal will be the statutory date of termination.

Employers should not be encouraged to drag out appeals procedures in the hope that the employee may miss the relevant time limit for complaining to a tribunal. In such circumstances, it is possible that the tribunal may hold that it was not reasonably practicable for the employee to present his case in time; see The escape clause p248.

5.3 Statutory minimum notice period

Excluded categories

The right to receive and the obligation to give statutory minimum notice do not apply to:

- certain overseas employments;
- certain merchant seamen;
- certain short-term and part-time employees;
- Crown servants;
- employees with less than one month's continuous service.

The right

Once an employee has been continuously employed for one calendar month, the minimum notice required by section 49 of the 1978 Act to be given by an employer is:

1. not less than one week's notice if the employee's continuous service is less than two years;

2. not less than one week's notice for each year of continuous service if the period of that service is two years or more but less than twelve years; and

3. not less than twelve weeks' notice if the period of continuous service is twelve years or more.

However, an employer is only entitled by statute to one week's notice from an employee who has been employed for one month or more and the sliding scale set out above does not apply.

The statutory notice periods are minimum periods only, and it is, of course, possible for the parties to agree on longer notice periods.

Equally, either party can accept payment in lieu of notice. It is not, however, possible to contract out of the minimum notice period.

The particular problems arising in insolvency cases are discussed in section 5.5 Insolvency of the employer p62 and the rules on claims for damages in respect of failure to give minimum notice are set out in Chapter 6.

5.4 Statutory minimum pay during notice

Excluded categories

As summarised in section 5.3 Statutory minimum notice period – Excluded categories p60. Note also the restrictions listed in Restrictions on the right, below.

The right

A qualifying employee is entitled to minimum remuneration during the statutory notice periods summarised in section 5.3 Statutory minimum notice period – The right p60, even if longer notice is actually given and whether or not the notice is given by the employer or the employee.

  The parties cannot contract out of the right, but section 50(3) of the 1978 Act provides that the right does not arise where the contract requires the employer to give notice at least one week longer than that required by the Act. The right does not arise either if notice is not given. An employee dismissed without notice cannot claim under the statute, although he can sue on his contract. In assessing the value of his claim, the court can take into account his loss of the rights that he would have had if proper notice had been given.

Restrictions on the right

The employer may not be liable for payment during the whole of the statutory notice period, ie. if:

1. he grants leave of absence during the notice period, whether or not he does so pursuant to the employee's statutory right to time off;

2. if the employee gives notice and then goes on strike;

3. if the employee is validly dismissed without notice during the notice period.

Amount of entitlement

Where an employee has normal working hours (see section 22.5 A week's pay p226) and actually works those hours, his position is governed by the terms of his contract.

Where he does not work some or all of these hours, Schedule 3 paragraph 2 of the 1978 Act provides that he is still entitled to be paid for them if he is:

1. ready and willing to work, but given no work; or

2. incapable of work through sickness or injury; or

3. taking his lawful holidays.

For each of those hours he is entitled to be paid at the rate of his week's pay (see section 22.5 A week's pay p226) divided by the number of his normal working hours. The position is basically similar where the employee does not have normal working hours. In both cases, contractual or statutory sick pay, holiday pay, and certain state benefits can be deducted from the amount due.

5.5   Insolvency of the employer

Excluded categories

The following categories of employee are excluded from the statutory rights in respect of the insolvency of the employer:

*   an employee whose spouse is the employer;

*   certain seamen;

*   certain overseas employments;

*   police service employees;

*   Crown servants.

None of the rights depends upon a qualifying period of continuous employment. This section sketches the rules; the detail is to be found in company and insolvency legislation, which should be read in conjunction with the 1978 Act.

Definition of insolvency

Self-evidently, an employee whose employer is not insolvent is not entitled to insolvency rights. Less obviously, for these purposes, an employer is not insolvent merely because he is unable to pay his debts as they fall due.

Broadly, an employer is 'insolvent' if:

1. being an individual, he has become bankrupt;

2. being an individual, he has died and his estate is being administered as an insolvent estate;

3. being a company, a winding-up order has been made or a resolution for voluntary winding up has been passed, or a receiver has been appointed or possession of company property taken by debenture holders under a floating charge.

Preferential debts

The following debts of an employer to an employee are preferential; in other words, they are paid out in preference to ordinary creditors:

1. arrears of wages for up to four months before the commencement of winding up or the date of the receiving order. The maximum claim that can be made at the time of writing is £800; any excess will rank as an ordinary debt;

2. accrued holiday pay due on termination of employment before or by reason of the insolvency;

3. unpaid pension contributions for up to four months prior to the insolvency.

The following payments are included in the definition of wages for these purposes:

1. a guarantee payment;

2. payment during medical suspension;

3. payment for time off for carrying out trade union duties, to look for work in redundancy cases and for ante-natal care;

4. payment due under a protective award;

5. statutory sick pay.

Guaranteed debts

The following debts of an insolvent employer can be claimed by an employee from the State:

1. arrears of pay (including the five specific types of payment referred to in Preferential debts, above) not exceeding eight weeks' pay in total;

2. minimum pay during notice calculated as set out in section 5.4 Statutory minimum pay during notice p61;

3. up to six weeks' holiday pay due within the last 12 months of employment;

4. any unfair dismissal basic award calculated as set out in section 24.3 The basic award p237;

5. any reasonable sum by way of reimbursement of the whole or part of any fee or premium paid by an apprentice or articled clerk;

6. certain unpaid contributions to an occupational pension scheme or a personal pension scheme.

In the case of the first four items, the maximum rate per week guaranteed is limited, albeit subject to review. At 1 April 1990 the limit was £184 per week per item. The limit applies to the employee's gross weekly wage (before any deductions for tax or national insurance are made).

Payment of guaranteed debts

Payment of guaranteed debts is made by the State and tends in practice not to be made quickly. If payment is refused in whole or in part, the employee can apply to an industrial tribunal.

The application must be made within three months of the date of communication of the Secretary of State's decision. If that is not reasonably practicable, it should be made within such further period as is reasonable.

If the tribunal finds that the payment should have been made, it must declare the liability and the amount due. The tribunal will, however, have regard to the employee's duty to mitigate his loss. That duty is discussed more fully in the context of compensation for wrongful dismissal; see Mitigation of loss p71.

6

Claims for Breach of Contract

6.1 Introduction

Claims relating to a breach of contract often arise in connection with dismissals. Such claims come in a variety of forms. This is an area where employers, as well as employees, sometimes resort to litigation.

Long before the unfair dismissal regime was introduced, employees sacked without proper notice were able to seek compensation for wrongful dismissal in the ordinary civil courts – the County Court or the High Court.

'Wrongful dismissal' is the name given to the common law action for a breach of an employment contract, and it is often confused with unfair dismissal. People mistakenly believe that the two concepts are the same but in fact they differ in many important respects. An employee who has not been guilty of conduct justifying summary dismissal (ie dismissal without proper notice) is entitled to bring a claim of wrongful dismissal even if, for example, he has not been employed for long enough to have unfair dismissal rights.

Wrongful dismissal has in recent years often been overshadowed by the development of unfair dismissal law. An employee who qualifies for the right not to be unfairly dismissed may complain to a tribunal even if proper notice has been given. Unfair dismissal law is governed by statute and it will be considered in detail later.

Yet actions for wrongful dismissal continue to be important, especially for senior employees who may find that the arbitrary ceiling on unfair dismissal compensation limits the value of an unfair dismissal complaint.

Moreover, claims for breach of an employment contract are likely to have a new lease of life in future. This is because in March

1990 the Government announced that it proposed to allow claims for damages for breach of an employment contract to be brought before an industrial tribunal, provided that:

1. the claim arises or is outstanding on the termination of the employee's employment; and

2. the claim arises in circumstances which also give rise to proceedings already or simultaneously brought before an industrial tribunal under other statutory provisions.

This will not deprive the ordinary civil courts of the power to hear claims relating to a breach of an employment contract. Moreover, industrial tribunals will not be allowed to deal with claims for compensation for personal injury.

At the time of writing, the rules bringing this important change into effect have not been published. Initial reaction to the proposals was that:

1. it appears likely that it will be up to the employee to choose whether to pursue a claim in the industrial tribunal or the ordinary civil courts;

2. the requirement that other proceedings must be brought before the matter can be dealt with in the tribunal may lead to an increase in spurious complaints, for example, in respect of unfair dismissal.

In practice, many employees have been deterred in the past from bringing wrongful dismissal claims because of their unfamiliarity with court procedure. Even though legal aid is not available for presenting a complaint to an industrial tribunal (whereas it may be available for a claim in the ordinary courts), it seems certain that once the new system becomes widely known, many employees will seek to take advantage of it.

6.2 Notice of termination

Either party to a contract of employment can bring it to an end by giving notice to the other. The length of the notice required to bring the contract to an end is a matter for agreement between the parties, subject to the minimum periods laid down by statute and discussed in section 5.3 Statutory minimum notice period p60.

A fixed-term contract may not be lawfully terminated before the end of the agreed term, unless the employee is in breach of its provisions. Any such termination will entitle the innocent party to claim damages.

If no period of notice is expressly agreed, then the contract may be terminated upon the giving of reasonable notice. The problem in any particular case is to assess what is 'reasonable notice'. It will not be less than the statutory minimum period, but it may be considerably more. Relevant factors may include the employee's

● seniority;

● length of service;

● remuneration;

● skill and qualifications.

While it is sometimes suggested that the courts will rarely imply a right to more than six months' notice – possibly twelve months' notice in the case of a senior company director – generalisations are unhelpful when so much depends upon the facts of each specific case.

6.3 Restrictions on the employer's right to give notice

Occasionally, it is argued that in the circumstances the employer has restricted his own power to dismiss the employee. In such a case, so the argument runs, an employee may be able to sue for wrongful dismissal for a reason other than inadequate notice.

An example may be where the employee has procedural safeguards against dismissal. Such safeguards might be expressly stated in the contract or incorporated from a collective agreement. Sometimes, too, the employer may limit the substantive grounds (other than gross misconduct; see section 14.3 Breaches of discipline p150) for which he can dismiss. In that event a dismissal might be fair under unfair dismissal law and yet wrongful, even though proper notice was given.

An employer's right to dismiss prematurely will be restricted where he has agreed to employ the employee for a fixed term. Employment 'for life' may even be agreed, in which case any prior termination would amount to wrongful dismissal. In practice, the courts are likely to be slow to come to the view that a contract guaranteed a lifetime's employment.

More commonly, the question is whether an employer who specifies a 'probationary period' for a new employee is entitled to dismiss him before the expiry of that period for reasons other than gross misconduct. Everything here will depend on how the contract is interpreted. In *Dalgleish v. Kew House Farm Ltd* (1982), the letter of appointment said: 'Your position will be probationary for a period of three months, at the end of which time your performance will be reviewed and if satisfactory you will be made permanent.' The employee was dismissed after three weeks with one week's pay in lieu of notice. The Court of Appeal decided that the employer had not fettered his power to dismiss within the stated three-month period.

6.4 Where summary dismissal is justified

'There is no rule of thumb to determine what misconduct on the part of a servant justifies summary termination of his contract'

according to the Court of Appeal in *Wilson v. Racher* (1974). In that case, an employee who was dismissed after using 'obscene and deplorable' language in the presence of his employer's wife and family nevertheless succeeded in a wrongful dismissal claim.

There are no rigid rules in this area, but it can be said that the employee's breach must be serious to justify summary dismissal. An analogy can be drawn with the concept of gross misconduct in unfair dismissal law.

Gross negligence – negligence which is especially serious in nature – may on occasion justify summary dismissal. However, an employer needs to think carefully before sacking someone on the spot for gross negligence. The case of *Dietman v. London Borough of Brent* (1988) is salutary. Ms. Dietman was a social worker criticised for her part in the tragic and well-known case of the death of Jasmine Beckford. An inquiry ruled that by her non-intervention she was grossly negligent, but the list of examples of gross misconduct in her contract all involved an element of intention and conduct which was either dishonest or disruptive. The Court of Appeal ruled that, in the circumstances, she had been wrongfully dismissed without notice, in breach of her contract.

When an employer becomes aware that an employee has been

guilty of conduct justifying summary dismissal, he must decide within a reasonable time whether to dismiss. If he delays unduly, he may be deemed to have waived his right to terminate the employment. In contrast to the position under unfair dismissal law, however, an employer may rely upon gross misconduct discovered *after* the dismissal to justify a summary dismissal.

6.5 Damages

The measure of damages for wrongful dismissal is governed by general legal principles. The employee will be entitled to recover his loss arising as a reasonable and probable consequence of the breach of contract. Normally, this will be restricted to the amount of remuneration that he would have received had proper notice been given.

Quantifying the amount of that remuneration sometimes gives rise to problems. Depending upon the terms of the contract, it may include the value of a wide range of contractual benefits such as:

• a company car;

• pension rights;

• private health care;

• bonus and commission;

• rights under share incentive schemes.

This is important, because many employers who wrongfully dismiss employees assume incorrectly that their only liability is in respect of take home pay for the notice period. However, in many cases, especially where senior executives are concerned, the value of non-cash perks over a lengthy notice period may be very high.

Injured feelings

Normally, no compensation will be recoverable for injury to feelings or the manner of dismissal. This stringent – some would say harsh – principle was laid down by the House of Lords in *Addis v. Gramophone Co Ltd* (1909). There are some exceptional cases where there may be an entitlement to damages, such as where an entertainer's reputation and future work prospects are damaged

70

by the manner of dismissal. Some have suggested that a claim may be made where hurt feelings should have been contemplated as a probable consequence of the manner of dismissal, but this view was criticised by the Court of Appeal in *Bliss v. South East Thames Regional Health Authority* (1985).

Mitigation of loss

The employee is under a duty to mitigate, or minimise, his loss. The relevant legal principles are:

1. he cannot recover for loss consequent upon his employer's breach of contract where he could have avoided suffering that loss by taking reasonable steps;

2. if he in fact avoids or reduces his loss, he cannot recover for the avoided or reduced amount, even if the steps that he took were more than could reasonably be required of him;

3. he may recover loss or expense incurred in taking reasonable steps to mitigate his loss.

A wrongfully dismissed employee should therefore seek alternative employment at the earliest opportunity. He has to give credit for wages he earns or could reasonably have earned during the notice period. Whether or not he can reasonably be expected to take employment of a different kind or at a lower rate of pay will depend upon the circumstances. The rules are not rigid. In some cases there may be no immediate duty to accept alternative employment of a substantially inferior status. If so, a plaintiff may seek work of the same status and pay for a reasonable time, without suffering a reduction in damages as a result.

Other deductions

If the court awards damages, it will also make deductions to take account of the accelerated payment, the normal vicissitudes of life, the implications of taxation and the employee's national insurance contributions. No account will be taken of any unfair dismissal basic award made at an earlier tribunal hearing: *Shove v. Downs Surgical Plc* (1984).

The detailed rules on taxation, in particular, are horrendously complex. Suffice it to say here that there is more than one possible

71

approach. However, no income tax is deducted from awards under £30,000 (a figure which may from time to time be reviewed). One view is that if an award is over £30,000, the ex-employee may be taxed subsequently on the amount by which the damages exceed £30,000: *Bold v. Brough, Nicholson & Hall Ltd* (1964). Alternatively, notional deductions for tax may be made from the full amount of the award; the amount of income tax to which the ex-employee will be liable on the excess over £30,000 is calculated and added to the sum to be awarded: *Stewart v. Glentaggart* (1963). Because of the complexities, it will usually be wise to take expert advice before offering a substantial sum to settle or forestall a wrongful dismissal claim.

6.6 Injunctions and judicial review

The conventional remedy for wrongful dismissal is damages. Courts have long been unwilling to grant an employee an injunction to restrain his employer from terminating his contract without proper notice. The traditional thinking was expressed in a Victorian case involving the legendary showman Phineas T. Barnum; it was said that to order the continuation of a contract of employment would be to 'turn contracts of service into contracts of slavery'.

Contemporary thinking was expressed differently by the High Court in *Alexander v. Standard Telephones & Cables Ltd* (1990). Judicial reluctance to grant injunctions to restrain a breach of contract was said to be based on the fact that it is not practicable to make an employer and employee work together in circumstances where one of the parties is not prepared to continue the relationship:

> 'Once an employer has lost confidence in an employee, nothing a court says or orders will correct that view and the relationship will have broken down ... in such circumstances the employee's redress is damages.'

Yet the High Court acknowledged that this general principle can lead to difficulties. There have been a number of special cases where injunctions have been granted in recent years. In *Irani v. Southampton & South West Hampshire Health Authority* (1985), an employee was granted an injunction against employers who apparently still had 'perfect faith' in his honesty, integrity and loyalty. There was also a job available for him to do. This was described in *Alexander* as a 'borderline case' where the judge felt that the relationship had not broken down and that it was practicable to delay dismissal pending application of an existing disputes procedure. In contrast, *Alexander* was a redundancy case where the judge considered that the relationship had broken down – the employer believed that there was no work for the plaintiffs to do. The employers would suffer detriment if the plaintiff's employment was continued, as other workers considered more capable would then have to be dismissed. No injunction was granted.

An employee may also be entitled to remedies under public (ie administrative) law, as well as private (ie employment or contract) law. Thus in *R v. East Berkshire Health Authority ex parte Walsh* (1984), an employee claimed unfair dismissal and also applied under Order 53 of the Rules of the Supreme Court for judicial review; what he was requesting was an order quashing the alleged dismissal, prohibiting the continuance of an appeal hearing and quashing any decision reached at that hearing. The Court of Appeal accepted that if a public authority was required by Parliament to create rights for an employee under the terms of his contract, but failed to do so, public law remedies would be available. However, if, as in the present case, private law remedies were available, a breach of contract gave rise to no remedies under public law.

In those rare cases where a public remedy is available, judicial review may be granted in cases involving, for instance, a failure to observe natural justice. This was the case in *R v. Secretary of State for the Home Department, ex parte Benwell* (1985). A prison officer was dismissed on the basis of evidence of which he was unaware and upon which he was given no opportunity to comment. He was therefore able to obtain judicial review.

Such cases remain, however, very much the exception rather than the rule.

6.7   Overlap with unfair dismissal

Most claims for compensation for dismissal are complaints of unfair dismissal, which must be brought before an industrial tribunal. Tribunal procedures may be open to criticism in some respects, but in comparison to proceedings in the civil courts, they are informal, speedy, cheap and easily accessible. This is why allowing an employee to present a breach of contract claim to a tribunal is likely to encourage an increase in such claims. But, even prior to the introduction of the new system, employees pursued the old common law remedy in a number of cases and for a variety of reasons:

1. where the maximum compensatory award for unfair dismissal (see section 24.4 The compensatory award p237) would not cover the loss of a highly-paid employee for his contractual notice period;

2. because costs are seldom awarded against the employer by a tribunal (see section 25.10 Costs p256), whereas costs are quite likely to be awarded against an employer who unsuccessfully defends a wrongful dismissal claim.

3. because no deduction will be made in an award for wrongful dismissal if the employee has contributed by his own fault to his dismissal;

4. because legal aid is not available for an industrial tribunal hearing but may be for a case in the civil courts;

5. where the employee cannot bring an unfair dismissal claim, for example, because he has insufficient continuous service or is over the normal retiring age.

6. where the dismissal was clearly fair.

Where both an unfair dismissal and a wrongful dismissal claim are made, the tribunal may exercise its discretion to postpone an unfair dismissal hearing pending the outcome of the wrongful dismissal case in the County Court or High Court if, for example, there are complex issues common to both proceedings. Almost always in practice, however, an employee presents his unfair dismissal claim first because of the much shorter time limit on instituting proceedings.

6.8 The Wages Act

The Wages Act 1986 entitles workers to complain to an industrial tribunal if an unlawful deduction is made from their wages. The rules are summarised in section 15.4 Claiming money from an employee p171. There has been an enormous upsurge in the number of Wages Act claims, partly because some employees and their advisers see the 1986 Act as offering a means of bringing what is, in effect, a wrongful dismissal action in the industrial tribunal via the 'back door'. At the time of writing, different divisions of the EAT had expressed conflicting views as to whether or not non-payment of wages in lieu of notice constitutes a deduction from wages, thus enabling a worker to present a claim to a tribunal, and clarification from the higher courts is needed.

A cynic might even wonder whether it is this trend which prompted the government announcement with regard to extending tribunals' jurisdiction, as outlined in section 6.1 Claims for breach of contract – Introduction p66. Be that as it may, the new regime – when it is introduced – may in practice lead to fewer claims being brought under the 1986 Act.

6.9   Claims against incompetent employees

Occasionally an employer may wish to claim that a negligent employee's incompetence has amounted to a breach of contract and to sue for damages for any loss occasioned thereby. This possibility is discussed in section 15.4 Claiming money from an employee p171.

6.10   Claims for breach of a restrictive covenant

An employer who feels that a dismissed employee is about to compete unfairly and unlawfully with his business may wish to seek redress in the form of damages or – more urgently and sometimes more importantly – an injunction. The increasing fierceness of commercial competition probably explains why this has been a growth area for litigation in recent years.

A detailed analysis of the law in this area cannot be provided here. Briefly, an employer who has clear grounds for believing that an ex-employee intends to use or disclose a trade secret which he obtained through his old job may be able to obtain an injunction to prevent this. Yet in practice it is usually difficult to judge what kind of business information will be protected by the courts, especially if there has been no breach of an express contractual duty of confidentiality. The Court of Appeal suggested useful

75

guidelines in this area in *Faccenda Chicken Ltd v. Fowler* (1986), where relevant factors were said to include the nature of the job and the information. However, even that was a case in which the employers' claim for an injunction against a former salesman who set up in competition proved unsuccessful. In *Johnson & Bloy (Holdings) Ltd v. Wolstenholme Rink plc and Fallon* (1987), however, the Court of Appeal did grant an injunction to restrain an ex-employee from using or disclosing confidential information contained in documents he had removed from his old company.

A wise employer will ensure that key executives are bound by suitably worded covenants in their contracts which restrict them from certain competitive activities for a period of time after the end of their employment. An employee who refuses to agree to such covenants may be fairly dismissed, even if the covenants did not form part of his original contract; see Dismissal for refusal to agree to a change p208.

A restrictive covenant is, however, *prima facie* unenforceable at common law. For it to be enforceable, the clause must:

1. be reasonable as between the parties;

2. be reasonable when the public interest is taken into account; and

3. go no further than is reasonable for the protection of the company's legitimate business interests.

Thus restrictions often contain limits on freedom to compete within a particular geographical area and a particular period of time.

Many reported cases show how the courts have reviewed the reasonableness or otherwise of particular covenants. An employer who wrongfully dismisses an employee may, however, find that a court then refuses to allow him to enforce a restrictive covenant which he hoped would be binding upon that employee.

Thus in *Briggs v. Oates* (1990), the High Court ruled that an employer's breach of contract in dismissing a solicitor put an end to that contract – including the obligations of the solicitor under his contract not to compete with his ex-employer within a five-mile radius.

7
The Meaning of Redundancy

7.1 Introduction

Redundancy law is complex. Although it has become increasingly familiar during periods of economic recession, it still gives rise to many headaches for employers, employees and their advisers.

The law is set out in Part VI of the Employment Protection (Consolidation) Act 1978, supplemented by some unrepealed parts of the Employment Protection Act 1975. Three areas have to be considered:

1. redundancy payments;

2. redundancy consultation and notification provisions;

3. unfair dismissal by reason of redundancy.

In order to understand the relevant principles, the meaning of 'dismissal by reason of redundancy' must first be understood. Unfortunately, the concept of redundancy is easily misinterpreted.

A voluntary redundancy, in the sense in which that phrase is usually understood, will amount to a dismissal, because it is not a termination by mutual consent but rather an agreement that the employer will dismiss: *Burton Allton & Johnson Ltd v. Peck* (1975).

There is a difference between voluntary redundancy in that context and the position where an employee applies to retire under an early retirement scheme and his application is accepted. In the latter case, where there is no compulsion, the employment comes to an end by mutual agreement and there is no dismissal; see section 3.5 Mutual consent p37.

7.2   The statutory definition

Redundancy is defined in section 81(2) of the 1978 Act. It covers a dismissal attributable wholly or mainly to:

1.   a) the fact that the employer has ceased, or intends to cease, to carry on the business for the purposes of which the employee was employed by him; or
    b) the fact that he has ceased, or intends to cease, to carry on that business in the place where the employee was so employed; or

2. the fact that the requirements of the business for employees to carry out work of a particular kind, or for employees to carry out work of a particular kind in the place where the dismissed employee was so employed, have ceased or diminished or are expected to cease or diminish.

For the purposes of this definition, the employer's business and that of any associated employer are to be treated as one, unless redundancy would be established without including the other business(es). If, therefore, the employer's business is expanding, but an associated employer's business is contracting, and a long-serving employee of the associated employer is transferred to work for the employer, resulting in the dismissal of one of the employer's own employees, that may constitute redundancy. This is so even if there is no cessation or diminution of the employer's business as such.

Cases which do not fall within the statutory definition do not amount to redundancy. The commonly-used phrase 'redundancy situation' does not appear in the legislation. Although it is convenient shorthand, care must be taken when using the phrase, as it is easy to lose sight of the precise legal position.

An intriguing example of a non-redundancy reason for dismissal occurred in *Vaux and Associated Breweries Ltd v. Ward* (1968). The Divisional Court held that to replace a 57-year-old barmaid with a 'bunny-girl' doing essentially the same job (whether or not in a more glamorous manner) was not to make the barmaid redundant. Several more prosaic situations which do not amount in law to redundancy are discussed in section 7.6 Non-redundancy dismissals p83.

7.3   Cessation of business

The position in the case of a cessation, or intended cessation, of the business is quite straightforward. However, where the reason for the cessation is that the employer has transferred his undertaking to another, then there may be no dismissal because of the operation of the Transfer of Undertakings (Protection of Employment) Regulations 1981; see Chapter 20.

7.4   Moving the place of business

Where the place of employment is moved, the terms of the employee's contract will be important. An employer may, in accordance with the contract, require the employee to transfer to another of his places of business. If so, the mere closing of the place where the employee actually worked will not in itself give rise to redundancy.

On the other hand, if there is no express or implied provision in the contract requiring the employee to be mobile and if the employer is ceasing business at every place where the employee could be required to work, the employee will be redundant. The value of anticipating such matters well in advance, when drafting the contract, is clear.

7.5   Reduction in work

Work of a particular kind

Dismissals arising from a reduction in work may cause a number of difficulties. People used to think that there was redundancy where the employer's business no longer required the same number of employees. In the light of the decision of the EAT and the Court of Appeal in *Cowen v. Haden Carrier Ltd* (1982), it seems that the position is more complicated than was originally thought.

The facts of the case were quite simple. The employee was promoted from the position of regional surveyor to divisional contracts surveyor. Later, the company found it necessary to reduce the number of staff employed. The employee was not willing to accept demotion and was dismissed. The employee argued that he was not redundant, because there was other work available within the terms of his contract of employment. Before the EAT, his argument succeeded. The EAT said that it is not sufficient, in order to establish redundancy, to show merely that the employer's requirement for employees to carry out work of a kind in which the dismissed employee was actually engaged has ceased or diminished. It is necessary to show such diminution or cessation in relation to *any* work that he could have been required to do under the terms of his contract. The EAT was clearly reluctant to reach this conclusion, saying that, in the experience of the members deciding the case, in practice a redundancy 'is accepted as having been shown where it is demonstrated that the actual job which the claimant was carrying out has ceased to exist'.

The Court of Appeal overruled the decision of the EAT on the facts but did not overrule the EAT's interpretation of the law. That view of the law has been criticised by a number of commentators but has nevertheless been followed in subsequent cases. It is not therefore enough to examine merely whether the same number of employees is still needed to carry out the work which an allegedly redundant employee was actually carrying out. Instead, it is necessary to look at whether there is a reduction in the requirement for an employee to perform the particular kind of work which he could be obliged to perform under the terms of his employment contract. In practice, this may create complications for the employer who drafts his contracts – and in particular the clauses relating to job duties – in broad terms.

'Bumping'

'Bumping' – sometimes referred to as 'transferred' or 'translated' redundancy – is a well-recognised industrial practice. 'Bumping' takes place when an employee's work disappears, but he is retained and another employee is dismissed instead.

If an employer's business is expanding, but an associated employer's business is contracting and a long-serving employee of the associated employer is transferred to work for the employer, resulting in the dismissal of one of the employer's own employees, that dismissal may be by reason of redundancy. This is so, even if there is no cessation or diminution of the employer's business as such. The practice of 'bumping' has survived the decision of the EAT in *Cowen v. Haden Carrier Ltd* (see above), although the EAT acknowledged that its decision to apply the 'contractual' test of redundancy could render very difficult any case based on 'bumping'.

In *Babar Indian Restaurant v. Rawat* (1985), an employee who worked in a restaurant owned by two partners was dismissed to make room for an employee who worked for a separate business owned by the two partners. The EAT took the view that the scope and extent of the business in which a redundant employee has been employed is a question of fact. In some cases, partners who operate more than one enterprise may be regarded, for redundancy purposes, as operating a single business. In other cases, such as where the work done in each enterprise is dissimilar and there is little or no interchangeability between members of the staff of each enterprise, the two businesses may be regarded as separate.

On the facts, this dismissal fell within the latter category and therefore the reason for dismissal was not redundancy. The EAT added that even where there was an overall redundancy situation so that 'bumping' could amount to redundancy, the handling of the dismissal must nevertheless be reasonable within the terms of section 57(3) of the 1978 Act; see Chapter 13.

Reorganisational redundancy

It was long thought that a mere redistribution of duties without any reduction in the number of employees required or the amount of work to be done did not amount to redundancy. A different view was adopted by the Court of Appeal in *Murphy v. Epsom College* (1984). The college employed one plumber and then took on the applicant as a second plumber. Part of his job was to work on the college's heating system and some of his work was of a kind more normally associated with a heating engineer than with a plumber. Initially, he carried out those wider duties, but following a dispute with the college, he declined to do anything but plumbing unless properly supervised. The college then reviewed its requirements and decided to appoint a heating engineer who would also do some general plumbing work and to make the applicant redundant.

The EAT held that there can be redundancy as a result of reorganisation which does not give rise to a reduction in work, in other words, where the overall number of employees in the business doing work of a particular kind is not reduced. The EAT gave the example of implementing new technology which requires the recruitment of an employee with a new skill. His job might necessarily include some or all of the functions formerly performed by existing employees. If, in consequence, the employer no longer requires the services of the employee(s) who formerly carried out those functions, the EAT said that dismissal might be by reason of redundancy.

This approach represents a development of the law which is interesting and potentially far reaching. Subsequently, however, the Court of Appeal adopted more conventional reasoning in upholding the dismissal. It held that as a heating engineer is a different kind of tradesman from a plumber, the college's requirements for plumbers had reduced from two to one. The dismissal was therefore properly categorised as a redundancy, even though

1. the dismissed plumber had carried out some duties of a kind more normally associated with a heating engineer;

2. the heating engineer would also do some general plumbing work; and

3. the overall number of employees employed did not change.

Spreading or sub-contracting the work

There may be a redundancy situation even where the requirements of the business for work of the particular kind remains the same. This will be the case if the same work is done by fewer employees, or by no employees at all.

Thus, as part of a cost-cutting exercise, an employer may simply ask some of the existing employees doing a particular job to absorb the work of colleagues who are then no longer required and are consequently made redundant. This happened in *Carryall Motors Ltd v. Pennington* (1980), where the company merged the posts of transport clerk and depot manager because the depot was thought to be over-staffed. The transport clerk was dismissed and the EAT accepted that the reason for dismissal was redundancy; although the output was the same, the company needed fewer employees to achieve it.

A popular means of saving costs is to reduce the workforce and hire independent sub-contractors to perform the same duties. In the typical case of *Bromby and Hoare Ltd v. Evans* (1972), a firm of builders decided that it was more effective and economical to use self-employed tradesmen than employees. The company therefore dismissed the last two directly employed decorators and it was held that they were entitled to redundancy payments, as their employer's requirements for employees to carry out decorating work had ceased.

7.6   Non-redundancy dismissals

Up-grading and new technology

By no means every dismissal occasioned by business reorganisation is due to redundancy. An employer may upgrade the requirements of a job or introduce new technology and, in the course of time, dismiss those employees who cannot meet the new standard. Such dismissals are only likely to be classified as being caused by redundancy if the changes were such as to transform the work, so that it became so different that it no longer fell within the scope of the employee's contractual duties.

Even if there is no redundancy situation, an employer in such circumstances may be able to show both that the dismissal was for a potentially fair reason and that it was fairly handled. Frequently, a dismissal can be categorised as being for 'some other substantial reason of a kind such as to justify the dismissal of an employee holding the position which that employee held' under section 57(1)(b) of the 1978 Act; see Chapter 21. The question will then be whether the handling of the dismissal was fair in all circumstances.

Changing the contract terms

While unilaterally changing an employee's terms of employment may amount to constructive dismissal, the reason for that dismissal will not necessarily be redundancy. This is the case even if the reason for imposing the change is a decline in the fortunes of a business.

This principle emerges from the case of *Chapman and Goonvean v. Rostowrack China Clay Co Ltd* (1973). The employers provided a free bus service to employees who lived far away from the works but, as more local labour was recruited, it became uneconomic to maintain the bus service and it was terminated. Those employees who could no longer get to work left, claiming that they had been constructively dismissed by reason of redundancy. The Court of Appeal took the view that the dismissal occurred as a result of the employer's desire to run the business cost-effectively, and not because of a reduction in the number of employees needed to carry out a particular function.

A similar approach was adopted by the Court of Appeal in *Johnson v. Nottinghamshire Combined Police Authority* (1974). Two telephonists were dismissed after refusing to change from normal office hours for five days a week to working either an early or late shift six days a week. Their redundancy payment claims failed because the dismissals arose, not from a reduced requirement for telephonists, but from a desire to improve efficiency through reorganisation.

Again, in *Lesney Products & Co Ltd v. Nolan* (1977), the Court of Appeal held that a group of machine setters who were required to work a double day shift system rather than a conventional day shift plus overtime were not redundant. The employers successfully argued that the change was made in order to reduce costly overtime, rather than because there was a reduction in the requirement for employees setting up the machines. It was also significant that those who left or were dismissed were replaced by new recruits.

Employers should not read into these cases a general principle that a change in hours worked cannot ever amount to a change in the kind of work being done. In *Macfisheries Ltd v. Findlay* (1985), a night shift worker refused to transfer to day working. His contract did not oblige him to work on the day shift if required, but there was no evidence to show that day work would differ from night work. The industrial tribunal found that night work was 'work of a particular kind', which had disappeared, so there was a redundancy. The EAT accepted that the tribunal would have been wrong to think that work done by night was in itself work of a particular kind – this would be inconsistent with the *Johnson* decision – yet the EAT did not accept that the tribunal had made such an error. It was equally possible that the tribunal had considered other factors such as the actual content of the different shifts.

Expiry of fixed term coupled with replacement

Where an employee's fixed-term contract comes to an end and is not renewed, the reason for dismissal may be redundancy.

However, if the employee is replaced by another employee – say, of a lower grade and commanding less pay – there is unlikely to be a redundancy.

An interesting example of the way in which the law operates is provided by *North Yorkshire County Council v. Fay* (1985). An English teacher in a comprehensive school claimed that she had been unfairly made redundant when her fixed-term contract was not renewed. One factor which led her to believe that she was redundant was that, during the currency of her contract, a teacher was transferred to her department from another school in the area which was understaffed.

The Court of Appeal decided that the industrial tribunal had been entitled to hold on the evidence that the teacher was not dismissed on grounds of redundancy. There was no suggestion that within the school where she worked there was a reduction in the requirement for English teachers. Nor was there any evidence to show that the local authority's wider requirements for English teachers had diminished. Nor was this a case of an employee who had lost her job directly because of 'bumping'. All that she lost because of the arrival of the other teacher was the chance of applying for, and getting, that particular job. That was not the cause of her dismissal.

Thus the outcome differed from that in *Lee v. Nottinghamshire County Council* (1980), where a college lecturer was taken on for two years to fill a vacancy which had arisen while the college was in the process of being run down prior to closure. The employer's argument that the dismissal was not due to any reduction of demand for employees, apart from that which had been anticipated at the outset of the contract, was rejected. Failure to renew a contract will give rise to redundancy where the statutory definition is satisfied, even though this can be foreseen at the outset. An employer who finds this prospect unsatisfactory should consider including in the fixed-term contract a clause excluding the employee's statutory rights; see section 23.2 Fixed-term contracts p229.

7.7 Business transfers

For some time it was suggested that when an employee is dismissed as a consequence of a business transfer to which the Transfer of

Undertakings (Protection of Employment) Regulations 1981 apply (see Chapter 20), the reason for dismissal is no longer that of redundancy, as had been the case prior to the introduction of the 1981 Regulations.

Obscure as the 1981 Regulations were, it seemed strange that a measure designed to increase employee protection should to some extent reduce it. Fortunately, the forced interpretation which gave rise to that conclusion has now been rejected by the EAT. In *Gorictree Ltd v. Jenkinson* (1984), it was held that a dismissal may be on the grounds of redundancy where it falls within reg 8(2), which provides:

> 'Where an economic, technical or organisational reason entailing changes in the workforce of either a transferor or a transferee before or after a relevant transfer is the reason or principal reason for dismissing an employee . . . the dismissal shall . . . be regarded as having been for a substantial reason of a kind such as to justify the dismissal of an employee holding the position which that employee held.'

The EAT pointed out that redundancy is one of the most common of the 'economic, technical or organisational reasons entailing changes in the workforce' to which reg 8(2) applies. Where a potentially fair reason for dismissal exists, the tribunal will then consider the question of whether the dismissal was fair.

8
Redundancy Payments

8.1 Introduction

The right of an employee to a statutory redundancy payment was introduced in 1965. The intention was to reduce resistance to business reorganisation and to facilitate mobility of labour by compensating people for loss of job security.

An employee is entitled by law to a redundancy payment in two different sets of circumstances. In the typical case, the employee must be dismissed by reason of redundancy; see section 7.2 The statutory definition p77. Alternatively, an employee may become entitled to statutory redundancy payment if laid off or kept on short time to the extent specified in the legislation; see section 8.4 Lay-off and short time p92.

If the employer contests the employee's right to a statutory payment and the matter reaches an industrial tribunal, then once the employee has established that he was dismissed, there is a presumption that the dismissal was for redundancy. A claim for a redundancy payment can be combined with a complaint of unfair dismissal, but the time limits for making the two claims differ.

Statutory redundancy payments are calculated in accordance with the formula explained in section 8.6 Calculating redundancy payments p95. An employer may, of course, enter into a voluntary agreement with employees to pay a sum in excess of the statutory figure in the event of redundancy.

8.2 Excluded categories

The following employees are not entitled to a statutory redundancy payment:

- employees who do not have two years' continuous employment;

- employees who are below the age of 20 at the date of dismissal, ie because the two-year qualifying period excludes service prior to the age of 18;

- employees who at the date of dismissal have reached 'normal retiring age' (see section 10.4 Normal retiring age p111), if that age is less than 65, or in any other case the age of 65;

- Crown servants;

- registered dock workers;

- share fishermen;

- the spouse of a sole employer;

- domestic servants in a private household who are close relatives of the employer;

- employees who are outside Great Britain on termination of employment unless under the contract they ordinarily work in Great Britain;

- employees who ordinarily work outside Great Britain unless on termination they are in Great Britain on their employers' instructions;

- employees with overseas governments.

In addition certain office holders who are not, strictly speaking, employees are nevertheless entitled to a redundancy payment.

An employee can contract out of his right to a redundancy payment in certain circumstances, which differ slightly from the contracting-out provisions in unfair dismissal law; see section 23.2 Fixed-term contracts p229. He may lose his right to a payment if an offer of alternative employment is made (see section 8.3 Offer of alternative employment p89), if dismissed for misconduct (see section 8.5 Dismissal for misconduct after redundancy p95), or if, subject to very stringent conditions set out in the Redundancy Payment Pensions Regulations 1965, he is paid a pension instead.

8.3   Offer of alternative employment

The offer

An employer may offer either to renew the contract of a redundant employee or to give him alternative employment. In certain circumstances, such an offer will bar the employee's right to redundancy payment. The key rules are in sections 82 and 84 of the 1978 Act.

If the employee refuses an offer of alternative employment (which need not be made in writing), he will not be entitled to redundancy payment by reason of his dismissal if:

1. the offer was made before the ending of the original employment; and

2. the new contract was to take effect either immediately on the ending of the original employment or within four weeks thereafter; and

3. the employee's refusal was unreasonable; and

4. either:
    a) the provisions of the contract as renewed, or of the new contract, as to the capacity and place in which he would be employed, and as to the other terms and conditions of his employment, would not differ from the corresponding provisions of the previous contract; or
    b) the first-mentioned provisions would differ (wholly or in part) from those corresponding provisions, but the offer constituted an offer of suitable employment in relation to the employee.

If an employer wishes to contest liability to make a redundancy payment because an offer of alternative employment has been made, the onus is on him to satisfy those four conditions. The conditions may be satisfied even if the alternative employment offered is with an associated employer.

Whether the offer of employment is 'suitable' is an objective matter. Relevant factors in determining suitability will vary from case to case but may include:

- the nature of the job;
- its pay and benefits;
- the new place of work;
- the status of the job.

Whether a refusal is 'unreasonable' is a subjective matter, concerning reasons which may be personal to the employee, but similar factors may again be relevant. It may, for instance, be reasonable for an employee who genuinely believes he cannot do the new work to a satisfactory standard to refuse: *Spencer & Griffin v. Gloucestershire County Council* (1985).

Acceptance of offer on the same terms

If an employee accepts the offer of a new job on the same terms as the original job, then:

1. he is regarded as not having been dismissed at all;

2. there is no trial period (see Acceptance of offer on different terms (below));

3. he is not entitled to a redundancy payment;

4. he has continuity of employment throughout the period of the original job and the new job.

Acceptance of offer on different terms

If an employee accepts the offer of a new job on terms different from those of the original job, then the legislation provides for a trial period in relation to the renewed contract.

The trial period comes into effect automatically. It will normally be for four consecutive calendar weeks from the time when the employee starts to work under the new contract. The four-week period cannot be reduced, but it can be extended for the specific purpose of retraining the employee for new work, provided that any agreement to do so

1. is made before the employee starts work under the new contract;

2. is in writing;

3. specifies the date of the end of the trial period; and

4. specifies the terms and conditions of employment which will apply as at the end of that period.

If, during the trial period, the employee terminates the contract for any reason, then he will be treated as having been dismissed on the date on which his original employment ended and his entitlement to a redundancy payment will depend on the factors referred to in Acceptance of offer on the same terms p90.

If the employer dismisses the employee during the trial period, then the question is whether the dismissal is for a reason connected with or arising out of the changed terms of employment. If so, the employee is again treated as having been dismissed on termination of the original job and his entitlement to a redundancy payment will be dealt with as above. If not, that is a different matter, and the dismissal will be considered by an industrial tribunal on its merits.

The six-month time limit referred to in section 8.7 Industrial tribunal claims p97 for making a claim to an industrial tribunal will run from the date of the termination of the trial period rather than from the date of the termination of the original job.

The common law position

The statutory trial period concept fits uneasily with the principle that, under the common law, an employee whose terms of employment are changed has in any event a reasonable period in which to decide whether or not to accept those terms.

The position under the common law was summarised by the EAT in *Turvey and Others v. CW Cheyney & Sons Ltd* (1979), as follows:

1. if an employee is expressly dismissed, or his fixed-term contract expires without being renewed, and his employer offers him a new job, he will be entitled only to the statutory trial period commencing on the date he starts the new job;

2. if he is not formally dismissed, but simply told that his job is coming to an end and asked to undertake different work, then:
   a) if he agrees to do the new work, he will only be entitled to the statutory period;

b) if he agrees to do the new work on a trial basis for a specified time, he has that specified trial period under the common law and then, if he accepts a new job, the statutory trial period commences;

c) if he merely starts working under the new terms with no indication that he accepts or rejects them, he will have a reasonable time to accept the job either expressly or by implication, following which he will then have the statutory trial period in addition.

8.4   Lay-off and short time

Lay-off

The term 'lay-off' is often used vaguely and confusingly. In colloquial usage, it can mean either dismissal or a mere failure to provide paid work under the contract of employment.

Where a lay-off is in fact a dismissal, an employee is entitled to a redundancy payment if he satisfies the various qualifying conditions. An unfair dismissal claim may also be possible.

Where there is no express dismissal, the question is whether the terms of the contract entitle the employer to lay the employee off. If the employer is acting in breach of the terms of the contract, the employee will be able to claim that he has been constructively dismissed and is therefore entitled to a redundancy payment, and possibly that his dismissal was unfair.

Where the employer is acting in accordance with the terms of the contract, the employee may nevertheless be entitled to a statutory redundancy payment if the provisions of section 87(1) of the 1978 Act are satisfied, in other words, if:

1. the contract gives the employer an express or implied power to lay off the employee without pay; and

2. the employee has been laid off under such power and has not been paid; and

3. the employee is not being laid off under a guaranteed week agreement and receiving his full weekly wage under that agreement.

Short time

If an employer does not employ and pay an employee for his normal working week under the terms of the contract, the first question is again whether this is permitted by the terms of the contract. If not, the employee will be able to claim that he has been constructively dismissed and that he is entitled to a redundancy payment, and perhaps that he has been unfairly dismissed. If short time is permitted by the contract, the employee can make no complaint, unless the statutory provisions in relation to short time apply.

Short time for redundancy payment purposes is set out in section 87(2) of the 1978 Act as occurring where:

1. the contract gives the employer an express or implied power to reduce the employee's working week; and

2. there is a diminution of work; and

3. the employee's earnings drop to less than half a week's pay.

The rules for calculating half a week's pay for these purposes are set out in section 22.5 A week's pay p226.

Right to redundancy payment

An employee who wishes to claim a redundancy payment in respect of lay-off or short time must give notice in writing to his employer of his intention to do so. Section 88 of the 1978 Act provides that he must also satisfy the following conditions:

1. he must have been laid off or kept on short time *either* for at least four consecutive weeks (ending with the date of the notice or not more than four weeks before that date), *or* for a series of at least six weeks (of which not more than three were consecutive) within a period of 13 weeks (the last of the six weeks ending as provided above). No account is taken of any week where the lay-off or short time is wholly or mainly due to a strike or lock-out;

2. he must give the required notice of intention to claim no earlier than the last of the four or six weeks referred to above, but not later than four weeks from the last day of either of those periods;

3. he must terminate his contract by giving one week's notice (or such other minimum period of notice as may be required by his

contract). The notice need not be given at the same time as the notice of intention to claim and a longer period is allowed if the employer serves a counter-notice: see The employer's counter-notice (below).

If the employee is in fact dismissed, he will not be entitled to a redundancy payment pursuant to his giving notice of intention to claim. This will not, however, prejudice his right to claim a redundancy payment in the normal way by reason of his dismissal.

The employer's counter-notice

If the employee takes the steps set out above and satisfies all the qualifying conditions, he will be entitled to a redundancy payment, unless the employer gives a counter-notice within seven days of receiving the claim, indicating that he will contest that claim.

The defence open to the employer is to show that 'it was reasonably to be expected that the employee (if he continued to be employed by the same employer) would, not later than four weeks after' the date of service of the notice of intention to claim 'enter upon a period of employment of not less than 13 weeks during which he would not be laid off or kept on short time for any week'.

Although the counter-notice need not specify the work offered, it is desirable for it to do so. The intention to contest liability for redundancy payment must also be made clear.

If the matter reaches an industrial tribunal, the employer has to establish the reasonableness of his expectation of an end to the lay-off or short time. Much will depend upon the available evidence, but if the employee remained laid off on short time for the whole four-week period, the industrial tribunal is bound to find in favour of the employee. The employer need not, however, establish an expectation that the employee will return to full-time work. It is enough if the employee is restored to a position where he receives more than half a week's pay.

If the matter reaches a tribunal, and the employer has given a counter-notice, the employee does not have to give the required notice to terminate the contract immediately, although he can do so. He must, in any event, give such notice within three weeks of the tribunal notifying him of its decision.

Similarly, if the employer serves a counter-notice and then

withdraws it by subsequent notice in writing, the employee (who will then be automatically entitled to a redundancy payment) must give notice to terminate not less than three weeks after the service of the notice of withdrawal.

8.5 Dismissal for misconduct after redundancy

Sometimes, after an employee has been given notice of dismissal by reason of redundancy, his employment will be terminated because of his misconduct, such as theft or violence. In such a case, section 92(5) of the 1978 Act enables a tribunal to award the employee either the whole or such part of any redundancy payment as the tribunal considers 'just and equitable'. This provision does not apply where the dismissal is for taking part in a strike.

In *Lignacite Products Ltd v. Krollman* (1979), a man of 24 years' service who was summarily dismissed for stealing from the company while under notice was awarded 60 per cent of his redundancy payment entitlement. The EAT thought the figure high, but refused to interfere with the tribunal's exercise of its discretion.

8.6 Calculating redundancy payments

The amount of a statutory redundancy payment (see Appendix D for a convenient 'ready reckoner') is calculated as follows:

1. for each year of employment between the ages of 18 and 21 – half a week's pay;

2. for each year of employment between the ages of 22 and 40 – one week's pay;

3. for each year of employment between the ages of 41 and either the normal retiring age (if it is less than 65) or in any other case the age of 65 – one and a half week's pay;

4. employment for longer than 20 years is not taken into account;

5. the maximum amount of a week's pay taken into account was £184.00 per week at 1 April 1990, but this maximum figure is reviewed from time to time and the amounts currently applicable should be checked with the Department of Employment;

6. in the year before the employee's 65th birthday various provisions scale down the payment on a monthly basis; the amount is reduced by one-twelfth for each month by which his age approaches 65. These tapering provisions do not apply if the normal retiring age is 64 or lower;

7. no deduction is made for tax.

The relevant date for calculating an employee's pay is normally the date on which the employment would have terminated had proper notice been given under the 1978 Act, whether or not such notice was given. In effect, therefore, the redundancy payment is based on final earnings.

A week's pay is calculated in accordance with the rules summarised in section 22.5 A week's pay p226. Only pay to which the employee is contractually entitled will be taken into account. Thus, whether or not the following form part of the week's pay will depend upon the express and implied terms of the contract:

- overtime pay;

- bonuses;

- commission;

- tips and gratuities.

Expenses will not be taken into account unless they represent a profit to the employee. Payments in kind, such as a company car or free accommodation, are not taken into account.

The employer must give a written statement to the employee when making a redundancy payment, showing how the amount is calculated, unless the amount of the payment has already been fixed by the decision of the tribunal. Failure to give such a statement without reasonable excuse is a criminal offence.

If an employee is not given a statement, he may by right demand one by a specified date, giving the employer at least one week. If the employer fails to comply without reasonable excuse, that is a further criminal offence.

There is also a risk that, if the employer fails to give a written statement, any payment he makes to the employee may not be treated as being in discharge of the redundancy payment.

For many years it was possible for employers to claim rebates on redundancy payments made, but the Government has now set its face against subsidising job cuts and the rebate scheme has been abolished.

8.7   Industrial tribunal claims

A question as to whether an employee is entitled to statutory redundancy payment may be referred to an industrial tribunal. If it is established that the employee has in fact been dismissed, the 1978 Act raises a presumption that he was redundant.

Broadly speaking, there is a time limit of six months from the date of dismissal for making application to a tribunal. More specifically, an employee shall not be entitled to redundancy payment unless within six months from the date of the dismissal, one of the following events has occurred:

1. the payment has been agreed and paid;

2. the employee has made a claim for the payment by notice in writing to the employer;

3. the matter has been referred to an industrial tribunal under the 1978 Act;

4. an unfair dismissal application has been lodged with the tribunal.

The six-month time limit can be extended. A tribunal can deal with an application during a further six-month period if it appears to be 'just and equitable' that the employee should receive a redundancy payment. This decision is made with regard to his reasons for failing to take the necessary steps within the original six-month period, and all the other relevant circumstances.

9
Handling
Redundancies

9.1 Introduction

An employer who contemplates declaring redundancies should be fully aware of his duties of consultation and notification. Lack of consultation is one of the grounds upon which an industrial tribunal may regard a redundancy dismissal as unfair under the 1978 Act. Detailed guidance on this important area is given in Chapter 13.

In addition, the Employment Act 1975 ('the 1975 Act') imposes a duty to consult representatives of recognised trade unions about redundancy proposals, even where only a single employee is involved. The sanction for breach of that duty is called a 'protective award'. The 1975 Act also requires an employer to notify the Secretary of State if he plans to make ten or more employees redundant at one establishment within a specified period. The relevant provisions are contained in sections 99–107 of the 1975 Act.

The statutory duty to consult arises:

1. where the employer proposes to dismiss an employee as redundant; and

2. where he recognises an independent trade union as representing employees of that description.

The obligation arises even if none of the employees who are to go are union members. In this area, the law regards the recognised union as the exclusive representative of employees in respect of whom it is recognised.

9.2 Excluded categories

The obligation to consult and notify does not apply to the following classes of employment:

- certain categories of seamen;

- employment ordinarily involving work outside Great Britain;

- certain short-term workers;

- Crown servants and police service workers.

9.3 When is a trade union 'recognised'?

An employer need not consult representatives of a trade union which is not independent or which he does not recognise. A union is independent if it is not dominated, controlled or liable to undue influence by the employer.

'Recognition' in this context means recognition to any extent for the purposes of collective bargaining. 'Collective bargaining' is defined in the Trade Union and Labour Relations Act 1974 as meaning negotiations about:

1. terms and conditions of employment, or the physical conditions in which any workers are required to work;

2. engagement or non-engagement, or termination or suspension of employment or the duties of employment, of one or more workers;

3. allocation of work or the duties of employment as between workers or groups of workers;

4. matters of discipline;

5. the membership or non-membership of a trade union on the part of a worker;

6. facilities for officials of trade unions;

7. machinery for negotiation or consultation, and other procedures, relating to any of the foregoing matters, including the recognition by employers or employers' associations of the right of a trade union to

represent workers in any such negotiation or consultation or in the carrying out of such procedures.

In other words, a union may be recognised even if the employer does not formally acknowledge it. There will be recognition where the employer accepts that he is expected to *negotiate* with the union about any of the relevant items as a matter of course.

Recognition may therefore be implied by conduct. In practice this will usually involve a course of dealings between the employer and the union over a period of time.

Each case of alleged recognition by conduct will depend upon its precise facts. However, it is worth noting the decision of the Court of Appeal in *NUGSAT v. Albury Brothers Ltd* (1979) – that a limited amount of correspondence and exploratory discussions between the trade union representative and the employer did not constitute 'recognition'. This was despite the fact that the employers' national association had concluded a collective agreement with the trade unions.

9.4 Obligation to consult

The obligation to consult does not arise where one or more redundancies are contemplated as a mere possibility. Practical difficulties are most likely to arise where an employer is undertaking work or a contract of limited duration. In the building and construction industry, to take a classic example, there will come a time when the end of the work will be in sight, even if it was not in sight at the outset. The precise date when the work will end may not be predictable and the contractor may need to phase out his workforce over a period of time. It has been suggested that the obligation to consult arises when the employer becomes aware that the next move will be a reduction, and not an increase, in the number of men employed. A more satisfactory generalisation is that an employer 'proposes to dismiss as redundant' when he has come to a considered decision that a redundancy dismissal or dismissals are inevitable in the foreseeable and reasonably near future. This is the case even though an exact final date and an exact final number cannot be determined with certainty at the time.

Consultation must be with the recognised unions' representatives. A 'representative' is a person authorised by the union to negotiate with the employer. In practice, this will mean the shop steward, the district union official or even, in some cases, a regional or national official.

The employer must disclose *in writing* to the union representatives the following details:

1. his reasons for the proposed redundancies;

2. the descriptions of the employees he proposes to dismiss and the numbers involved;

3. the total number of employees of each such description employed at the establishment in question;

4. the proposed method of selection for dismissal;

5. the proposed method of carrying out the dismissals with due regard to any agreed procedure, including the period over which the dismissals are to take effect.

In due course, the employer has to consider any representations made to him by the union representatives and to give reasons if he rejects any of those representations. That is all. The employer is under no obligation to negotiate or reach agreement with the union.

9.5 Special circumstances

An employer who is in breach of his duty to consult may have a defence if there are 'special circumstances' which render it 'not reasonably practicable' for him to comply with the statutory requirements. In such a case, he must take whatever steps *are* reasonably practicable.

There is no statutory definition of 'special circumstances'. As so often, much will turn on the precise facts of each case. While this allows tribunals considerable discretion, it also means that employers lack much-needed authoritative guidance as to their position.

The problems are demonstrated by the decision of the Court of Appeal in *Clarks of Hove Ltd v. Bakers' Union* (1978), that 'special' must mean something out of the ordinary, something uncommon. The onus is on the employer to show the existence of such special circumstances in his particular case.

Insolvency is not necessarily a special circumstance, although it may be in the case of a sudden disaster. However, if there is a gradual rundown of the business, known to the directors, which eventually leads to insolvency, the company may have no defence against a failure to consult.

Unfortunately, it is sometimes difficult in practice for an employer faced with serious financial difficulties to comply with the statutory obligations. If he does comply, his plight may become known to creditors, bankers, customers, and so on, from whom he is trying, quite properly, to raise further finance in order to save the business. In some cases it can therefore be argued that complying with the law may even bring about premature redundancies or redundancies which might otherwise not have occurred.

9.6 Timing of consultation

The cardinal principle is that consultation must begin 'at the earliest opportunity'. Quite apart from this, there are a number of specific provisions applicable to larger-scale redundancies. These are minimum requirements which do not detract from the overriding duty to consult at the earliest opportunity.

When it is proposed to dismiss at one establishment:

1. 100 or more employees within a period of 90 days or less; or

2. 10 or more employees within a period of 30 days or less,

then consultations must take place at least 90 days (in the first case) or 30 days (in the second case) before the first dismissal takes effect.

If consultation has previously begun with regard to the proposed redundancy of other employees, those employees are not taken into account when determining the number of employees under the above rules. It is unclear whether this in effect permits employers to stagger redundancy exercises with a view to restricting their duty to consult. A tribunal might look at the reality of the programme and be unimpressed by a contrived attempt to skirt round the rules.

Consultation must not be a sham exercise. In *Transport and General Workers Union v. Ledbury Preserves (1928) Ltd* (1985), the EAT made it clear that:

'there must be time for the union representatives who are

consulted to consider properly the proposals that are being put to them. In the present case ... the meeting at which the consultation takes place was called at short notice and ... the union officials were somewhat taken by surprise, and yet, about half an hour after the meeting, the notices of dismissal were sent out.'

The EAT therefore remitted the case for a different tribunal to consider whether there had been consultation at the earliest opportunity.

When does a dismissal 'take effect'? In *National Union of Teachers v. Avon County Council* (1978), the EAT said that dismissal takes effect for this purpose when the employment terminates. Consequently, the minimum statutory consultation period 'is reckoned back from the effective date of termination'. Yet the EAT added that this could give rise to problems, because 'very often at the date of the beginning of consultation it is not known what will be the effective date of termination because obviously the notice of dismissal will not then have been given'. Perhaps the best solution is to give all employees concerned notice of dismissal simultaneously at the close of the consultation period, even though notice entitlement may differ and therefore their jobs may actually end at different times – unless, perhaps, they are paid in lieu of notice rather than working that notice out. Sometimes, by agreement, the consultation period itself can be translated into a cash 'buy-out' payment.

There is no statutory definition of 'establishment'. In *Barratt Developments (Bradford) Ltd v. UCATT* (1977), the EAT held that it was a question of fact for industrial tribunals to determine according to the circumstances of each case. The EAT said that it is 'difficult to say what the line is, but it is perfectly easy to say on which particular side of the line any particular set-up falls'. While this seems optimistic, in practice a commonsense interpretation of 'establishment' will usually be adopted. In the *Barratt* case itself, 14 house building sites administered from one base were held to constitute a single establishment.

A less fluid approach will be taken when identifying the 'employer' who is obliged to consult. This much is clear from the decision of the EAT in *E Green & Son (Castings) Ltd and Others v. ASTMS* (1984). Three companies, all operating from the same premises and all subsidiaries of one holding company, notified the trade union of proposed redundancies. Taking into account the terms of the relevant employment contracts, the EAT accepted that each company was a separate employer for the purposes of section 99. This mattered because the relevant consultation period was therefore 30 days, rather than 90 days, in each case. The EAT was unimpressed by an argument that the corporate veil should be lifted and that the three companies should, in the circumstances, be regarded as constituting a single employer.

9.7 Industrial tribunal claims

Where the employer is in breach of his statutory duty to consult, the trade union can make a complaint to an industrial tribunal.

The claim must be presented to the tribunal either before the proposed dismissal takes effect, or within three months from the date on which it did take effect. Where the tribunal is satisfied that it was not reasonably practicable to lodge the complaint within the three-month period, it can deal with the complaint out of time.

If the tribunal finds that the employer breached his obligations, it must declare this. It may also make a 'protective award' conferring certain rights upon the employees concerned.

9.8 Protective award

The effect of a protective award is to entitle the employees concerned to payment for a period of time, called the 'protected period'. That period begins on the date of the award or on the date when the first dismissal takes effect, whichever is the earlier.

The tribunal has discretion in fixing the length of the protected period, depending upon what is just and equitable, taking account of the seriousness of the employer's default. The maximum protected period will be:

1. in a case involving one hundred or more employees – 90 days;

2. in a case involving ten or more employees – 30 days;

3. any other case – 28 days.

How should the tribunal exercise its discretion? Two principles emerge from the case of *Talke Fashions Ltd v. Amalgamated Society of Textile Workers* (1977). First, the tribunal's paramount consideration should be to compensate the employee for being given short shrift by the employer. Secondly, the seriousness of the employer's default, in relation to the employee rather than the trade union, should be taken into account.

A rather different line was taken by the EAT in *Spillers-French (Holdings) Ltd v. USDAW* (1979). The EAT held that the tribunal could make a protective award even if there were no loss or hardship to the employees concerned. What has to be considered, said the EAT, is not the loss or potential loss of actual remuneration to employees, but the loss of days of consultation which has occurred.

The *Spillers-French* case gives rise to a question which has yet to be satisfactorily answered. Should the protected period be limited to the number of days that consultation would actually have lasted? In *GKN Sankey Ltd v. National Society of Metal Mechanics* (1980), which involved over 100 redundancies, the EAT upheld a 70-day protected period, even though, when added to the 34 days of consultation that had actually taken place, this gave a total period of 104 days. Ironically, the employees through their union had decided to forego further consultation after 34 days. Consultation was complete and indeed the employer altered his plans to accommodate the unions.

Each employee covered by a protective award is, subject to the exceptions below, entitled to a 'week's pay', calculated as indicated in section 22.5 A week's pay p226, for each week of the protected period and *pro rata* for a part of a week. The calculation date is the date of the protective award unless the employee was dismissed before that date, in which case it will be the same as the calculation date for redundancy payment purposes.

The following main exceptions should be noted:

1. no award will be made to an employee in respect of a period during which his employment continued, unless he would have been entitled to be paid either under his contract or under the statutory provisions regarding payment during his notice period (see section 5.3 Statutory minimum notice period p60);

2. an employee loses his right to a protective award if during the protected period he is fairly dismissed, other than by reason of redundancy, or unreasonably terminates his own employment;

3. if the employer offers alternative employment to the employee to take effect before or during the protected period, the offer is

treated in the same way as an offer of new employment in a 'typical' redundancy; see section 8.3 Offer of alternative employment p89.

Any contractual payment made to an employee in respect of the protected period will go towards discharging liability in respect of the protective award. If a payment in lieu of notice is made, it is the gross (not net) amount which should be offset against the protective award. Any *ex gratia* payment made, however, does not discharge liability.

An employee who is not paid his protective award can apply to an industrial tribunal within three months from the date in respect of which it is claimed that payment under the award was due. The time limit can be extended where it is not reasonably practicable to present the claim sooner.

9.9 Advance notification

An employer must – whether or not he recognises a trade union – notify the Department of Employment in writing of his proposal to make redundant either:

1. 100 or more employees at one establishment within a period of 90 days or less; or

2. 10 or more employees at one establishment within a period of 30 days or less.

The notification must be 90 or 30 days respectively before the first dismissal takes effect. If an independent trade union is recognised in respect of those employees, a copy of the notice must be given to the union representative.

The notice must be in the prescribed form (currently this is form HR1), and must include details of any consultations with trade unions, where there is a statutory duty to consult. The Department may require further information.

The employer may be excused if 'special circumstances' make it not reasonably practicable to comply, provided that he does his reasonable best. If that defence does not apply, he may be prosecuted and fined. Prosecution can only be initiated by, or with the consent of, the Secretary of State.

9.10   Time off in redundancy

The right

An employee who has been:

1. given notice of dismissal by reason of redundancy; and

2. continuously employed for two years by the date on which
   a) the notice is due to expire; or
   b) the date on which it would have expired had the statutory minimum period of notice been given, whichever is the longer,

has the right to 'reasonable' time off during his working hours to look for new employment or to make arrangements for training for future employment. The rules are contained in section 31 of the 1978 Act.

An employee who is allowed time off is entitled to be paid for that time at the appropriate hourly rate.

The remedy

If an employer unreasonably refuses to allow an employee to have time off when obliged to do so, the employee is entitled to be paid an amount equal to the remuneration he would have received had he been allowed the time off.

An employee can make a complaint to a tribunal if he is unreasonably refused time off or if he is not paid for time off. The complaint must be made within three months from the day on which it is alleged that time off should have been allowed, or within such further period as the tribunal considers reasonable if it was not reasonably practicable for the complaint to be presented within the time limit.

The tribunal may order the employer to pay remuneration:

1. for the period of absence; or

2. for the period during which time off should have been allowed; or both.

The maximum award cannot exceed two-fifths of a week's pay.

Any contractual remuneration paid to an employee for a period when he takes time off to seek or train for new work during the notice period goes towards discharging the statutory liability and vice versa.

10
Who can Claim Unfair Dismissal?

10.1 Introduction

The law of unfair dismissal is important and often controversial. Subject to various exceptions, section 54 of the 1978 Act provides that every employee shall have the right not to be unfairly dismissed.

In a classic passage in *W. Devis & Sons Ltd v. Atkins* (1975), the late Mr Justice Phillips, a former President of the EAT, once said that the phrase 'unfair dismissal' was

'in no sense a common-sense expression capable of being understood by the man in the street, which at first sight one would think it is. In fact . . . it is narrowly and to some extent arbitrarily defined. And so the concept of unfair dismissal is not really a common-sense concept . . .'

Many employers have over the years learned to their cost the truth of his remarks.

To say this is not to deny the necessity for unfair dismissal law. Some employers do treat their employees badly, and social justice demands that there should be a right of redress for unjust treatment. Nevertheless, even the most fair-minded and tolerant of employers have to be on their guard. The law is far from perfect and it contains a multitude of traps for the unwary. The first essential is to be aware of whether or not an employee has the right to complain of unfair dismissal.

10.2   Excluded categories

The following classes of employee are excluded from unfair dismissal rights:

● share fishermen;

● persons employed on UK-registered ships whose employment is wholly outside Great Britain or who are not ordinarily resident in Great Britain;

● police service employees;

● some Crown servants (although the vast majority of civil servants are not excluded);

● employees of certain international organisations;

Employees who would otherwise be protected may be excluded if they:

1. lack the requisite period of qualifying service;

2. are above normal retiring age;

3. ordinarily work outside Great Britain;

4. (in certain circumstances) were taking part in a strike or other industrial action at the time of dismissal.

The rules in these cases are outlined below. The position as regards dismissals and industrial action is considered in Chapter 18.

Section 67(2) of the 1978 Act provides that a tribunal cannot consider a complaint of unfair dismissal unless it is presented to the tribunal before the end of the period of three months beginning with the effective date of termination. If it was not reasonably practicable for the complaint to be presented within that time limit, it must be presented within such further period as the tribunal considers reasonable.

It is possible to contract out of unfair dismissal rights in the circumstances outlined in Chapter 23.

10.3 Qualifying service

Trade union-related dismissals

Where the reason for dismissal falls within section 58 of the 1978 Act as amended (see Chapter 19), there is no requirement of qualifying service. The employee is protected from the outset of his period of employment, but the burden is on the employee to prove that the reason for dismissal was his trade union involvement.

Medical suspension

There is a limited right under section 19(1) of the 1978 Act for an employee to be paid when suspended from work on medical grounds. If the employer dismisses the employee instead of paying him, the employee may claim unfair dismissal if he has four weeks' continuous employment.

The two year rule

In all other cases, an employee must have two years' continuous employment ending with the effective date of termination in order to claim unfair dismissal.

Employers therefore have ample opportunity to dismiss employees who are patently unsatisfactory before the first two years are up. But it is unwise – as well as bad industrial relations – to be too cavalier. No qualifying service is required to launch a sex or race discrimination claim. A short-serving black employee who is turfed out with no prior warning for a trivial breach of discipline, for instance, may understandably – even if wrongly – infer that he is being victimised because of his race. Defending a discrimination claim is, indeed, often more troublesome and traumatic than resisting a claim of unfair dismissal.

10.4 Normal retiring age

There is an age limit for unfair dismissal rights. At first sight, the rules seem simple. In practice, they have given rise to much complex litigation.

Briefly, an employee who has, on or before the effective date of termination,

1. attained the normal retiring age for an employee holding the position which he or she held; or, if there is no normal retiring age or the normal retiring age is sexually discriminatory,

2. (whether a man or a woman) attained the age of 65 years,

will not be able to claim unfair dismissal.

This exclusion does not apply if the employee has been dismissed for a trade union-related reason; see Chapter 19. To dismiss an octogenarian shop steward because of his trade union activities would be automatically unfair.

The meaning of 'normal retiring age' was considered by the House of Lords in *Waite v. Government Communications Headquarters* (1983). Where there is a contractual retiring age for all or nearly all employees in a particular position, that is presumed to be the normal retiring age. But the presumption can be rebutted by evidence that there is in practice some higher age at which employees holding the position are regularly retired, which they have reasonably come to regard as their normal retiring age. The test is: 'What would be the reasonable expectation or understanding of the employees holding that position at the relevant time?'

So, for example, the presumption may be rebutted even though some employees are retired at the contractual retirement age. Moreover, in *Swaine v. Health & Safety Executive* (1986), the EAT held that, for there to be a normal retiring age, there must be a specific age at which people normally retire. If people are retired at various ages within a particular age band, there is no 'normal' retiring age. Thus, the age limit of 65 for unfair dismissal rights applies, even though employees could not reasonably expect to be employed until that age.

In practice, however, the departure from a contractual retiring age will need to be quite significant in order to rebut the presumption. Statistics may be relevant, even though the legal test is not merely statistical. Statistics tend to show, as the EAT pointed out in *Whittle v. Manpower Services Commission* (1987), what happens in practice and that is often crucial in determining what is a 'reasonable expectation' of those holding the relevant position.

Mauldon v. British Telecommunications plc (1987), was a case where the presumption was rebutted. More than nine-tenths of the staff were kept on beyond the contractual retiring age of 60. They retired at various ages; the EAT therefore found that there was no 'normal' retiring age and the appropriate age limit for making a claim was thus 65.

If there is a change in policy on the employer's part with regard to retirement, tricky questions can arise. The House of Lords offered guidance in *DHSS v. Hughes* (1985), but a degree of uncertainty remains.

Briefly, the position appears to be this. If an employer communicates a policy to employees leading them reasonably to expect to retire later than their contractual retirement age, and that policy is operated in practice, then the presumption that the contractual retirement age is the normal retiring age will be rebutted − at least while the policy remains in force. However, if the change in policy lowers the normal retiring age, and this is communicated to employees, their original expectations will be destroyed and replaced by new expectations as to the earliest date at which they can be compelled to retire under the new policy. It seems at least arguable that under the present state of the law an employer may, through a change of policy, fix a new retiring age *below* that stipulated in the contract which is legally effective and may not even give rise to a valid claim for breach of contract on the part of the employees affected.

10.5   Work outside Great Britain

Section 131(2) of the 1978 Act excludes employees who under their contracts ordinarily work outside Great Britain from unfair dismissal rights. If, however, an employee is working within Great Britain under the terms of his contract at the time of dismissal, he does not forfeit his right merely because during his previous two years of service he at one stage ordinarily worked outside Great Britain: *Weston v. Vega Space Systems Engineering Ltd* (1989).

In *Wilson v. Maynard Shipbuilding Consultants AB* (1978), the Court of Appeal indicated that the proper approach is:

1. to examine what the terms of the employee's contract require, rather than what actually happened during the period for which the contract was in existence; and

2. in cases where the employer has a discretion as to where the employee should work, to ask what is the employee's 'base', as indicated by the contractual terms. In the absence of special factors, the base is likely to be the place where he ordinarily works, even though in fact he spends more time away from this base than he spends there – as with, for example, many long-distance lorry drivers.

Two subsequent Court of Appeal decisions have cast doubt on the 'base' test. In *Todd v. British Midland Airways Ltd* (1978), the employee was a pilot who worked for a British airline company but spent more than half his flying days outside Great Britain. He was allowed to claim unfair dismissal, but one judge suggested that the question of the employee's 'base' was merely one of several factors for consideration.

Similarly, tribunals were cautioned against paraphrasing the legislation in *Janata Bank v. Ahmed* (1981). The 'base' test, it was said, provides a likely and common-sense inference from the facts, but no more.

Once again, therefore, it must be emphasised that although many of the statutory provisions are opaque, and judicial guidelines are helpful, the latter should not be regarded as a substitute for the terms of the legislation.

11
The Reason for Dismissal

11.1 Introduction

If, in a wrongful dismissal action, the employer shows a sufficient reason for a summary dismissal, he has a complete defence. This is so even if, for example, he did not know until after the dismissal that the employee had been guilty of serious misconduct justifying dismissal without notice.

If an employee claiming a redundancy payment establishes that he has been dismissed, there is a presumption that the reason for dismissal was redundancy.

The position is different in unfair dismissal law. There are two basic questions for the tribunal:

1. Has the employer established that the principal reason for the dismissal fell within the category of reasons specified as potentially fair (see section 11.8 Potentially fair reasons p121)?

2. Did the employer act reasonably in all the circumstances in treating that reason as sufficient to dismiss?

Consequently, ascertaining the real reason for the dismissal is crucial.

11.2 Written statement of reasons for dismissal

Excluded categories

The following categories of employee are not entitled to insist upon a written statement of reasons for dismissal:

- overseas employees;

- share fishermen;

- police service employees;

- employees with less than two years' continuous employment.

The employee's right

A dismissed employee may request a written statement giving particulars of the reasons for his dismissal pursuant to section 53 of the 1978 Act. He is not entitled to such a statement unless he makes the request. The request should be made within (in practice) three months of the date of dismissal. The request need not be in writing. The employee is entitled to receive the written statement within 14 days of the request.

A written statement of reasons may be used in evidence in any proceedings. It is common for a request for a written statement to precede a claim for a redundancy payment or for unfair dismissal.

The cautious employer will therefore think carefully before responding. He will wish to ensure that the contents of the written statement accord with any arguments that he may wish to advance at a subsequent tribunal hearing. He must, however, respond, since an employee can complain to a tribunal that:

1. the employer unreasonably refused to provide a written statement; or

2. the particulars given are inadequate or untrue.

The time limit for the presentation of a complaint is three months from the date of dismissal; the tribunal may extend the time limit when it is not reasonably practicable to comply. Such a complaint may be combined with an unfair dismissal claim.

If the tribunal finds the complaint well founded:

1. it may make a declaration of the employer's reasons for the dismissal; and

2. it must make an award that the employer pay the employee twice his 'week's pay', calculated as specified in section 22.5 A week's pay p226.

Providing reasons

The apparently straightforward rules set out in section 53 have given rise to much debate. The following general principles can be gleaned:

1. even if an employer supplied a written statement of reasons prior to an employee's request, he may still be guilty of an unreasonable refusal to provide a written statement in compliance with a request: *Marchant v. Earley Town Council* (1979);

2. mere failure to comply within 14 days of a request does not necessarily amount to unreasonable refusal: *Lowson v. Perry Main & District Social Club & Institute Ltd* (1979);

3. there is no objection to the written statement referring to additional documents but the documents which the employee receives should contain at least a simple statement of the essential reasons for the dismissal: *Horsley Smith & Sherry Ltd v. Dutton* (1977);

4. failure to supply a written statement may, depending upon the circumstances, amount to a refusal to do so: the *Marchant* case;

5. a refusal to supply a written statement is not necessarily unreasonable: the *Marchant* case;

6. a refusal to supply a written statement because dismissal is denied may be unreasonable but is not necessarily so – it depends largely upon the reasonableness of the belief that there was no dismissal: *Broomsgrove v. Eagle Alexander Ltd* (1981);

7. a terse statement may be inadequate but, on the other hand, the employee is not entitled to press for particulars so detailed that they resemble a full case history of his employment. What is 'adequate' is a question of fact in the circumstances;

8. even if the particulars are incorrect, they are not necessarily 'untrue'. They are only untrue if an employer who dismissed for one reason falsely claims to have dismissed for another: *Harvard Securities plc v. Younghusband* (1990).

11.3   References

The right to a written statement of reasons for dismissal is limited in scope. It is not clear, for example, why any qualifying service – let alone a two-year period as for unfair dismissal rights – should be required.

The EAT has said that the right is supposed

'to enable the employee to have a piece of paper setting out the reasons for his dismissal which he could show to other employers to explain the reason why his previous employment had come to an end'.

However, such a piece of paper may not always be a great help in obtaining a new job.

Dismissed employees will, for these and other reasons, frequently ask their employers for a reference. Here the law is clear. There is no duty upon an employer to supply a reference, either to a prospective employer, or on a general 'to whom it may concern' basis.

An employer who, possibly out of kindness, supplies a reference sometimes finds that its glowing terms contradict arguments (eg as to the employee's capability or conduct) that he may later wish to advance at a tribunal hearing. The same applies to information given to government departments when enquiries are made after the employee has applied for state benefits.

In any event, an employer must not allow his heart to rule his head so that he runs into difficulties with the general law. Any reference given must not be defamatory. Nor must it be deceitful or carelessly worded – if it is, the result may be a claim for compensation, either from a maligned ex-employee or a duped prospective employer. Negative as it may seem, the safest course is often to supply no reference at all.

11.4   The real reason for dismissal

If there is more than one reason for the dismissal, it is the principal reason which is relevant for unfair dismissal purposes. Occasionally, the principal reason may be a 'composite' reason comprising a number of potentially fair reasons, all equally important in the mind of the employer.

The tribunal will not necessarily accept a mere assertion by the employer as to why the employee was dismissed. This may become an important practical matter where, for example, the employer denies an allegation that an employee was dismissed for a trade union-related reason; see Chapter 19.

The employer should therefore be in a position to produce evidence to demonstrate the genuine principal reason for dismissal.

In ascertaining the principal reason, the tribunal will disregard events occurring after the dismissal or events which happened before the dismissal but which were unknown to the employer when he dismissed. This was made clear by the House of Lords in *W. Devis & Sons v. Atkins* (1977).

The tribunal will therefore assess the reasonableness of the dismissal in the light of the facts known to the employer at the time of dismissal. Therefore, an unfair dismissal will not become fair simply because the employer subsequently becomes aware of something which would have justified the dismissal had it been known earlier.

It has been suggested that the *Devis* principle may amount in some cases to a 'rogue's charter', but the criticism is overstated. Information which becomes available after the dismissal may be relevant in a number of ways, ie:

1. if it helps to prove the accuracy or otherwise of evidence given in relation to incidents prior to the dismissal;

2. if it was taken into account in confirmation of the original dismissal during an internal appeal;

3. if it is just and equitable for the tribunal to take account of that information in assessing how much compensation (if any) should be awarded to an unfairly dismissed employee; see Contributory fault p242.

11.5 Industrial pressure

One exceptional case should be mentioned. Section 63 of the 1978 Act provides that, in determining whether a dismissal is fair, no account shall be taken of any industrial pressure exerted on the employer to dismiss. If the employer can show no other reason for the dismissal, he will be held to have acted unfairly. As the EAT has said:

'It does not sound fair, it does not sound right, but that is what Parliament has decided should be the position.'

'Industrial pressure' for these purposes need not involve official trade union action. It must, however, be pressure to dismiss rather than to take some action short of dismissal. The EAT suggested in *Ford Motor Company Ltd v. Hudson* (1978), that an appropriate test would be:

'Was the pressure exerted on the employers such that it could be foreseen that it would be likely to result in the dismissal of those employees in respect of whom the pressure was being brought?'

In certain circumstances where workers have pressured the employer to dismiss an employee for not being a union member, the employer may join them to the proceedings and they may have to reimburse some or all of any compensation which he is ordered to pay.

11.6 Automatically fair reasons

It is automatically fair to dismiss for the purpose of safeguarding national security.

Certain 'closed shop' dismissals used automatically to be fair. That is no longer the case: see section 19.8 Dismissal and the closed shop p196.

11.7 Automatically unfair reasons

The following five reasons for dismissal are automatically regarded as unfair:

1. dismissal of an employee for a conviction which is 'spent' pursuant to the Rehabilitation of Offenders Act 1974 (unless the employee is excluded from the scope of the Act);

2. dismissal of a woman for a reason connected with her pregnancy, subject to the rules outlined in Chapter 17;

3. dismissal of an employee for trade union membership or activity or for non-membership of a trade union; see Chapter 19;

4. dismissal for a reason connected with the transfer of an undertaking or part thereof within the meaning of the Transfer of Undertakings (Protection of Employment) Regulations 1981, subject to certain exceptions specified in the Regulations; see Chapter 20;

5. selection for redundancy for a trade union-related reason or in breach of a customary arrangement or agreed procedure, unless special reasons justified departing from that arrangement or procedure; see section 13.2 Automatically unfair selection p132.

11.8 Potentially fair reasons

The following reasons are specified by section 57(1) and (2) of the 1978 Act as potentially fair:

1. a reason related to the capability or qualifications of the employee for performing work of the kind which he was employed by the employer to do;

2. a reason related to the conduct of the employee;

3. the fact that the employee was redundant;

4. the fact that the employee could not continue to work in the position which he held without contravention, either on his part or his employer's, of a duty or restriction imposed by or under an enactment;

5. some other substantial reason of a kind which would justify the dismissal of an employee holding the position which that employee held.

An industrial tribunal must be satisfied that the reason for the dismissal was one of those potentially fair reasons before it will consider whether the dismissal was actually handled fairly. There is no formal burden of proof on the employer, but in practice he will need to be able at least to explain why the dismissal decision was taken. Once that has been resolved, the crucial question arises – did he act reasonably in all the circumstances?

12
Handling Dismissals Fairly

12.1 Introduction

When is a dismissal fair? The question is much more easily asked than answered. 'Fairness' in the context of unfair dismissal is a legal concept. Too often employees and employers confuse it with their own perception of what is morally fair. Perhaps this explains why they are so frequently disappointed or surprised by the outcome of a particular case.

The all-important test of fairness is set out in section 57(3) of the 1978 Act, ie:

> '. . . the determination of the question whether the dismissal was fair or unfair, having regard to the reason shown by the employer, shall depend on whether in the circumstances (including the size and administrative resources of the employer's undertaking) the employer acted reasonably or unreasonably in treating it as a sufficient reason for dismissing the employee; and that question shall be determined in accordance with equity and the substantial merits of the case.'

Tribunals therefore have a considerable discretion in determining the fairness of dismissal. Perhaps this is inevitable. However, the employer who wishes to anticipate in advance whether or not his actions are likely to be considered reasonable is faced with a number of difficulties. The EAT has from time to time set out certain guidelines on the interpretation of the test in section 57(3), but its attempts to clarify the law have met with mixed results.

Judicial guidelines, like the contents of relevant Codes of

Practice, are useful aids to decision-making, provided they are not treated as holy writ. The possible existence of an exception to a general 'rule' should always be recognised. Similarly, although key principles are discussed below and there is more specific comment in relation to particular types of dismissal in later chapters, it must always be remembered that each case requires consideration on the basis of its own facts.

12.2 The approach of the tribunal

The correct approach for a tribunal to adopt in answering the question posed by section 57(3) is as follows:

1. the starting point should always be the words of section 57(3) themselves;

2. in applying the section, a tribunal must consider the reasonableness of the employer's conduct, not simply whether they (the members of the tribunal) consider the dismissal to be fair;

3. in judging the reasonableness of the employer's conduct, a tribunal must not substitute its decision as to the right course to adopt for the decision of the employer;

4. in many (though not all) cases there is a 'band of reasonable responses' to the facts within which one employer might reasonably take one view, and another quite reasonably might take another;

5. the function of the tribunal is to determine whether, in the particular circumstances of each case, the decision to dismiss fell within the band of responses which a reasonable employer might have adopted. If the dismissal falls within the band, the dismissal is fair; if the dismissal falls outside the band, it is unfair.

This analysis was first proposed by the EAT in *Iceland Frozen Foods v. Jones* (1982), and it was approved by the Court of Appeal in *Hereford and Worcester County Council v. Neale* (1986). Lord Justice May emphasised the realities of this branch of industrial relations: 'Deciding these cases is the job of industrial tribunals and when they have not erred in the law, neither the appeal tribunal nor this court should disturb their decision unless one can say in effect, "My goodness, that was certainly wrong".'

12.3   ACAS guidance

Nevertheless, an industrial tribunal must take into consideration relevant provisions of any Code of Practice that has a bearing upon the case before it. Especially important in many cases is the ACAS Code on 'Disciplinary Practice and Procedures in Employment'. The current edition of that Code first appeared in 1977, and much has happened to affect the behaviour of management and employees at the workplace since then. Indeed, it was the absence of regular updating of Codes of Practice on employment matters that led the then President of the EAT to say in *Grundy (Teddington) Ltd v. Plummer and Salt* (1983):

> 'It is a proper and useful part of our function in a limited number of cases to give guidance as to the general approach to what constitutes reasonable conduct by an employer.'

Unfortunately, this view has not always been shared by his successors.

ACAS did issue a consultative document on a revised draft Code of Practice intended to replace the 1977 Code, and also those paragraphs of the 1972 Industrial Relations Code of Practice which deal with redundancy. The Government rejected the draft, arguing that what was needed was something shorter and simpler, which placed more emphasis on the obligations of employees in the maintenance of harmonious industrial relations.

The response from ACAS was interesting. In late 1987, it issued an 'advisory handbook' called *Discipline At Work*. This booklet was intended to complement the 1977 Code by providing 'more practical guidance', taking account of developments since 1977 with a view to helping employers and employees handle matters of discipline, absence and sub-standard work.

Because the handbook, which was amended in 1989, is purely advisory and lacks the legal status of a Code of Practice, it is not mandatory for industrial tribunals to take its recommendations into account when applying the section 57(3) test. It may be, however, that industrial tribunals will allow themselves to be influenced – even if only sub-consciously – by the views of ACAS as to what constitutes fair practice when commonly encountered employment problems arise.

12.4   Terms of the contract

The terms of the employee's contract of employment are likely to have a direct bearing on whether or not it was fair to dismiss him. Consequently:

1. the employer should set up and implement appropriate terms and conditions of employment, including detailed disciplinary rules and procedures. This will involve attempting to anticipate the problems that may arise later;

2. those terms, rules and procedures should be specifically incorporated into the contracts of employment of all employees. Of course, the terms may vary substantially from one employee to another. The important point is that all relevant matters should be considered carefully from the outset;

3. the employer should ensure that his actions in practice do not conflict with the terms of the contract.

12.5   The employer's size and resources

An employer who runs, say, a small grocery business cannot fairly be judged by the same standards of industrial relations practice as a powerful multi-national corporation with vast personnel resources. The law recognises this by providing that the tribunal shall take into account the size and administrative resources of the employer's undertaking when determining the fairness of the dismissal.

This may sometimes have the effect of enabling an employer to justify a dismissal even where there has been a procedural oversight. In some cases, it may hardly be practicable for a small firm to comply with all the canons of industrial relations fairness. In a very small business, for example, it is hardly realistic to provide for an internal appeal against a decision of the sole active director.

Nevertheless, the fact that a business is small does not give it *carte blanche* to flout accepted standards of reasonable behaviour. Thus in *Henderson v. Granville Tours Ltd* (1982), the EAT refused to accept that the size of the business could excuse the employer's failure to investigate properly a complaint made against the employee, when that complaint led to his dismissal.

125

The fact that the tribunal will take into account the employer's size and resources also means that a large company will find it difficult to justify a lapse from a proper procedure. An employer with a substantial personnel department will have little excuse for a failure to handle dismissals properly.

12.6   Length of service

The length of service of an employee will usually be taken into account in deciding whether or not it was fair to dismiss.

There may be cases where it might be within the band of reasonableness to dismiss a relatively short-serving employee, but where it is unfair to dismiss an employee with many years' service. This will be all the more so if the long service has been blemish-free. On the other hand, there may be cases where, for example, misconduct such as dishonesty) is so serious that the employee's past record has little relevance.

In cases of alleged lack of capability also, length of service will often be relevant. The longer the employee has served, for example, the more time a reasonable employer will allow him to (say) recover from sickness or achieve a performance target.

Length of service is also important as a factor to be taken into account when selecting employees for redundancy; see Length of service p136.

12.7   Investigation, consultation and warnings

A reasonable employer will make all relevant investigations *prior* to taking a decision affecting the employee's employment. He will also discuss the matter with the employee himself and (where appropriate) his union representative. Except in a case of gross misconduct or negligence, where summary dismissal is justified, he will warn the employee of the consequences if there is no improvement in the situation.

In different ways, the themes of investigation, consultation and warnings are relevant in a number of different cases, including dismissals for conduct, capability and redundancy. To take a classic example, the case law on suspected misconduct (see The legal test p153) indicates that, where a proper procedure involving reasonable investigations into the facts is followed, dismissal may be justified even where the employee is subsequently acquitted by a criminal court of the alleged misconduct.

An employer is entitled, moreover, to have regard in a misconduct case to the fact that an employee has received a previous warning in deciding whether or not to dismiss. This is so even where, said the EAT in *Auguste Noel v. Curtis* (1990), that previous warning related to behaviour which was different from that which is the potential basis for dismissal.

12.8 Consistency

Handling dismissals fairly entails treating employees consistently. Inconsistency may arise where two or more employees are treated differently even though their circumstances are genuinely similar.

Thus, although the dismissal of multiple suspects in a misconduct case may be fair (see Multiple suspect cases p154), it is likely to be unfair to dismiss one employee and not another where both are equally under suspicion.

Problems of consistency may also arise where a previously tolerant employer finally loses patience with a recalcitrant employee. Where a number of disciplinary offences have in the past escaped with little or no reprimand, it may well be unfair if, without warning, the employer finally decides that 'enough is enough' and responds to a further breach of rule by dismissing the employee concerned.

In short, acting reasonably does not involve turning a blind eye to misconduct. Rather, it necessitates a just, measured and predictable response, in fairness both to other employees and to the employee concerned.

12.9 Appeals

A reasonable employer will almost always allow an employee the right to appeal against a decision which is adverse to him. Permitting an appeal against a dismissal decision is especially important. Even if the terms of employment set out the appeals procedure in some detail, it is good practice to remind the employee specifically of his rights at the time of dismissal.

It is desirable for the appeal to be heard by a manager (usually, although not necessarily, senior in status to the manager who took the dismissal decision) who was not involved in the dismissal decision.

The procedure to be followed at the appeal hearing will depend upon the circumstances but some of the points suggested in Chapter 26 in relation to disciplinary interviews may usefully be borne in mind.

An employee who fails to exercise his right to appeal cannot be said thereby to have accepted that his dismissal was fair. However, in *Hoover Ltd v. Forde* (1980), the EAT suggested that such a failure might amount to a failure to mitigate loss (see Mitigation of loss p244), although a contrary view was expressed by the EAT in Scotland in *William Muir (Bond 9) Ltd v. Lamb* (1985).

Failure to allow an employee to appeal against a dismissal decision will not necessarily in itself justify a finding that a dismissal was unfair. However, it may reinforce a finding on other grounds that the dismissal was improperly handled.

12.10 When to test fairness

The statutory test of fairness need not necessarily be applied at the precise date when an employee is told that he or she is being dismissed. Where appropriate, matters which come – or could have come – to light subsequently, for example, during the course of an internal appeal hearing, may be taken into account in assessing the reasonableness of the employer's action in dismissing.

This was made clear by the decision of the House of Lords in *West Midlands Co-operative Society Ltd v. Tipton* (1986). The question there was whether an employer's refusal to allow an employee to exercise his contractual rights of appeal against summary dismissal could render that dismissal unfair. The Court of Appeal had decided that the only relevance of post-dismissal events lay in the evidence they provided of an employer's state of mind and general attitude towards the employee at the date of dismissal. However, the Law Lords unanimously rejected that approach.

Moreover, even where there is no attempt to appeal against dismissal, the fairness of that dismissal is not necessarily judged only at the time when the employee was first given notice of termination of employment. *Stacey v. Babcock Power Ltd (Construction Division)* (1986), concerned an employee who was given notice in February 1984 that his employment would be terminated by reason of redundancy the following May. In April the company unexpectedly obtained new contracts which might have made it possible for the employee to be kept on; unfortunately, his notice was allowed to expire without further action and the company proceeded to recruit new employees. The EAT held that, where an employee is given notice, the process of dismissal is not complete until that notice has expired. The company's failure to offer a long-serving employee the chance to stay at work rendered unfair a dismissal which was incontestably fair at the time when notice was originally given.

12.11   When do procedural errors affect fairness?

In the early years of the unfair dismissal regime, industrial tribunals were apt to view stringently any failure on the part of an employer to observe fair procedures in arriving at a dismissal decision. The harshness of this approach was mitigated by the decision of the EAT in *British Labour Pump Ltd v. Byrne* (1979), which introduced the so-called 'no difference test'. Briefly, it was said that if an industrial tribunal was satisfied that the employer would have dismissed had his procedure been correct, and that such a dismissal would be in the circumstances have been reasonable, then the dismissal would be fair in terms of section 57(3).

This doctrine was laid to rest by the House of Lords in the exceptionally significant case of *Polkey v. A. E. Dayton Services Ltd (formerly Edmund Walker (Holdings) Limited)* (1987). The House of Lords held that, in applying section 57(3), there is no scope for an industrial tribunal to consider whether, if the employer had acted differently, he might have dismissed the employee. It is what the employer did that is to be judged, not what he *might* have done. Thus the 'no difference test' and all decisions supporting it were inconsistent with the statute and would be overruled.

This does not mean that a procedural lapse automatically renders a dismissal unfair. Whether in any particular case it did so is a matter for the tribunal to consider in the light of the circumstances known to the employer at the time of dismissal. Moreover, the question of whether a different approach would have affected the employee's fate remains highly relevant when the question of his remedy for unfair dismissal – typically, financial compensation – is considered; see section 24.4 The compensatory award p237.

Nevertheless *Polkey* is a decision which has helped many employees to succeed in unfair dismissal claims which they might previously have lost. Its significance is illustrated by *Spink v. Express Foods Group Ltd* (1990), where the EAT stressed that fairness requires that someone accused of misconduct should know the case to be met; should hear or be told the important parts of the evidence in support of that case; and should have an opportunity to criticise or dispute that evidence and to adduce his own evidence and argue his case.

According to a subsequent short report in *The Times*, Mr Polkey ultimately received compensation of about £5,500, but the employers found themselves having to foot a bill approaching £100,000 for legal costs. Considering that the law of unfair dismissal and the industrial tribunal system is intended to be speedy, cheap, informal and accessible, this is sobering news.

13
Unfair Redundancies

13.1 Introduction

Amazingly, some employers still believe that if, because (for example) of a downturn in work, an employee is made redundant and given his statutory redundancy pay, there can be no question of a finding of unfair dismissal. That belief is mistaken and frequently proves expensive for employers.

Given levels of unemployment in Great Britain in recent years, it is perhaps inevitable that there should have been significant developments in the law of unfair dismissal so far as it relates to redundancies. Unfortunately, courts and tribunals have not been wholly consistent in their approach to claims of unfair redundancy.

It is therefore essential for employers to devote considerable care to the handling of individual redundancy dismissals. Sometimes this is easier said than done when urgent economic or commercial pressures make redundancy inevitable. Nevertheless, the cost of failure to observe the principles of good industrial relations practice can be very high.

Clearly, if an employer fails to establish that the principal reason for dismissal was redundancy, the dismissal will be unfair. This may not be the decision if he can show that the true reason was one of those others specified by the legislation as potentially fair and the tribunal accepts that he acted fairly in dismissing for that reason.

The technical definition of redundancy, especially as it relates to cases of reduction in work, (discussed in Chapter 7), may lead to problems here. Some circumstances which at first sight seem akin to redundancy do, in fact, fall outside that definition.

The cautious employer will therefore sometimes plead not only redundancy when defending an unfair dismissal claim but also, in the alternative, 'some other substantial reason' justifying the dismissal; see Chapter 21. In the event that the redundancy defence fails, he may still be able to show that the dismissal was fair in the circumstances of business reorganisation.

The basic principle is that an industrial tribunal will not sit in judgement on the wisdom of the employer's decision to implement redundancies.

Nevertheless, the employer ought to be able to produce evidence to the tribunal to show that redundancy was the real reason for the dismissal and that a proper business decision was reached. This may entail producing figures showing declining profitability. In *Orr v. Vaughan* (1981), the EAT ruled that in implementing redundancies, an employer must act on reasonable information reasonably acquired.

Even if redundancy is established as the reason for the dismissal, the dismissal may nevertheless be unfair if:

1. selection was due to trade union membership, non-membership or activities; or

2. selection was in contravention of a customary arrangement or agreed procedure; or

3. implemented unreasonably, eg because an unreasonable selection procedure was adopted, consultation was lacking or there was a failure to consider alternatives to redundancy.

13.2   Automatically unfair selection

The basic principle

Section 59 of the 1978 Act provides that where:

1. the reason or principal reason for the dismissal of an employee was his redundancy; and

2. the circumstances applied equally to one or more other employees in the same undertaking who held positions similar to that held by him; and

3. those other employees were not dismissed by the employer; and

4. a) the reason or principal reason for his selection was his membership or non-membership of a trade union or his trade union activities; or

b) he was selected in contravention of a customary arrangement or agreed procedure relating to redundancy and there were no special reasons justifying a departure from that arrangement or procedure in his case,

then the dismissal will be automatically unfair.

It will be a question of fact in each case as to whether other employees hold positions similar to the complaining employee. The relevant group may not necessarily, however, be restricted to employees in the same department as the complaining employee.

Selection for trade union involvement

A redundancy dismissal is automatically unfair if selection is for a trade union-related reason; see Chapter 19.

In practice, employees often find it difficult to prove that they have been selected for redundancy for trade union-related reasons. The evidence supporting a claim on that basis will usually be circumstantial, but may, for example, include one or more of the following matters:

1. conduct by the employer which is inconsistent with his alleged reason for dismissal;

2. the timing of selection, for example, if it occurred at about the same time as the employer became aware of the fact of the employee's trade union membership;

3. a history of anti-union statements and actions on the part of the employer.

Agreed procedures and customary arrangements

An agreed procedure will be an arrangement which deals specifically with the handling of redundancies. Normally, it will be made between the employer and a recognised trade union. It need not necessarily be in writing, although in practice that is usually the case. The agreed procedure may form part of an existing collective agreement between management and the union.

A customary arrangement may be regarded as, in effect, an

implication of agreed procedure. It is often claimed that the customary arrangement is 'last in, first out' or ('LIFO'). However, the tribunal will not automatically accept that the LIFO principle was the customary arrangement in the particular industry concerned.

An 'agreed procedure' may exist even if it is not set down in any formal shape or expressly agreed: *Henry v. Ellerman City Liners Ltd* (1984). In practice, however, there will often be an express agreement between the employer and recognised trade union and the 'agreed procedure' may form part of an existing collective agreement.

It is unwise to rely too heavily upon an argument based upon 'special reasons' justifying departure from an agreed procedure or customary arrangement. For example, in *Reid and others v. Cross International* (1985), the Court of Appeal upheld an industrial tribunal's decision on the facts that a serious downturn in trade caused by the loss of a valuable contract did not justify a departure from the agreed procedure of 'last in, first out'.

Customary, or agreed selection criteria may sometimes be unlawful, for example, in a case where they are sexually discriminatory (see Unlawful selection criteria p138). Although there is no direct authority on the point, it is realistic to assume that the unlawful nature of the criteria will usually be regarded as a 'special reason'.

Finally, it should be noted that redundancy selection in the context of a business transfer is fraught with difficulty as a result of the operation of the Transfer of Undertakings (Protection of Employment) Regulations 1981; see Chapter 20.

13.3 Unreasonable selection

Identifying the selection group

The unit of selection may not comprise just those employees who actually do the work which is ceasing or diminishing and so giving rise to the need for redundancy: *Cowen v. Haden Carrier Ltd* (1982). Management must look both at the work that the employees do, and that which they could be required to do under the terms of any 'flexibility' provisions which may be contained in the contracts of employment, before deciding whether or not certain employees can be excluded from consideration. Even if there is no other work available which they can contractually be required to undertake, dismissed employees may be able to argue that the selection group should include all those other workers whose job they are capable of performing and could contractually be asked to perform.

In general terms, tribunals are inclined to look at the workforce as a whole, without dividing it arbitrarily into separate units. However, a company may wish to put the various contracts upon which it is engaged into distinct compartments, and to deal with the employees working on each contract separately. An employer who adopts this approach needs to be able to justify it by producing clear evidence that there were sound business reasons for concentrating for redundancy purposes upon certain parts only of the workforce. Similarly, where employees are doing comparable work but at different times, for example, where a shift system operates, it may be unreasonable to restrict a selection group to employees carrying out work at a particular time or on a particular shift.

Fair selection criteria

Choosing selection criteria
An employer must be prepared to explain how he reached his decision to select a particular individual for redundancy. While length of service will almost always be a highly relevant factor, in the absence of an agreed procedure, customary arrangement or contractually binding system of selection, he will usually be entitled to take a variety of other matters into account. Any such factors must be objective, rather than subjective. This is, according to the EAT in *Williams v. Compair Maxam Ltd (1982)*,

'to ensure that redundancy is not used as a pretext for getting rid of employees which some manager wishes to get rid of for quite other reasons, eg for union activities or by reason of personal dislike'.

Provided that he avoids a subjective approach, the employer who draws his redundancy selection criteria loosely will tend to have more discretion than one who does not. Thus in *BL Cars Ltd v. Lewis* (1983), the overriding factor laid down by the employer was the need to retain a balanced workforce. In the circumstances, it was wrong to hold that a long-serving employee was to be treated as having some 'priority' and that, in order for the employer to

135

select fairly, he had to find major shortcomings in the employee's performance if that were to outweigh the factor of length of service.

Naturally, the criteria that are relevant will vary from company to company and from time to time. Those referred to below are often applied.

Length of service

The importance of length of service has already been noted. Yet redundancy will often imply major organisational change in the business and it might be inappropriate to rely solely on service as the selection criterion. Other factors may be taken into account and they may, cumulatively, outweigh length of service in particular cases. Rarely, it may even be unreasonable to rely solely on length of service as a guide to selection. This might be the case, for example, if doing so entailed retaining an employee past retirement age at the expense of a much younger employee.

Skill and qualifications

Skills and qualifications that may reasonably be taken into account in redundancy selection can range from the sophisticated – such as the ability to operate unfamiliar technology – to the relatively mundane – such as the possession or non-possession of a driving licence. The important question will be whether the skills concerned are relevant to the redundancy exercise.

Efficiency/ability/flexibility

The job performance of members of the redundancy selection group is likely to be a major consideration. Job performance may involve matters such as efficiency, ability and flexibility, which are closely allied but distinct. The most capable employee, for example, may not be the most adaptable. However, it should be borne in mind that a 'gut feeling' that an employee with a superficially good track record is in fact severely limited, and will not easily adapt to the reorganised structure following redundancy, will often be hard to justify objectively.

Attendance Record

A poor attendance record may legitimately be taken into account in arriving at a decision on redundancy. In *Gray v. Shetland Norse Preserving Co Ltd* (1985), it was held to be reasonable to select an employee for redundancy on the basis of a poor attendance record, despite the fact that he had never been warned that he risked losing his job if his attendance did not improve. The EAT distinguished between poor attendance as a selection criterion and dismissal simply for poor attendance. In the latter case a pattern of warnings would almost always be necessary to justify dismissal.

An employer should not, however, automatically take attendance records at their face value. The EAT emphasised in *Paine and Moore v.Grundy (Teddington) Ltd* (1981), that it is desirable to ascertain the reasons for the absences, so that management is in possession of all the relevant facts before the selection decision is made.

Discipline and loyalty
An employee's disciplinary record may legitimately be taken into account when selecting for redundancy. More controversially, management may sometimes have regard to the loyalty of particular employees who in the past stayed at work while others were on strike. This would be the case especially if the adverse effect of the strike gave rise in itself to the need to implement redundancies, or if it is reasonable to believe that to dismiss the loyal employees would cause friction and unrest. Loyalty in this sense may be a legitimate selection criterion, but seldom will a reasonable employer allow it to assume overriding importance.

Personal circumstances
To what extent should an employer take into account the personal circumstances of redundancy candidates in making his decision? Inevitably, an employer who bases his decision on factors wholly unrelated to employment, such as marital status or domestic or financial circumstances, embarks on a risky course. To select on the assumption that a married man is the family breadwinner, for example, might not only be unfair but also amount to unlawful sex discrimination.

Yet it would be equally unwise to ignore personal circumstances altogether. Thus, in *Seymour v. British Airways Board* (1983), the EAT held that a person who is both disabled, and registered as such, is entitled to special consideration, which includes considering his personal circumstances before deciding to dismiss him. Once again, however, the ultimate question concerns the reasonableness of the employer's approach. In *Seymour*, the employers had a policy for assessing the effectiveness of disabled workers and for considering suitable alternative employment for them; they were held to have acted fairly in selecting a disabled worker for redundancy. Indeed, there may be cases where the special consideration given to a registered disabled employee will be outweighed by his low productivity.

Pay/expense

Financial considerations are likely to play an important part in determining the need for redundancies in the first place. Long-serving employees are apt to have higher levels of pay, so it may be much more cost-effective to retain employees with less service. Nevertheless, a reasonable employer will consider all the relevant factors, including the possibility of offering longer-serving employees the choice of a pay cut rather than dismissal.

Unlawful selection criteria

Redundancy selection on the grounds of race or sex will be unlawful within the terms of the anti-discrimination legislation and is also likely to be unfair. A hidden danger is that selection criteria may be unlawful, even where they are not obviously so. For example, a female employee who works part-time and who is selected precisely because she is a part-timer may be able to claim that she has been unlawfully discriminated against on the grounds of her sex and therefore unfairly dismissed, although it was not the employer's intention to discriminate on such grounds.

Such a claim may succeed even where the redundancy selection procedure has been specifically agreed with the recognised trade union. Thus in *Clarke and Howell v. Eley (IMI) Kynoch Ltd* (1982), the agreement provided that part-timers would be selected for redundancy before full-timers, who would then be selected on the basis of length of service. It was held that the requirement to work full-time was one with which a smaller proportion of women than men could have complied. On the facts, one of the two applicants could not have complied with the requirement because of her domestic situation. This was unlawful sex discrimination, as well as being unfair under the 1978 Act.

Nevertheless, selection on the basis of 'part-timers first' may be justified, for example, where fitting part-timers into standard shift patterns is neither efficient nor economic: *Kidd v. DRG (UK) Ltd* (1985). The EAT declined to interfere with an industrial tribunal's refusal to assume that selecting part-timers first is discriminatory. Moreover, the EAT accepted that, even if the selection procedure was indirectly discriminatory, it was justifiable in the circumstances. This view was based on the 'marginal advantages' put forward by the employers of retaining one shift of full-time rather than two shifts of part-time workers. As the EAT itself pointed out, the case illustrates the flexibility of the concept of indirect discrimination. Nevertheless, employers would still be wise to think long and hard before implementing a selection procedure based on 'part-timers first'.

Applying selection criteria

Just as selection criteria must be reasonable, so must they be objectively and rationally applied. Some selection factors can be much more easily assessed than others. Questions of length of service, remuneration and disciplinary records are likely to be more straightforward than matters such as job performance. If performance is to be taken into account, it will usually be appropriate to seek the view of the immediate superiors of the employees in the selection group. A company which operates a system of regular job appraisals should find it easier to assess job performance fairly. On the other hand, if such a system exists, it will be difficult to argue that an employee whose appraisals reveal no significant criticisms is a poor performer.

In many cases, some factors will point towards retaining one particular employee, while others will work in favour of one of his colleagues. A difficult balancing operation is called for. One way to measure the relevant factors is to devise a 'points system', in which the various selection criteria which are to be taken into account are identified and points are attributed to employees within the selection group under each heading. Such an approach is particularly desirable with larger employers, where the selection group is sizeable. It must be kept in mind, however, that an employee who fares badly in comparison with others under review may have been a loyal and diligent worker. The task of management in making comparisons is often difficult. The best approach combines a degree of detachment with a carefully thought-out selection procedure.

13.4   Fairness and consultation

The importance of consultation

The importance of proper consultation as an element of any redundancy exercise can scarcely be over-estimated. Lack of consultation is one of the grounds upon which an industrial tribunal may regard a redundancy dismissal as unfair under the 1978 Act. All too often, employers who scrupulously consult recognised trade unions about redundancy proposals (in accordance with the 1975 Act), find themselves losing unfair dismissal claims brought by individual employees who are aggrieved because they were not consulted personally!

Observing current industrial practice

An employer who fails to consult a recognised trade union about proposed redundancies will risk not only a claim for a protective award, but also complaints that the redundancies were unfair under section 57(3) of the 1978 Act. The 1972 Industrial Relations Code of Practice makes clear the importance of consultation and the point is further developed in *Redundancy Handling*, a useful booklet which ACAS first issued in 1988.

In the well-known case of *Williams v. Compair Maxam Ltd* (1982), the EAT tried to set out (albeit in very general terms) the principles which, in current industrial practice, a reasonable employer would be expected to adopt when implementing redundancies.

The two lay members of the EAT indicated that generally, where employees are represented by an independent trade union, a reasonable employer will:

1. seek to give as much warning as possible of impending redundancies;

2. consult the union as to the best means by which the desired management result can be achieved fairly and with as little hardship to the employees as possible. In particular, the employer will seek to agree redundancy selection criteria with the union and consider with the union whether selection decisions have been made in accordance with those criteria;

3. in any event, seek to establish selection criteria which can be

objectively checked against such things as attendance records, efficiency on the job, experience or length of service;

4. consider any union representations with regard to such selection; and

5. ascertain whether, instead of dismissing an employee, he could offer him alternative employment.

The EAT was no doubt conscious of the possibility that later attempts might be made to interpret the judgment as laying down binding rules of law, so it specifically stated that the five principles were not immutable and also that they were merely standards of behaviour:

'Therefore, in future cases before this Appeal Tribunal there should be no attempt to say that an industrial tribunal which did not have regard to or give effect to one of these factors has misdirected itself in law.'

Regrettably, *Compair Maxam* has been much misunderstood. This led the EAT in Scotland, in *A Simpson & Sons v. Reid and Findlater* (1983), to describe *Compair Maxam* as a case

'which is becoming over-worked and increasingly misapplied . . . it was certainly never intended that the five so-called principles should be considered in each and every redundancy case, should be ticked off as in a shopping list as to whether or not they have been complied with. . .'.

More recently, the EAT, in *Rolls Royce Motors Ltd v. Dewhurst* (1985), gave vent to its own exasperation, complaining that 'no decision of this court seems to give greater trouble than *Compair Maxam*'.

It is important to keep the criticisms of *Compair Maxam* in perspective. In seeking to act reasonably when handling redundancies, most employers will find it useful to consider specifically the points suggested in that case. It is unacceptable, however, to seek to appeal against an unwelcome decision of an industrial tribunal simply on the ground that *Compair Maxam* has not been applied to the facts of the case in question.

The need for individual consultation

All too often, employers – even those who conscientiously observe the rules regarding trade union consultation – overlook the need to discuss their redundancy proposals fully with the employees who are directly affected. Consultation with a recognised trade union is essential, but not in itself sufficient. Certainly, it does not release an employer from the obligation to make sure that each employee is personally aware of the position. Thus in *Wall's Meat Co. Ltd v. Selby* (1989), where there was consultation with the union but not with the employee concerned, the Court of Appeal accepted that the dismissal was unfair, although such a dismissal would not automatically be unfair in every single case.

Employers should take special care when redundancy candidates include both union members and non-members. The EAT pointed out in *Lafferty Construction Ltd v. Duthie* (1985) that it is likely to be unfair to non-members if they are disadvantaged because they do not receive the same prior warning of redundancy proposals as union members.

The clearest statement of the importance of individual consultation in recent years appeared in *Freud v. Bentalls Ltd* (1982), where the EAT proclaimed that 'consultation is one of the foundation stones of modern industrial relations practice'. The EAT added that a general policy not to consult with employees of, say, a particular grade runs contrary to fundamental principles of good industrial relations. Although the nature of consultation may differ, according to whether the employee is a shop-floor worker and a member of a recognised union, or a member of management not represented by a union, the desirability of consultation applies to employees of all kinds.

There seem to be three main reasons why employers sometimes take a deliberate decision not to consult. First, there may be a view that consultation will do little more than depress and demoralise an employee who is bound to receive the redundancy as a *fait accompli*. Secondly, in some industries, the employer may fear sabotage from disgruntled redundancy candidates – a typical example is the fear that a computer programmer will extract some kind of revenge by introducing a 'logic bomb' into the computer system. Thirdly, the situation of the business may be so grave, and the selection of the individuals concerned so inevitable that consultation would make absolutely no difference to the outcome.

Non-consultation may sometimes be justified on one or more of these grounds, but it is generally unsafe to rely upon any of them, other than in the most exceptional circumstances. Even where vital commercial considerations explain a failure to consult, an employer may be held to have acted unfairly. The problems are illustrated by *Holden v. Bradville Ltd* (1985). In that case the EAT overturned an industrial tribunal's decision that it was not practicable to consult where 33 redundancies were required urgently at a time when takeover negotiations were being conducted in secret. The EAT considered that multiple interviews 'could readily have been arranged without inconvenience or dislocation to the company', and that there was insufficient evidence that the need for secrecy precluded consultation.

Consultation implies a dialogue, not a monologue. In *Barratt Construction Ltd v. Dalrymple* (1984), the EAT suggested that it is incumbent upon a senior employee to express interest in junior positions as an alternative to redundancy at the time of his projected dismissal, and not merely at the industrial tribunal hearing. It was held that an industrial tribunal had gone too far in presuming that, because there was no evidence of a search for jobs throughout the group of companies of which the employer was a member, the dismissal was inevitably unfair. A tribunal should not give the benefit of the doubt to either party, but rather must review the fairness of the dismissal decision on the evidence as presented.

In essence, consultation involves giving the employee the chance to have a say in his own destiny. If he fails to respond, that is his own affair, but the employer should provide the opportunity for full discussion. That discussion may result in the employee challenging the basis of his selection. In such cases, it may make sense to review the selection criteria and how they were applied. It is also possible that hitherto unconsidered possibilities of redeployment may emerge. If not, the employer may wish to offer constructive help; companies whose resources are not too depleted may assist by financing outplacement counselling, for example.

Would consultation have made any difference?

For over a decade industrial tribunals and the EAT took the view that where there is a procedural flaw in the handling of redundancy, such as a lack of consultation, a failure to take into account all relevant selection criteria or a failure to make reasonable efforts to find alternative employment, it is still necessary to consider what would have been the likely result had that been done which ought to have been done. If handling the matter correctly would not have made the slightest difference, and the claim would have been dismissed, it was said that it was open to the tribunal to say either that the dismissal was fair or unfair with an award of no compensation.

As has been mentioned in Chapter 12, the House of Lords decided in *Polkey v. AE Dayton Services Ltd (formerly Edmund Walker (Holdings) Ltd)* (1987) that this approach was misconceived. For a dismissal to be fair, an employer must have followed a proper procedure in arriving at the dismissal decision. Failure to consult with Mr Polkey about his redundancy cost the company dear.

13.5 Alternatives to redundancy

Before implementing redundancies, a reasonable employer will consider whether an alternative course of action is open to him. Although there may be a need to cut overheads, including labour costs, redundancy is not necessarily inevitable.

Possible alternatives will depend upon the circumstances. They may be temporary or permanent, and might include short-time working, pay cuts or seeking volunteers rather than imposing compulsory redundancies at the outset.

An employer who is challenged on the point will have to convince the tribunal that he gave genuine thought to the alternatives to redundancy. It will seldom be enough simply to assert that consideration was given but that there were clearly no alternatives. The manager making the dismissal decision should ensure that he is in possession of all relevant information. For example, it is a classic mistake to assume that an employee who, in normal circumstances, would not entertain demotion, would reject the possibility out of hand. This may not be the case if the only other alternative is unemployment.

Where a company is part of a group, the obligation to seek alternatives to enforce redundancies may be extensive. In the well-known case of *Vokes Ltd v. Bear* (1973), the employer made no attempt to see if the employee concerned could be fitted in elsewhere within a group of 300 companies. There was evidence that at least one of these companies was advertising for people to fill comparable positions shortly after the employee's dismissal. The employers did not offer help to him prior to the dismissal, nor was he given time off work to seek a new job. The dismissal was held to be unfair.

That decision has been much quoted over the years, and in *MDH Ltd v. Sussex* (1986), the EAT had to make it plain that it is an error of law to treat *Vokes* as giving rise to a binding principle. The industrial tribunal had heard no evidence as to whether any alternative employment was available, *Vokes* had not been cited to it and it appeared to be unduly impressed by the fact that MDH Ltd and Vokes Ltd were both part of the Tilling Group of companies. There are no grounds for criticising the decision of the EAT, but nevertheless it would be unwise for employers to confine their search for vacancies for potentially redundant employees solely to their own business when other group members may well be able to accommodate those workers.

The importance of considering alternatives underlines the need to consult with employees and their representatives about redundancy proposals. Tribunals tend to take the view that the consultation process itself may throw up alternatives to redundancy that, without consultation, the employer might not have considered or thought practicable.

14
Misconduct and Dismissal

14.1 Introduction

In every business, no matter how well it is run, employees will occasionally commit acts of misconduct, and managers need to know how to deal with such incidents firmly and effectively. To turn a blind eye to indiscipline is foolish, yet to over-react or to respond too hastily before the facts are clear is equally unwise. Not only does this represent bad industrial relations, but it may expose the business to a potentially expensive claim of unfair dismissal.

There are many different types and degrees of disciplinary problem, and several of the more common and more serious are examined here. First, it is important to appreciate that, sometimes, apparent indiscipline proves on investigation to be nothing more than a misunderstanding. Even if it is established that the employee was at fault, the appropriate action for management to take may be to counsel the employee rather than simply to impose some sort of penalty. Dismissal should be regarded as a last resort.

A certain type of conduct on the part of an employee is a potentially fair reason for dismissal. Although the legislation does not define 'conduct', it is usually clear whether a dismissal is for a reason relating to 'conduct'; although, occasionally, cases involve an element of 'capability' too, as with sub-standard performance. The key question in practice tends to be whether the employer acted reasonably in deciding to dismiss.

In assessing the fairness of a dismissal for misconduct, an industrial tribunal will take into account the principles set out in the ACAS Code of Practice relating to disciplinary practice and procedures. Every employer should be familiar with this Code of Practice. Although failure to observe its provisions does not in itself render a person liable to proceedings, an employer who is unaware of those provisions, or who ignores them in a particular case, is unlikely to be able to handle disciplinary matters in a way that will be regarded as fair by a tribunal. The handbook *Discipline At Work* offers useful supplementary guidance.

14.2   Disciplinary rules and procedures

The importance of rules and procedures

It is essential for an employer to set up and implement proper disciplinary rules and procedures, which should be incorporated into the contract of each employee. There may, of course, be different rules and procedures for different categories of employee. The Code of Practice should be seen merely as laying down minimum standards for the fair handling of disciplinary matters. Many employers will wish to anticipate practical problems which may arise in their particular line of business and draft detailed rules accordingly.

It almost goes without saying that, having established disciplinary rules and procedures, an employer must comply with them. It will be embarrassing or, at worst, disastrous, if a tribunal finds that clear rules were disregarded in a particular case.

Natural justice

No disciplinary action should be taken until the complaints have been fully investigated. Natural justice requires that:

1. the employee should know the nature of the complaint made against him;

2. he should have an opportunity to state his case; and

3. the employer should act in good faith.

Although there are occasionally clear-cut cases where strict compliance with every aspect of natural justice is unnecessary, the proper handling of the disciplinary hearing and any appeal hearing in accordance with the contractual disciplinary rules and procedures should enable the employer to comply with these requirements. Each case should be treated on its own merits.

Warnings

The Code of Practice makes it clear that, unless an employee is guilty of gross misconduct, it will generally be unfair to dismiss him for a first breach of discipline. Proper disciplinary procedures will provide for the giving of warnings in respect of minor disciplinary offences.

A first warning will often be oral. Sometimes there will be no need formally to confirm the position in writing to the employee. Many employers doubt whether to do so is conducive to good industrial relations. This is particularly the case where the oral warning is intended simply to improve conduct, rather than to act as a first step in a procedure that might lead to more severe sanctions. Nevertheless, some record should be kept of formal verbal warnings and the employee should be made aware of any such entry on his personnel file. If no written evidence of the warning is available and the employee denies that the verbal warning was given, a tribunal may believe the employee.

There is no strict rule about the number of warnings which should be given prior to dismissal. A second minor offence, or a first offence of a more serious nature, will usually call for a formal written warning. This should record, at the very least, the nature of the offence and the likely consequence of a further offence.

Further misconduct may warrant a final warning. If intended as a last step prior to dismissal, such a warning should again record the nature of the offence and make it clear that a further offence will leave the employer with no alternative but to dismiss.

A warning should be just that. It is unwise to try to soften the blow by expressing the complaint vaguely, and generalised criticism alone is insufficient. An employee who is not specifically warned of the risk that he runs by committing a further offence may justifiably complain that he was unfairly treated if dismissal follows a repetition.

Where an employee is given a written warning, he should be asked to acknowledge receipt, even if he disputes the need for that warning. If he refuses to do so, the fact should be noted. This is not unnecessary bureaucracy. It is by no means unknown for employees to deny at a later date having received warning letters. Where a warning letter is sent by post, it may be prudent for it to be sent recorded delivery.

Arguably, the need for formal warnings is less important in the case of senior employees. Formal warnings are often thought to de-motivate executives in key positions. In any event, senior managers (by the nature of their jobs) may reasonably be expected to be fully aware of what is required of them. Again, however, the question will be whether the employer has acted reasonably in the circumstances of a particular case. In cases of doubt, it is prudent to set out the position as clearly as possible.

A formal disciplinary procedure should make it quite clear how long a warning will last. A delicate balance has to be struck. On the one hand, if warnings are removed from the record within a very short period of time, intermittent but persistent offenders may create problems for management. On the other hand, it will not be fair to keep warnings 'alive' for excessive periods.

The length of time for which a warning should remain on record usually depends on the seriousness of the offence. In practice, it will be appropriate for most warnings to expire after three months at the earliest and after two years at the latest. A procedure which keeps even a final warning for a serious offence on record for more than two or at most three years will in most cases be regarded as unfair. Past 'expired' warnings may still be of marginal relevance in the case of a long-serving employee with a history of disciplinary offences who seeks unwisely to convince a tribunal that, prior to the final incident which led to dismissal, he had an unblemished work record.

Alternative disciplinary sanctions

In preparing and implementing disciplinary rules and procedures, employers sometimes overlook the fact that warnings or dismissal are not the only possible sanctions for misconduct.

It may be worth considering whether any of the following penalties are available under the terms of the contract and, in any event, whether they represent an appropriate sanction:

- suspension with pay;
- suspension on reduced pay;
- suspension without pay;

- demotion;

- transfer;

- loss of privileges.

Whilst warnings or dismissal are certain to remain the most widely-used disciplinary sanction, an employer who has available a range of possible penalties may find it easier to ensure that the punishment properly fits the crime.

14.3 Breaches of discipline

Gross misconduct

Whether a single breach of discipline justifies summary dismissal will depend upon the precise circumstances. It is unwise to adopt too rigid an approach. Disciplinary rules usually set out a list of offences which will be regarded as gross misconduct, but the examples given are not usually exhaustive, and that should be made clear.

Here a number of the most common examples of gross misconduct are considered. It must be emphasised that, even if it seems clear at first sight that the employee is guilty of gross misconduct, the matter must be thoroughly investigated and a proper disciplinary procedure followed.

Disobedience

If an employee deliberately disobeys a reasonable and lawful instruction given by an authorised superior, that will generally amount to gross misconduct justifying summary dismissal.

The crucial question tends to be whether the instruction was reasonable, and the terms of the contract may be relevant here. If an employee refuses to perform a task which he is clearly required to do by the contract, dismissal will often be justified.

Problems may arise if an employee with a comprehensive job description is asked to undertake work not specifically referred to in that description. The best solution in practice is to try to anticipate such problems when drafting the terms of employment and, where necessary, to provide that the contents of any job description do not include every task which the employee might be asked to perform.

Violence

An act of violence towards the employer, a fellow employee or a customer will usually amount to gross misconduct. The EAT said in the case of *C.A. Parsons & Co. Ltd v. McLoughlin* (1978) that the dangers associated with fighting at the workplace are sufficiently accepted for an employer to rely on them as justifiable and reasonable grounds for dismissal, even where there is nothing in the contract which specifically refers to dismissal for fighting.

In practice, however, it would be wise to make specific reference to violence – and, indeed, threats of violence – in the list of examples of gross misconduct set out in the disciplinary procedure. Furthermore, even where an employee has undoubtedly become involved in a fight, it is unwise to dispense with a proper and full investigation of the facts. For example, it may emerge that the employee was not actually fighting, but attempting to break up an altercation between colleagues. Alternatively, he may have been subjected to such outrageous provocation that dismissal would be too harsh a penalty.

Bad language

Whether or not bad language will justify summary dismissal will depend upon the particular circumstances.

The nature of the employment is certainly relevant. In many industries, the use of earthy language is part and parcel of the working environment. It may also be relevant to consider where, when and to whom the bad language was used and the extent of the offence actually caused. For example, offensive language directed at the employer's most valued customer may be regarded as much more serious than the use of similar words towards a fellow employee.

Drunkenness

While drunkenness at work will be misconduct, it will by no means always justify summary dismissal. The following factors are often relevant in determining whether a single instance of drunkenness amounts to gross misconduct:

1. the works rules;

2. whether safety was endangered;

3. whether company property was endangered;

4. whether the employee misbehaved seriously while drunk;

5. whether any subsequent apology by the employee reduces the seriousness of the offence.

Lateness and absenteeism

It will be very unusual for a single instance of lateness or absence from work to justify summary dismissal. Generally, it will be necessary for a proper warnings procedure to be followed. As ever, the employer should ensure that appropriate rules are incorporated into the employee's contract of employment.

In this area, the size and resources of the employer may be particularly relevant. For example, in the case of a very small business, a single unauthorised absence from work may be regarded, quite reasonably, as much more serious than a comparable absence on the part of an employee in a much larger concern, where the absence has little effect on the smooth running of the business.

Dishonesty

Cases of dishonesty frequently give rise to difficulties. Dishonesty may, for example, involve:

1. stealing company property;

2. stealing from fellow employees;

3. clocking offences;

4. time sheet or expenses frauds.

There is no reason why any of the above forms of dishonesty

should not justify dismissal, but the contract of employment and disciplinary rules and procedures should deal with the position specifically.

Tricky problems occur where there is no proof of dishonesty (as is often the case), or where the act of dishonesty is not directly connected with the employment. The relevant principles, which apply generally to cases of misconduct, are discussed below.

14.4 Suspected misconduct

The legal test

If an employee is caught red-handed in an unequivocal act of theft from his employers, that will generally be a clear case of gross misconduct justifying summary dismissal. Unfortunately for employers, proof of dishonesty is often hard to find. If a suspected employee denies his guilt, the question arises whether he may nevertheless be fairly dismissed.

The answer is yes, provided the employer acts reasonably in all the circumstances and makes all reasonable inquiries. This was made clear by the Court of Appeal in *W. Weddell & Co. Ltd v. Tepper* (1980), where a passage from the judgment in *British Home Stores Ltd v. Burchell* (1978) was quoted with approval. That passage laid down the following standards of fairness as being normally (but not always) applicable to dismissals for suspected misconduct, including suspected dishonesty:

1. the employer must honestly believe in the guilt of the employee;

2. the employer must have in his mind reasonable grounds upon which to sustain that belief;

3. at the final stage at which he formed that belief, on those grounds, the employer must have carried out as much investigation into the matter as was reasonable in all the circumstances of the case.

In practice, the first and second of these elements of fairness may often be combined – did the employer hold a reasonable belief in the employee's guilt? Belief in guilt will not be reasonable if unsupported by objective evidence.

Reasonable investigation is the cornerstone of a fair dismissal.

Where the employer's investigation has not been completed and may continue for some time, he should consider suspending the employee, in the interests of both the business and the employee. Unless the employee's contract of employment permits suspension without pay during disciplinary investigations, the suspension should be with pay. Otherwise, the employee will be entitled to resign and claim that he has been constructively dismissed.

A suspected employee should be informed of the complaints against him and be allowed an opportunity to give his own version of events to the person who will decide whether or not he should be dismissed. Informing an employee of the substance of the complaints against him may entail supplying him with details of statements made by witnesses in order to enable him properly to put forward his explanation; see The investigative process p160.

Multiple suspect cases

Particular difficulties arise where more than one employee is suspected of an act of misconduct. In *Monie v. Coral Racing Ltd* (1981), the Court of Appeal held that the dismissal of one of a pair of suspects was fair in the circumstances of the case. Money had disappeared from the employer's safe and there were strong grounds for believing that either the appellant or another employee had taken it. The company could not pinpoint the culprit and therefore dismissed both individuals.

The Court of Appeal took into account the fact that the employer, having conducted a reasonable investigation into the matter, could not be expected to retain a suspected employee who occupied a position of trust. The judges accepted that their decision involved a departure from the first and second limbs of the *Burchell* test. Where the employer reasonably believed in the guilt of one of the two employees, but was unable in fairness to decide which was guilty, it would be 'perverting a valuable guideline . . . into an inflexible rule' to hold that, as there was no unequivocal and reasonable belief in the guilt of one particular employee, it was unfair to dismiss him.

It is not clear how far this approach can be pressed. A classic example of the problem created by multiple-suspect cases is that of losses suffered in bar takings, apparently as a result of dishonesty, where the employer cannot pinpoint which of numerous members of his bar staff is responsible. Inevitably, much will depend on the particular facts, but it is surely possible for the *Monie* principle to be stretched to cover even the dismissal of, say, half a dozen employees, provided that:

1. there have been full investigations into the circumstances of the losses; and

2. dismissal of suspects is the only means of preserving the employer's interests, especially if losses are continuing to mount; and

3. dismissal is applied as a consistent penalty to all those individuals who are reasonably suspected of dishonesty.

The vital question in these cases was summarised simply by the EAT in *Parr v. Whitbread plc* (1989): 'Is there anything more a reasonable employer should have done?' If the answer is negative, dismissal will usually be fair.

14.5 Criminal charges

Pending criminal proceedings

It is vital to grasp the difference between the requirements of fairness in industrial relations and the principles of criminal law. For example, reasonable belief in the employee's guilt may be based upon a confession made by the employee, even if that confession would be inadmissible in a criminal trial. In *Morley's of Brixton Ltd v. Minott* (1982), a dismissal based upon such a confession was upheld as fair by the EAT.

It is well established that a dismissal may be fair, despite a lack of proof that the employee actually committed the alleged act of misconduct – and even if he has in fact been acquitted at a criminal trial concerning the same matter, as in *Saeed v. Greater London Council* (1986). The same is true if, for example, the employee is, after the dismissal, acquitted on a criminal charge relating to the alleged incident. Evidence which comes to light after the dismissal will generally not be relevant.

An especially acute problem arises where an employer wishes to question an employee about an incident which is the subject of police inquiries and possible criminal charges. The mere fact that an employee has been charged with criminal conduct allegedly committed during his employment is not by itself usually sufficient to justify summary dismissal. The employee charged may be advised by his representatives to say nothing. In such a case, can it be fair to dismiss when the employer has not had an opportunity to consider the employee's version of events?

The Court of Appeal in *Harris and Shepherd v. Courage (Eastern) Ltd* (1982), upheld a dismissal in such circumstances. It is essential for the employer to give the employee a chance to explain and to make him realise that dismissal is contemplated.

There is, however, no hard and fast rule that, once a man has been charged with a criminal offence, his employer cannot dismiss him on suspicion of having committed that offence if the employee chooses not to make a statement, even if he is acting on legal advice. At that stage the reasonable employer is entitled to consider whether the material he has is sufficiently indicative of guilt to justify dismissal without warning. If it is so indicative, a decision to dismiss may be fair.

Involving the police

Employers should avoid abandoning their own investigations and relying solely upon the outcome of police inquiries. In *Read v. Phoenix Preservation Ltd* (1985), the EAT said it would be 'wholly improper' for an employer to allow the police to be present at an internal hearing without the employee's foreknowledge and consent. In any event, a police officer should not be allowed to conduct the disciplinary hearing on behalf of the company.

Offences unconnected with work

The Code of Practice sets out the basic principles relating to criminal offences committed outside the employment. It states that such offences should not be treated as automatic reasons for dismissal, regardless of whether the offence has any relevance to the duties of the individual as an employer. The main consideration should be whether the offence is one that makes the individual unsuitable for his type of work or unacceptable to other employees. Employees should not be dismissed solely because a charge against them is pending or because they are absent through having been remanded in custody.

It is not always easy to decide whether criminal dishonesty will make the individual unsuitable for continued employment. Much will depend upon the nature of the employment. In *Moore v. C and A Modes* (1981), a section leader in a retail store with 20 years' service was dismissed for shoplifting at another store. In a job where the opportunities for dishonesty were plentiful, the EAT held that it was fair to dismiss an employee who was 'reasonably believed to have been stealing just down the road', notwithstanding a long past record of honest and trusted service.

Rehabilitated offenders

The Rehabilitation of Offenders Act 1974 provides that a spent conviction or the failure to disclose a spent conviction shall not be a proper ground for dismissing a person from any office, profession, occupation or employment. A conviction is 'spent' for these purposes if the convicted person successfully completes a 'rehabilitation period', the length of which depends upon the nature of the sentence imposed.

In *Property Guards Ltd v. Taylor and Kershaw* (1982), two security officers were dismissed when it was discovered that some years previously they had been convicted of offences involving dishonesty. The convictions were 'spent' under the terms of the Act. Despite the high degree of trust which a security firm invests in its staff, security officers are not – oddly – within the classes of workers excluded from the provisions of the Act and the EAT held that the dismissals based on spent convictions were unfair.

Employers concerned about the effect of this decision may anticipate the point by requiring employees under their contract of employment to disclose any spent convictions. Unfortunately, such a provision is unlikely to justify dismissal for non-disclosure, since section 4(2)(b) of the Act provides that a person 'shall not be subject to any liability or otherwise prejudiced in law' by reason of failing to disclose a spent conviction.

14.6 Fair procedures in practice

Basic principles

The importance of procedural matters in unfair dismissal law was emphasised by the House of Lords in the *Polkey* case. Lord Bridge made it clear that, even where an employer has *prima facie* grounds to dismiss an employee for misconduct, he will not, in most cases, act reasonably in treating that reason as sufficient for dismissal unless and until he has taken the necessary 'procedural' steps. Thus, Lord Bridge said,

> 'the employer will normally not act reasonably unless he investigates the complaint of misconduct fully and fairly and hears whatever the employee wishes to say in his defence or in explanation or mitigation'.

Since then, in a number of cases judges have provided interesting and useful guidance on matters of disciplinary procedure. A case which arose out of the miners' strike, *McLaren v. National Coal Board* (1988), saw the Court of Appeal stress that 'no amount of heat in industrial warfare can justify failing to give an employee an opportunity of giving an explanation for misconduct'. Even where a serious offence is admitted, at least a hearing will enable the employer to consider any mitigating factors before deciding what action to take.

Moreover, before an employer sets disciplinary procedures in train, he must first have reason to believe that a breach of discipline has occurred. The case of *Laughton and Hawley v. Bapp Industrial Supplies Ltd* (1986), shows that it is a mistake to assume too readily that any act by an employee which, on the surface, seems hostile to his employer's interests justifies a disciplinary penalty.

The employees were a warehouse manager and his deputy who knew details of the company's suppliers, customers and pricing. In November 1984, they wrote to ten suppliers, stating that they intended to start trading the following January and asking for product lists and other terms. In December, the company found out and, in an interview, the men admitted that they planned to set up in the same line of business. They were summarily dismissed. An industrial tribunal held that they had been guilty of gross misconduct; their intention to set up in competition was in itself a breach of the implied duty of loyalty.

They appealed successfully. While the EAT thought it understandable that an employer should be suspicious in such circumstances, dismissal was only justified if he had reasonable grounds for believing that a wrongful act had been, or was about to be, committed. According to the EAT, an employee who plans to compete with his employer, either on his own account or on behalf of another organisation, does not thereby breach his contract, unless he is in breach of a specific term which does not fall foul of the doctrine of restraint of trade, or is intending to misuse trade secrets. There were no solid grounds for supposing that this was the case here, nor was there any suggestion that the two men did not devote their working time or their talent during that time to their employer's business.

It is impossible to provide a checklist of all the procedural mishaps which may amount to a breach of natural justice. A thought-provoking example of such a breach occurred in *Campion v. Hamworthy Engineering Ltd* (1987). The Court of Appeal said that it was a serious breach of natural justice for a person hearing an appeal by an employee under his employer's disciplinary procedure against dismissal to have a private discussion, before deciding the appeal, with the person who had taken the original decision to dismiss, or who had presented the employer's case at the appeal.

Significantly, in *Campion* the private discussion took place after the appeal was heard, but before its determination. The Court of Appeal acknowledged that, in the practical circumstances of industrial life, an appeal pursuant to a disciplinary procedure cannot be conducted 'with the formal rigour appropriate to an appeal in the Supreme Court'. Nevertheless, holding such a private discussion involved impropriety that was a matter of substance, not just of form.

The same principle would apply to a private discussion which prejudiced the fair handling of the original disciplinary hearing itself.

Delay

Even where an employee's conduct plainly merits dismissal, an employer who delays excessively in taking steps to deal with the matter may be acting unfairly. This is the lesson of *Royal Society for the Prevention of Cruelty to Animals v. Cruden* (1986). An industrial tribunal found that the employee, an RSPCA inspector, had been guilty of 'gross misjudgment, and idleness, quite incompatible with the proper performance of his duties'. Had the RSPCA acted promptly, dismissal would have been reasonable. However, although the incidents complained of occurred in February and March, for a variety of reasons which did not satisfy the tribunal as legitimate, it was not until October that formal disciplinary proceedings were commenced. The tribunal thought that this rendered the eventual dismissal unfair, a decision which the EAT declined to overturn, although Mr Cruden's contributory fault resulted in a nil compensation award.

The investigative process

The danger of jumping to conclusions is shown by the case of *ILEA v. Gravett* (1988). According to the EAT, the *Burchell* test requires an employer to prove, on the balance of probabilities, two things. First, he must prove that he believed – again on the balance of probabilities (not beyond reasonable doubt, as in a criminal trial) – that the employee was guilty of misconduct. Secondly, he must prove that in all the circumstances based upon the knowledge of and after consideration of sufficient relevant facts and factors, he could reasonably hold that belief.

The EAT accepted that the situations which arise upon the second limb of this 'test' can and will be infinitely variable. At one extreme there will be cases where the employee is virtually 'caught in the act'. At the other, there will be situations where the issue is one of pure inference. As the scale moves towards the latter end, so the amount of enquiry and investigation which may be required, including questioning of the employee, is likely to increase. At some stage, the employer will need to face the employee with the information which he has. That may be during an investigation prior to the decision that there was sufficient evidence upon which to form the view, or it may be at an initial disciplinary hearing. In some cases, it may be that, after hearing the employee's version, further investigation ought fairly to be made.

To say this is not to suggest that it is incumbent upon a reasonable employer to carry out a quasi-judicial investigation, with a confrontation of witnesses and cross-examination of witnesses. This was made clear by the Northern Ireland Court of Appeal in *Ulsterbus Ltd v. Henderson* (1989).

However, employers need to take care. In *Louies v. Coventry Hood & Seating Co. Ltd* (1990), at both the disciplinary and the appeal hearing, the employers said that they had two independent statements from witnesses suggesting that the employee had been guilty of gross misconduct. On neither occasion was he allowed to see the statement; no reason was given. This was held to be unfair.

Relying on information received

Sometimes employers rely upon facts supplied by informants in pursuing a disciplinary investigation. It is not uncommon for an informant to refuse to allow his identity to be disclosed – perhaps because of fear of intimidation. This is what happened in *Linford Cash & Carry Ltd v. Thomson* (1989), in which the EAT suggested a number of helpful guidelines for employers faced with similar problems in the future. A careful balance must be maintained between the desire to protect informants who are genuinely in fear and providing a fair hearing of issues for employees who are accused of misconduct. For example, the information given by the informant should be put in writing and in taking a statement from an informant, the following points are important:

1. the date, time and place of each or any observation or incident;

2. the opportunity and ability to observe clearly and with accuracy;

3. circumstantial evidence, such as why certain small details are memorable;

4. whether the informant has suffered at the hands of the accused or has any other reason to fabricate, whether from a personal grudge or any other reason or principle.

Conduct of the hearing

In both large and small businesses, it will not always be easy to decide who should conduct a disciplinary hearing and take the decision whether or not to dismiss an employee on the grounds of misconduct. In *Slater v. Leicestershire Health Authority* (1989), the Court of Appeal held that a nurse's dismissal was not rendered unfair by the fact that the manager who had carried out a preliminary investigation also conducted the disciplinary hearing and took the decision to dismiss.

The Court of Appeal accepted that it is a general principle that a person who holds an enquiry must be seen to be impartial. However, the rules of natural justice do not form an independent ground upon which a dismissal decision may be attacked, although a breach of those rules will clearly be an important matter when an industrial tribunal considers the question of fairness. It is noteworthy, however, that one judge considered that it was ill-advised for the manager concerned to conduct the disciplinary hearing after he had been involved in the preliminary investigation.

In small concerns, it will often be inevitable that the same member of management (possibly the managing director himself) will be personally involved throughout. In larger organisations, however, it will make sense to arrange matters so that it can be shown that the person who conducted the disciplinary hearing did so with an independent and open mind.

Similar problems arise if a witness to an incident later seeks himself to discipline an employee because of it. In *Moyes v. Hylton Castle Working Men's Social Club and Institute Ltd* (1986), the club's chairman and assistant secretary observed an incident in which, it was alleged, the club steward sexually harassed a barmaid. Complaints about the steward were investigated by a sub-committee of five officials, including the chairman and assistant secretary. Both men also participated in a subsequent meeting at which it was decided to dismiss the steward.

The EAT held that it was a breach of natural justice, rendering the dismissal unfair, for the two officials to be both witnesses and judges. Any reasonable observer would conclude that in view of that dual role, justice did not appear to be done, nor was it done. The EAT acknowledged that there will inevitably be cases in industrial relations where a witness to an incident will be the person who has to make the decision to dismiss. However, in *Moyes* it was entirely unnecessary.

The Code of Practice says that disciplinary procedures should give employees 'the right to be accompanied by a trade union representative or by a fellow employee of their choice'. Sometimes employees ask if they can be accompanied by their solicitor or other legal adviser. An employer must judge each such request on its merits. There is no hard and fast rule that a solicitor must always be allowed to attend. Indeed, in some cases this may be positively unhelpful, especially if the solicitor is inexperienced in industrial relations matters and seeks to adopt an excessively legalistic approach in purported defence of his client's interests. However, there are cases when it might be unfair to deny an employee legal representation: misconduct cases potentially including a criminal offence are one example.

Consistency

The importance of consistency in disciplinary proceedings is noted in *Discipline At Work*. The handbook makes it clear, however, that:

> 'this does not mean that similar offences will always call for similar disciplinary action: each case must be looked at on its merits and any relevant circumstances taken into account'.

A good illustration of how this principle works in practice is provided by the decision of the Court of Appeal in *Securicor Ltd v. Smith* (1989). Mr Smith's dismissal resulted from an incident in which he and his team leader breached one of Securicor's strict rules governing the handling and transit of cash. Initially, both employees were dismissed and their dismissals were affirmed upon appeal. After that, both men lodged further appeals. At that stage, it was decided that the team leader was less at fault than Mr Smith. The team leader's appeal therefore succeeded and he was reinstated with a final warning, but Mr Smith's appeal failed.

The Court of Appeal considered that Securicor did not act unreasonably in accepting the appeal panel's decision that Mr Smith was more culpable than his team leader. The appeal panel's view was rational and based on clear reasons and the industrial tribunal found no facts to indicate that the factual basis of the appeal panel's decision was wrong. Indeed, had Securicor refused to accept the findings of the appeal panel and not reinstated the team leader, he would have had 'an unanswerable case that his dismissal was unfair, since the employers would have rejected a reasonable finding by the very panel which they themselves set up'.

Deciding the penalty

Courts and tribunals have long emphasised that, for a dismissal to be fair, the penalty of dismissal must not be disproportionate to the offence. It must 'fit the crime'. This theme is taken up in *Discipline At Work*, which includes a separate section about deciding on and implementing disciplinary action. For instance, an act of dishonesty will, as mentioned above, usually be regarded as gross misconduct warranting summary dismissal (provided a reasonable disciplinary procedure is followed). The question is sometimes asked whether the same principle would apply in the case of an employee who, say, filches an office biro.

A similar point arose for consideration in *Rentokil Ltd v. Mackin* (1989), in which the EAT in Scotland accepted an industrial tribunal's view that an employer had reacted too harshly to a trivial offence of dishonesty. Two employees were summarily dismissed after their employers were informed that they had helped themselves to milk-shakes while working in the kitchen of a client company. The men did not deny the offence and offered to pay for the drinks, maintaining that the client's manager had allowed them to help themselves in his previous employment. The industrial tribunal and the EAT accepted that the employees were in a position of trust and that the fact that the value of the milk-shake was small was not decisive. Taking the milk-shake amounted to theft but, within the spectrum of such conduct, it was 'at the lower end'. Dismissal was not reasonable, although the compensation awarded to the employees was reduced by 40 per cent to reflect their contributory fault.

Appeal procedures

Discipline At Work provides useful guidance on the holding of appeals. This is particularly helpful with regard to the stress laid by the House of Lords in *West Midlands Co-operative Society Ltd v. Tipton* (1986) on the importance of recognising an employee's right of appeal. More recently, the EAT emphasised the following in *Whitbread & Co plc v. Mills* (1988):

'Appeal procedures form part of the process of ensuring that a dismissal is fair and both the original and the appellate decisions of the employer are necessary elements in the overall process of terminating a contract of employment. It follows that the fairness issue must be decided after the appeal procedure has been completed.'

Sometimes a defect in an employer's disciplinary procedures can be remedied at the appeal stage. If some act or omission has brought about an unfair disciplinary hearing, whether or not an appeal has rectified the situation will depend upon the degree of unfairness of the original hearing. If the original decision is scrapped and the matter is re-heard from the beginning, the fault may be corrected. However, if there is to be a correction by the appeal, then that appeal must be comprehensive in nature, in other words, essentially a re-hearing rather than a mere review.

Even if an employee has a contractual right of appeal, to deny him that right does not *automatically* render his dismissal unfair, according to the EAT *Post Office v. Marney* (1990). It is, however, to say the very least, risky to commit such a breach of contract and sound industrial relations practice.

15
Poor Performance and Dismissal

15.1 Introduction

It is potentially fair to dismiss an employee for a reason relating to his capability or qualifications for performing his work.

'Capability' in this context is assessed by reference to the employee's skill, aptitude, health or any other physical or mental quality.

'Qualifications' means any degree, diploma or other academic, technical or professional qualification relevant to the position which the employee held.

Capability dismissals tend to give rise to problems, which are exacerbated by the overlap in some cases between the capability of the employee and his conduct. For example, if an employee is not doing his job properly, it may be because of his lack of co-operation and poor attitude, a lack of the necessary ability, or both.

In such cases, it is not easy to decide to what extent a formal disciplinary procedure needs to be followed. As a general rule, however, disciplinary procedures as such should not be used to deal with a mere lack of capability. The handbook *Discipline At Work* provides useful suggestions for the handling of these often tricky cases.

The special problems which arise where ill-health absence gives rise to a lack of capability are discussed in Chapter 16.

15.2 Incompetence

The problem

Before recruiting an employee, the employer will have tried to

166

assess whether he is sufficiently skilled or has the aptitude for the work in question. Clearly, it will not be until the employee has actually performed the job for a period of time that the employer will be sure that the appropriate standard of work is being achieved.

As the qualifying period for unfair dismissal rights is generally two years, it will usually, by means of proper monitoring processes, be possible to weed out unsuitable employees before they are eligible to make a complaint of unfair dismissal to a tribunal. Personnel policies should take this into account.

Difficulties arise, however, where a longer-serving and previously satisfactory employee demonstrates a lack of skill or aptitude. This can arise for one or more of a number of reasons, such as:

1. the job may change and become more demanding;

2. he may be unable to cope with new technology;

3. his attitude to the job may deteriorate;

4. he may be over-promoted and unable to perform satisfactorily in a more senior position.

Evidence of incompetence

Establishing a lack of skill or aptitude will not always be easy. An approach often followed by tribunals is to ask whether the employer honestly and reasonably held the belief that the employee was not competent and whether there was a reasonable ground for that belief. To be able to satisfy the tribunal, the employer should investigate the matter fully.

Regular job appraisals, properly operated, may provide helpful evidence. A failure to achieve reasonable productivity or sales targets may also demonstrate incompetence. On the other hand, there may be a number of commercial or other factors beyond the employee's personal control which account for an apparent decline in performance. Complaints from customers or fellow employees will also merit serious investigation to find out whether they have any substance.

Employers should bear in mind that a letter of commendation sent to the employee, or a substantial wage rise given to him shortly before a warning or dismissal for incompetence, may strike a tribunal as inconsistent with the argument that the employee was lacking in capability. A glowing and carelessly-worded reference may create similar problems.

Dealing with incompetence

In appraising the problem, it is important to bring the criticisms to the employee's attention and to seek his comments. The handbook *Discipline At Work* offers useful guidance and emphasises that proper training and supervision are essential to the achievement of satisfactory performance. Inevitably, the appropriate action to be taken following full and sympathetic discussion with the employee will depend upon the facts. It might, for example, involve:

- re-training;
- additional training;
- additional support or back-up;
- assistance with domestic problems;
- medical treatment;
- changing the employee's duties.

It would be pointless and indeed misleading to suggest here a precise period of time which should be given to an employee to demonstrate a sustained improvement in his level of skill or aptitude. Relevant factors may include:

- the nature of the job;
- the employee's length of service;
- his status;
- his past record;
- the seriousness of his shortcomings;
- the interests of the business.

The employer has to make a *bona fide* judgement of what is reasonable in the circumstances.

The employee should be warned of the consequences of a failure to improve, so that there is no confusion. Sometimes it is suggested that there is no need to give a senior employee a warning that his job is in jeopardy – it will usually be clear that he is under-performing. On the other hand, the case of *McPhail v. Gibson* (1976), suggests that an explicit warning for senior employees is especially important. Certainly, it must be plain to the employee, somehow or other, that his job is seriously at risk if dismissal is to be fair.

Occasionally, a single act of gross negligence will suffice to justify dismissal. The sin may be one of omission or commission. Everything will depend upon the circumstances. It will be comparatively rare – except in the case of high-risk employees (see below) – for an employer to be able to justify dismissal without giving the employee a second chance.

A checklist for the handling of dismissals for incompetence is included in Chapter 26.

High-risk employees

There are a number of exceptional activities in which the degree of skill required is so high, and the potential consequence of the smallest departure from that standard so serious, that a single failure to perform as required is enough to justify a dismissal.

In *Alidair Ltd v. Taylor* (1976), examples were given of the passenger-carrying airline pilot, the scientist operating the nuclear reactor, the chemist in charge of research into the possible effect of drugs, the driver of an express train and the driver of an articulated lorry full of sulphuric acid. With all such employees, one error can bring about a major disaster.

Over-promotion

Particular care must be taken in the case of apparent over-promotion. If the employee is clearly not able to perform the new job adequately, it may be unfair to dismiss rather than to allow him to return to his old job, or another, more suitable position in the organisation. It is in any event wise (as in all cases of apparent incompetence) to ascertain whether there are any jobs which the employee could perform competently before taking a dismissal decision.

Blanket dismissals

Suppose serious employee negligence occurs, potentially justifying dismissal, but the employer, in investigating what went wrong, finds himself unable to pinpoint precisely who was responsible. Are his hands tied?

The case of *McPhie and McDermott v. Wimpey Waste Management Ltd* (1981), shows that they are not. A gear box in a company vehicle seized up because it had not been filled with oil. Two fitters were responsible for topping up the oil but management could not ascertain which of them was specifically at fault. Both were dismissed. Applying the principles suggested in *Monie v. Coral Racing Ltd* (1980) (see Multiple suspect cases p154), both dismissals were fair, although the EAT accepted that those principles should not be pressed too far in cases other than of suspected dishonesty.

Nor, interestingly, was dismissal too severe a punishment for this single instance of negligence. In reaching this conclusion, the EAT was influenced by the following considerations:

1. the vehicle had been damaged;

2. if an unserviceable vehicle had been discovered on the road, the company's licence was liable to be revoked;

3. a vehicle in such a state could have caused a serious accident.

The *Monie* principles may be relevant in cases – far from uncommon – involving stock or cash discrepancies at pubs, clubs and off-licences. *Whitbread & Co plc v. Thomas* (1988) is an illustration. Serious stock losses occurred at an off-licence and, although three part-time assistants in the branch were warned about the losses, the losses continued. Ultimately, the three assistants were dismissed. The EAT accepted that dismissal was an option reasonably open to the company in the circumstances; on the facts, to have transferred the assistants to other shops subject to a warning would merely have been 'postponing the inevitable'.

15.3 Lack of qualifications

Sometimes an employer will recruit an employee on the basis that the employee must obtain certain necessary or desirable qualifications within a defined period of time. If so, it will be important to record the position clearly in writing at the outset of the employment. If the employer fails to obtain the required qualifications within the agreed time limit, dismissal will usually be justified.

Occasionally, the employer will decide that an employee who is already a member of staff requires a particular qualification for the proper performance of his job. If the employee fails to obtain such qualification within a reasonable period of time, it is possible for dismissal to be fair if the employer can show that the qualification is essential and that only with such a qualification can the employee do the job properly.

It will usually be difficult to establish these points to the satisfaction of an industrial tribunal. It is also conceivable in such circumstances that a dismissed employee might be entitled to a redundancy payment, if his revised job specification amounts to a different kind of work.

15.4 Claiming money from an employee

Incompetence sometimes has expensive consequences. An employer who suffers financial loss through negligence may wish to seek recompense from the individual concerned.

The Wages Act 1986 protects workers from unlawful pay deductions and fines. Even where a worker, in writing or under the terms of his contract, agrees in advance to a deduction being made from his wages, special safeguards apply if he works in 'retail employment' and his employer makes a deduction or imposes a fine because of cash shortages or stock deficiencies. The employer must, before receiving the first payment of any particular shortage, notify the worker in writing of the full amount owed. Any deduction – even if it is due to alleged dishonesty – must not exceed 10 per cent of the gross amount of wages payable on any pay day. However, this limit does not apply to the worker's final payment of wages on termination.

An employer may sue an employee or ex-employee for compensation for losses incurred by the company because of the individual's negligence. An employee owes an implied contractual duty to his employer to exercise reasonable care and skill in carrying out his job. Thus, in *Janata Bank v. Ahmed* (1981), the Court of Appeal upheld a judgment ordering a former bank manager to compensate his former employers to the tune of more than £30,000 in respect of losses caused by his negligence.

In practice, however, many incompetent employees are, in the financial sense, 'men of straw'. To sue them may simply be to throw good money after bad.

16
Sickness and Dismissal

16.1 Introduction

Employee sickness often gives rise to human problems. Furthermore, when someone is away from work for more than a short time due to ill-health, his or her job may eventually be placed in jeopardy. There is a widely-held belief that an employer is debarred from dismissing an employee whose sickness is genuine, and who is no malingerer. That belief is misconceived. Unfortunately, the legal rules in this area have long been a source of confusion, both to employers and employees.

16.2 Frustration of employment by sickness

It is possible – but unusual – for long-term sickness to bring an employee's contract to an end by operation of law. This is the doctrine of 'frustration', discussed in section 3.6 Frustration of the contract p38.

In most cases an employer will not be able to rely on frustration. He must therefore take care to act reasonably.

16.3 How long must an employer wait?

The EAT stated, in *Spencer v. Paragon Wallpapers Ltd* (1976), that the basic question in such cases is: In all the circumstances, can the employer be expected to wait any longer and, if so, how much longer?

In answering that question, the employee's length of service will be relevant. In the case of long-serving employees, an employer

173

should be slow to dismiss on account of a single period of sickness absence, especially if that absence is viewed in the light of a previously good attendance record.

The terms of the contract may also have to be considered. The contract may provide for full or part payment of wages for a specified period of sickness absence. It may be unfair to dismiss an employee during that period, but not necessarily. Conversely, it is not necessarily fair to dismiss once that period has expired – everything will depend on the facts of the case.

The nature of the employee's job and the interests of the business may also be highly relevant. Even if there is no guarantee that the employee will be able to return to work within the very near future, it will not always be fair to dismiss. Much will depend upon the particular requirements of the business. A large organisation may be able to cope with an absent employee for a considerable period of time. On the other hand, the absence of a single worker may soon cause profound difficulties if the department is small and the absence puts great strain on other people who have to do the work. Similarly, the absence of a senior employee may be much more damaging than, say, that of an industrial worker on the factory floor.

The type of illness and prospect of recovery in the light of any available medical opinion will be critical factors, although the decision whether or not to dismiss should not be a purely medical one. This emerges from the decision of the EAT in *East Lindsey District Council v. Daubney* (1977), in which it was said:

'While employers cannot be expected to be, nor is it desirable that they should set themselves up as, medical experts, the decision to dismiss or not to dismiss is not a medical question, but a question to be answered by the employers in the light of the available medical advice. It is important, therefore, that when seeking advice employers should do so in terms suitably adjusted to the circumstances.'

The EAT added the following: 'Unless there are wholly exceptional circumstances, before an employee is dismissed on the ground of ill-health it is necessary that he should be consulted and the matter discussed with him, and that in one way or another steps should be taken by the employer to discover the true medical position.'

The handbook *Discipline At Work* provides guidance on the practicalities of dealing with absence procedures. It includes in an appendix a suggested form of letter to an absent employee's GP enquiring about the medical position.

Problems arise where there is a conflict of medical opinion, for example, where the employee's GP takes the view that he is, or soon will be, fit to return to work, while a 'company doctor' disagrees. It is not necessarily unfair to accept the report which is less favourable to the employee. The 'company doctor' will often be more familiar with the requirements of the job and his opinion may therefore carry more weight. It may be prudent, however, to refer more difficult cases to an independent specialist.

16.4   Access to medical reports

Unless the employee's contract of employment makes it clear that the employer is entitled to have the employee undergo a medical examination, the employee's consent is required before an examination can take place or medical information is disclosed. The Access to Medical Reports Act 1988 introduced a number of new procedural safeguards where a medical report is obtained for employment purposes from a medical practitioner 'who is or has been responsible for the clinical care of the individual'.

Briefly, the Act requires employers to notify their employees if they intend to apply to a medical practitioner for a medical report and to obtain the employee's consent to the application. The notification must also inform the employee of his or her rights under the Act.

If an employee refuses to give consent, however, an employer who follows a reasonable disciplinary procedure may nevertheless be able fairly to dismiss the employee, acting on such information as is available.

16.5   Assessing the position

It is important to discuss the position with the employee and take account of his representations. The EAT pointed out in the *East Lindsey* case that discussions and consultation will often bring to light facts and circumstances of which the employers were unaware, and which will throw a new light on the problem. If the employee is not consulted, and given an opportunity to state his case, an injustice may be done.

Where a disabled employee is concerned, it may also be appropriate to take account of the views of his welfare officer. Again, a question arises as to whether a failure to consult and consider representations will always render a dismissal unfair.

It was suggested in *Taylorplan Catering (Scotland) Ltd v. McInally* (1980), that an employee may, on occasion, be able to escape the consequences of failing to follow a fair procedure if he can convince the tribunal that to have handled the problem correctly would have made no actual difference to the final outcome. This 'last resort' defence is no longer available following the Law Lords' ruling in the *Polkey* case (see Chapter 12).

It is worth noting that in the *Taylorplan* case, the employers' need for a fit and healthy employee was an important factor in rendering the dismissal fair. Where the terms of the contract themselves specifically emphasise this requirement, the employer will tend to be in a stronger position than where the contract is silent on the point.

16.6 Alternatives to dismissal

Finally, the employer should consider whether any alternative to dismissal is available. Thus, in *Garricks (Caterers) v. Nolan* (1980), the employer was held to have acted unreasonably in not giving sufficient consideration to finding the employee a job in circumstances where, although he was not fit enough to do shift work, he could have done a day job. Similarly, if an employee has become incapable of manual work, it may be possible to allocate lighter duties to him, even if this means asking him to accept a pay cut rather than imposing a dismissal.

16.7 Persistent intermittent absences

A different kind of problem arises where an employee is frequently absent, but only for short periods of time. Considerable disruption may be caused and again the difficulties will be particularly acute where the employee works in a small department or occupies a key position. *Discipline At Work* emphasises that persistent absence should be dealt with promptly, firmly and consistently, so that employees realise exactly where they stand.

Because of the intermittent nature of this kind of absenteeism, medical reports may be of little assistance. There might be a variety of different reasons for the absences and any medical symptoms of illness only transient.

While it will usually be prudent to consider whether or not a medical report would help, it is clear in any event that an employer cannot be expected to tolerate persistent intermittent absenteeism indefinitely. Dismissal will not necessarily be unfair just because each absence is covered by a medical certificate.

The following factors are likely to be relevant:

1. the employee's age, length of service, performance and absence record as a whole (including the lengths of the various absences and the periods of good health between them);

2. the reasons given for the absences and the likelihood of an improvement;

3. the position occupied by the employee and whether or not suitable alternative work is available;

4. the effect of the absences upon other workers and upon the interests of the business;

5. the employee's representations;

6. whether or not the employee has been given a reasonable opportunity to improve his record.

In *International Sports Co Ltd v. Thomson* (1980), the employee had an absence record of 25 per cent for the year preceding her dismissal. She had been given various warnings, but no investigation of the medical position was obtained at the point of dismissal. Although the EAT thought that the dismissal related to conduct, or possibly 'some other substantial reason', rather than capability, it nevertheless held that the dismissal was fair. What was required was a fair review of the attendance record and the reasons for it and also appropriate warnings, after the employee had been given an opportunity to make representations. In the absence of an adequate improvement in the attendance record, dismissal would then usually be justified.

In *Lynock v. Cereal Packaging Ltd* (1988), the EAT emphasised that it was possible for the dismissal of a man with a poor attendance record to be fair, even though there was no medical evidence and the employee was fit at the time of the dismissal. An employer's approach in such cases should, however, be based on 'sympathy, understanding and compassion'.

16.8 Malingerers

Sometimes, employers believe that an employee who claims to be absent because of illness is in fact malingering. If the employee's doctor has provided a sick note, it will usually be difficult to persuade a tribunal to accept an allegation of this kind, but it is not impossible, as the case of *Hutchinson v. Enfield Rolling Mills Ltd* (1981) shows. The employee was off sick but travelled to Brighton to take part in a trade union demonstration. He was sacked and an industrial tribunal held that the dismissal was unfair on the basis that the employer should simply have accepted the sick note and that what the employee did during his absence was therefore irrelevant. The employer's appeal succeeded. It is therefore clear that, in the unusual case where there is evidence to show that the employee is fit to work, despite being covered by a medical certificate, the employer can seek to rely upon that evidence to justify a dismissal.

16.9   Ill-health caused by work

Even where the employee's ill-health is caused directly by the nature of his job, dismissal may be fair if handled properly. That was the case in *Glitz v. Watford Electric Co Ltd* (1979), where the vapour given off by fluid used on the employee's machine gave her headaches, but she refused an alternative job in another department. Nevertheless, the employer must take all reasonable steps to eliminate the dangers to health stemming from the work.

   Dismissal may also be justified even where there is only a risk of illness, such as the risk of a heart attack to a sole wireless operator on a sea-going ship. In *Harper v. National Coal Board* (1980), dismissal was held to be fair when the employee's epilepsy made him a danger to his fellow workers. Failing eyesight or hearing, arthritis or mental illness will also be possible grounds to justify dismissal in these circumstances.

16.10   Disabled workers

A registered disabled person cannot be dismissed, according to section 9(5) of the Disabled Persons Registration Act 1944 (unless the employer 'has reasonable cause for doing so'), where the result is to reduce the number of disabled workers in the business below the obligatory 3 per cent quota specified in the Act. It is unclear whether lack of efficiency or low productivity amount to 'reasonable cause'. The problem arises in a different form in the context of redundancy selection; see Personal circumstances p137.

178

17
Pregnancy Dismissals

17.1 Introduction

Dismissal for pregnancy, or for some reason connected with pregnancy, may be unfair in two situations, ie where a woman:

1. is dismissed for pregnancy or a connected reason before the expected date of confinement; or

2. is not allowed to come back to work after maternity leave, provided she has exercised validly her legal right to return.

In the former case, but not the latter, dismissal will be automatically unfair.

17.2 Dismissal for pregnancy

The basic principle

A woman is unfairly dismissed pursuant to section 60 of the 1978 Act if the principal reason for her dismissal is that she is pregnant or is any other reason connected with her pregnancy, unless:

1. at the effective date of termination of employment she is incapable, because of her pregnancy, of adequately doing the work which she is employed to do; or

2. she cannot, after that date and because of her pregnancy, continue to do that work without there being a contravention of some statute.

There is no statutory definition of the phrase 'any other reason connected with pregnancy'. It covers pregnancy-related illness, miscarriages, and abortions and is likely to be widely interpreted.
    The job security available to pregnant women has been increased

179

by the decision of the House of Lords in *Brown v. Stockton-on-Tees Borough Council* (1988). Mrs Brown was made redundant when the employment scheme on which she had worked came to an end. She applied for a post on a new scheme set up by her employers, but was not offered the job because she was pregnant and would require 14 weeks' maternity leave during the currency of the scheme. The House of Lords held that the selection of a woman for redundancy because she is pregnant and will require maternity leave is dismissal for a 'reason connected with her pregnancy' within the meaning of section 60 of the 1978 Act, and is therefore deemed to be unfair.

Significantly, Lord Griffiths said that section 60 'must be seen as a part of social legislation passed for the specific protection of women and to put them on an equal footing with men'. He did point out, however, that to make a pregnant woman redundant is not invariably unfair; there will be many redundancy dismissals which cannot be said to be connected with the woman's pregnancy. One example would be where she is made redundant because her job ceases to exist, and there is no possibility of offering alternative employment; similarly, if she is selected for redundancy by the application of a criterion such as last in, first out, dismissal will not be said to be connected with the pregnancy.

An equally liberal approach was adopted by the EAT in *Clayton v. Vigers* (1990). To dismiss a woman on maternity leave because it was impossible to find a temporary, rather than permanent, replacement for her was held to be automatically unfair.

The pregnant employee must have the requisite period of continuous service in order to claim that she has been unfairly dismissed under this head. However, a dismissed employee who believes her dismissal to be linked to her pregnancy, but who lacks the requisite period of continuous service, may be able to argue that her dismissal amounted to sex discrimination: *Webb v. Emo Air Cargo Ltd* (1990).

Offer of suitable alternative employment

Even if one of the two exceptions to the basic principle embodied in section 60 applies, the dismissal will still be unfair if, at the time of the dismissal, there was a suitable available vacancy but neither the employer nor any successor of his offered that vacancy before or on the termination date.

If such an offer is made, it must satisfy certain conditions in order to provide a defence, ie:

1. the new job must take effect immediately on the ending of the previous job; and

2. the work to be done must be both suitable in relation to the employee and appropriate for her to do in the circumstances; and

3. the terms as to the capacity and place in which she is to work and the other terms must not be substantially less favourable to her than the corresponding provisions of her previous contract.

17.3 The right to return to work

Conditions of entitlement

The law on the right to return to work following maternity leave is notoriously complex. There are a number of strict (and far from straightforward) conditions with which an employee who wishes to exercise her statutory right to return must comply:

1. she must continue to be employed by her employer (whether or not she is at work) until before the beginning of the eleventh week before the expected week of confinement;

2. she must at the beginning of that eleventh week have been continuously employed for two years;

3. she must inform her employer in writing at least 21 days before her absence or, if that is not reasonably practicable, then as soon as reasonably practicable:
   a) that she will be (or is) absent from work wholly or partly because of pregnancy or confinement; and
   b) that she intends to return to work; and
   c) of the expected week of confinement, or the date of confinement if it has already occurred;

4. if requested to do so by her employer, she must produce for his inspection a doctor's or midwife's certificate stating the expected week of confinement;

5. if at any time after 49 days from the beginning of the expected week of confinement notified (or the date of confinement), the

employer requests written confirmation from the employee that she intends to return to work, the employee must give that confirmation within 14 days of receiving the request (or, if that is not reasonably practicable, as soon as reasonably practicable). The request must be in writing and must make it clear that failure to confirm will disentitle her to return;

6. she must exercise her right strictly in accordance with the detailed requirements of section 47 of the 1978 Act: *Lavery v. Plessey Telecommunications Ltd* (1983). In particular, she must give written notice to her employer at least 21 days before the day on which she proposes to return and she must return within 29 weeks from the week of the actual confinement.

Exercising the right

The employer may postpone the return for up to four weeks. If he proposes to do so, he must notify the employee, giving reasons and specifying a date of return within the four-week period.

An employee on maternity leave can postpone her return for up to four weeks beyond the notified date of return, even if this takes the date beyond the 29-week period. This can only be done once and then only on medical grounds. The employee must provide the employer with a medical certificate stating that she will be incapable of work on the notified date of return.

If there is an interruption of work which makes it unreasonable to expect the employee to return, the 29-week period can be extended. A possible reason for such an interruption is industrial action. If a date of return has been notified she may return as soon as reasonably practicable after the interruption ceases. If not, she can return at any time within 28 days from the end of the interruption.

An employee who has a contractual right to return cannot exercise both contractual and statutory rights separately. She can, however, take advantage of whichever right is, in any respect, more favourable. The decision of the EAT in *Lucas v. Norton of London Ltd* (1984), indicates that where a woman does not exercise her statutory rights, failure to permit her to return after maternity will amount to a dismissal (which may be unfair) if it can be shown that her contract was not terminated when her absence began, but continued throughout.

The detailed application of the rules is fiendishly difficult in many cases, especially if an employee has a contractual right to return to work – the terms of which may sometimes not be entirely clear – as well as her statutory right. In this area, the courts have not so far tended to adopt such a flexible approach to interpreting convoluted facts to the benefit of employees as they have in other cases of pregnancy-related dismissal. The *Lavery* case in particular shows how a woman understandably confused by the tortuous legal requirements may forfeit her job if she makes a minor technical slip when trying to exercise her right to return to work.

Returning to work

The employee's right is to return to the original job on terms and conditions not less favourable than those which would have applied if she had not been absent. It need not be exactly the same job but must be of the same nature and capacity and at the same place. A full-time employee is not entitled to insist on being allowed to return to work only on a part-time basis, although it is possible in some circumstances for an employer who refuses to let her come back part-time to be guilty of sex discrimination, as in *Home Office v. Holmes* (1984).

The woman's prior employment will be deemed to be continuous with her period of employment after her return. For statutory purposes, for example, in relation to notice entitlement and redundancy pay, her period of maternity leave counts as part of her period of continuous employment; see Pregnancy or confinement p223.

If the employer fails to allow the employee to return, she is deemed to have been dismissed as from the notified date of return. The reason for the dismissal will be the reason for which she is refused re-employment. The dismissal will not necessarily be unfair, although in practice that will usually be the case.

If it is not practicable for the employer to allow the employee to return by reason of redundancy, she will be entitled to a redundancy payment, unless the employer (or his successor or an associated employer) offers alternative employment which satisfies the conditions set out below.

The mere fact of redundancy does not prevent the dismissal from being unfair, ie if suitable alternative employment exists and is not offered. Thus, there was an automatically unfair dismissal in *Community Task Force v. Rimmer* (1986), where a suitable alternative vacancy existed, even though the employers would have lost outside funding had they offered that vacancy to the employee. Considerations of what is 'economic' or 'reasonable' do not, according to the EAT, qualify the legal test of whether a job is 'available'. However, if an offer of suitable alternative employment is unreasonably refused, the employee will lose the right to a redundancy payment and the dismissal will be fair.

There are two exceptional cases where a refusal to allow an employee to return will not be deemed to constitute a dismissal:

1. if, immediately before her absence,
    a) the number of employees employed by her employer (and any associated employer) did not exceed five; and
    b) it is not reasonably practicable for the employer (or his successor) either to permit her to return to work in accordance with her statutory rights or to offer her employment under a contract satisfying the conditions set out below,

2. if it is not reasonably practicable for a reason other than redundancy for the employer (or his successor) to permit the employee to return to work pursuant to the statute, and the employer (or an associated employer) offers her employment under a contract satisfying the conditions set out below and the employee either accepts the offer or unreasonably refuses it.

The conditions referred to above are that:

1. the work to be done under the contract is suitable to the employee and appropriate for her to do in the circumstances; and

2. the provisions of the contract are not substantially less favourable than if she had returned pursuant to the statute.

The burden of proving all these matters is on the employer.

Dismissing a replacement

Normally there will be no difficulty in dismissing a temporary replacement for a woman absent on maternity leave, because the replacement will not have achieved sufficient qualifying service to be able to make an unfair dismissal claim.

In exceptional cases, for example, where a person temporarily replaces several employees in succession, the dismissal will normally (but not automatically) be fair if the employer notified the replacement in writing at the time of recruitment that the job would terminate once the last employee returned from maternity leave.

18
Dismissal and Industrial Action

18.1 Introduction

An industrial tribunal does not have the power to consider the fairness of a dismissal where, at the time of dismissal, the employer was conducting a lock-out or the employee was taking part in a strike or other industrial action, unless the employer discriminates between 'relevant employees' (see section 18.3 Discriminating between relevant employees p189), ie where:

1. one or more 'relevant employees' have not been dismissed; or

2. one or more such employees have been offered re-engagement and the employee concerned has not.

The relevant rules are set out in section 62 of the 1978 Act as amended. The reason why the tribunal has no jurisdiction in such matters is not entirely clear. It may reflect the policy, much eroded in recent years, of withdrawing the law from the field of industrial disputes. Surprisingly, section 62 will protect even an employer who has provoked the dispute. The tribunal will not inquire into the motives for his action or into whether or not the strike was justified.

The terms 'lock-out', 'strike' and 'other industrial action' are not defined in the legislation. This is unfortunate, because much turns on their precise meaning.

Special rules (discussed in section 18.4 Unofficial disputes p190) apply where an employee is dismissed while taking part in a strike or other industrial action which is unofficial.

18.2 Strikes, lock-outs and other industrial action

Strikes and lock outs

Whether industrial action in any particular case amounts to a strike or a lock-out is a question of fact for an industrial tribunal to determine, according to the Court of Appeal in *Express and Star Ltd v. Bunday* (1987). The fact that one of the parties to the dispute has committed a breach of contract is relevant but not decisive; thus, a lock-out can occur even if the employees locked out have not broken their terms of employment.

Other industrial action

A wide range of activities may be described as 'other industrial action', such as working to rule, a go-slow or picketing.

Tribunals again have considerable discretion in deciding whether a particular action amounts to 'other industrial action'. In *Faust v. Power Packing Casemakers* (1983), the Court of Appeal indicated that employees may be engaging in industrial action even if they are not in breach of contract. Three employees refused to work overtime because of a dispute over wages. Although there was no contractual obligation upon them to work overtime, the Court of Appeal concluded that the employees' action, in the circumstances, amounted to the application of pressure against the employer in order to extract some benefit from him. The employees therefore forfeited their right not to be unfairly dismissed.

An even trickier question is whether an employee is dismissed for taking part in trade union activities, eg by attending a union meeting during working hours without the employer's consent, or for taking part in other industrial action. No clear legal test has yet emerged, but the distinction is important. In the former case, the dismissal will be automatically unfair; see Chapter 19. On the other hand, in the latter case, the tribunal will have no jurisdiction.

Participation

Sometimes it is unclear whether or not a particular employee is taking part in a strike or other industrial action. The decision of the majority of the Court of Appeal in *Coates and Venables v. Modern Methods and Materials Ltd* (1982) suggests that the motives or reasons of a participating employee are not relevant.

In the *Coates and Venables* case, the employee in question did not go into work during a strike simply because she feared abuse from her colleagues if she did so. She was held to have taken part in the strike. The members of the Court of Appeal did not, unfortunately, speak with one voice but surely participation must be judged by actions, not motives. If it were otherwise, employers would find it impossible to tell which employees were participating and which were not.

Once an employee has clearly indicated that he will take part in a strike or take other industrial action, he will be regarded as having done so until the action is discontinued or he indicates an intention of ceasing to participate: *Williams v. Western Mail & Echo Ltd* (1980).

Thus, if an employee is on strike and one day has a cold which would have prevented him from going to work, he does not cease to take part in the strike, since he would have been on strike in any event. The same applies to participation in other industrial action. On the other hand, if an employee is off sick when a strike is called, he may never actually 'take part' in the strike within the terms of the legislation, even if he sympathises with its aims.

In practice, it can be difficult for an employer to know exactly how to deal with employees who are absent from work at the time of an industrial dispute. *McKenzie v. Crosville Motor Services Ltd* (1989) provides interesting guidance. During the course of a strike (in which he had worked normally at first) Mr McKenzie failed to turn up for work on two days, without contacting the company to explain why. The employers regarded him as being on strike and sacked him. He claimed unfair dismissal, putting forward certain rather flimsy reasons for his absences.

The EAT would not interfere with the tribunal's finding that, on the facts, Mr McKenzie was taking part in the strike. More significantly, the EAT said that in such a case it is incumbent on an employee who is away from work to provide his employer with information and a reason for his absence, 'so as to establish that he is not away from work as a result of withholding his labour', but for some permissible reason, such as sickness or holidays. An employer who is not given such information may be entitled to assume that the employee is taking part in the dispute.

18.3   Discriminating between relevant employees

Lock-outs

In the context of a lock-out, relevant employees are defined as those who are 'directly interested in the trade dispute in contemplation or furtherance of which the lock-out occurred'.

An employer is not protected by section 62 merely by dismissing all the employees he has locked out. All those directly interested in the dispute must be treated in the same way.

Strikes and other industrial action

Here, relevant employees are 'those employees at the establishment who were taking part in the action at the complainant's date of dismissal'.

The definition covers the case where an employer warns striking workers that he will dismiss those who fail to work normally at a given date. If some heed the ultimatum and return, the employer will be protected by section 62 if he dismisses all those on strike and does not discriminate between them, despite not having dismissed those who returned.

Non-discrimination

It is not necessary, in order for section 62 to apply, for the reason for dismissal to be the employee's participation in a strike or other industrial action. The employer simply has to show that all the relevant employees have been dismissed and that there has been no discrimination with regard to re-engagement. The reasons for the dismissals will not be taken into account.

The bar on discrimination between relevant employees does not mean that, if the employer offers them re-engagement, they must all be offered precisely the same terms. It is sufficient if the nature of the work and the capacity and place of employment are the same.

The extent to which the terms of re-engagement offered by the employer may vary between relevant employees will depend upon the circumstances. The fundamental principle is that there must be no victimisation.

189

An unfair dismissal claim based upon discriminatory re-engagement may only be made where a relevant employee has been offered re-engagement within three months of his dismissal. However, the dismissed employee has six months (rather than the usual three) in which to present his claim.

Selective re-engagement does not automatically render a dismissal unfair. Whether discriminatory selection is reasonable will depend upon the facts of the particular case.

18.4   Unofficial disputes

At the time of writing, the second Employment Bill of 1989 – expected to become the Employment Act 1990 – is passing through Parliament. The Bill extends section 62 by providing that an employee will have no right to complain of unfair dismissal if, at the time of the dismissal, he was taking part in an unofficial strike or other unofficial industrial action. Action will be unofficial in relation to an employee, unless:

1. he is a union member and the union endorses or authorises the action;

2. he is not a union member, but members of a union which has authorised or endorsed the action take part in the action; or

3. no trade union members are taking part in the action.

Membership of a union for purposes unconnected with the employment in question will be disregarded. Industrial action taken by a non-unionised workforce is not 'unofficial' for the purposes of these provisions; the normal section 62 rules will apply in such cases.

The main effect of the change introduced by the Bill is that, when faced with unofficial action, an employer may selectively dismiss any employee for any reason (except a specifically unlawful reason, such as discrimination on the grounds or sex or race), without any fear of an unfair dismissal claim.

19
Dismissal and Trade Union Involvement

19.1 Introduction

Dismissals for trade union membership, activity, or non-membership are covered by section 58 of the 1978 Act, as amended.

An employee dismissed for a reason specified in section 58(1):

1. will be able to claim unfair dismissal even if he has not achieved the period of continuous employment normally required to qualify for unfair dismissal rights or is over 'normal retiring age' or the age of 65;

2. may be able to claim interim relief pending the full hearing (see section 19.6 Interim relief p194);

3. will automatically be held to have been dismissed unfairly;

4. will be eligible for higher levels of compensation than those which are normally applicable.

A dismissal which is not for a trade union-related reason and therefore not automatically unfair may, of course, be unfair under the normal rules. However, the employee must, in such a case, have the requisite period of continuous employment in order to bring a claim. It is therefore important to be able to establish, for example, what can be described as 'trade union activities'.

It is unlawful under section 23 of the 1978 Act as amended, for an employer to take action short of dismissal to prevent or deter an employee from joining or refusing to join a union or from taking part in its activities.

19.2   Excluded categories

Employees falling within the following categories are not affected by the provisions dealt with in this chapter:

• where the employer is the husband or wife of the employee;

• share fishermen;

• employment where under his contract of employment the employee ordinarily works outside Great Britain;

• police service employees;

• where it is shown that the action complained of was taken for the purpose of safeguarding national security.

It is not possible to contract out of the statutory provisions.

19.3   Union membership

It is unfair to dismiss an employee because he is or proposes to become a member of an independent trade union. The rules contained in section 58 did not, however, apply in a case where an employee was dismissed after refusing to leave one union and join another: *Rath v. Cruden Construction Ltd* (1982).

More controversially, it seems that dismissal arising merely out of a claim by a union for recognition is not covered by section 58. Thus, in *Therm A Stor Ltd v. Atkins* (1983), a majority of shop-floor workers applied to join a union. The union requested recognition. The company decided in response to dismiss twenty employees. All those selected for dismissal were union members, yet the EAT would not accept the argument that victimisation of the group should be treated as action taken against each of the individuals within the group. Section 58 was considered to be restricted to dismissal for the personal action or proposed action of an employee.

19.4   Non-membership of a union

It is also automatically unfair to dismiss an employee because he is not a member of any union, or one of the number of particular unions, or refuses or proposes to refuse to become or remain a member. There are no exceptions to this rule, even if there is some form of 'closed-shop agreement' in force.

19.5   Union activities

It is unfair to dismiss an employee because he has taken part, or proposes to take part, in the activities of an independent trade union at any appropriate time. 'Trade union activities' are not defined in the legislation. The term does not cover industrial action, so there is no overlap between section 62 of the 1978 Act (discussed in Chapter 18), and section 58.

An employee does not have to be a union official in order to take part in union activities. On the other hand, a member who is acting in defiance of union policy on a particular issue is clearly not taking part in union activities.

A consistent judicial approach to the interpretation of 'trade union activities' has been lacking. In some cases, the term has been construed restrictively; in other cases, less so. Thus, an employee who complained about his employer's safety standards and had a petition signed by colleagues and vetted by a union official was held not to be taking part in union activities: *Chant v. Aquaboats Ltd* (1978).

However, in *Discount Tobacco & Confectionery Ltd v. Armitage* (1990), an employee who sought her union's help in obtaining written particulars of employment was held to have been dismissed on the grounds of union membership and not merely, as the employers tried to argue, for taking advantage of the union's services. The EAT held that she was protected by section 58.

The 'appropriate time' is time which is either:

1. outside the employee's working hours, ie hours when he is required in accordance with his contract to be at work; or

2. within his working hours but at which, in accordance with arrangements agreed with or consents given by his employer, it is permissible for him to take part in those activities.

The House of Lords indicated in *Post Office v. Crouch* (1974), that an employee may take part in union activities while on his employer's premises although not when actually working. On the other hand, a break period may be outside working hours even though the employee is paid for that period.

In some circumstances, tribunals may imply the consent of the employer to the employee's participation in union activities. The Court of Appeal, however, declined to imply consent in a case where the management merely remained silent when told of the proposed activities: *The Marley Tile Company Ltd v. Shaw* (1980).

19.6 Interim relief

Interim relief is made available by section 77 of the 1978 Act to employees who allege that trade union membership, non-membership or activity was the reason for their dismissal.

In order for interim relief to be granted, the following conditions must be met:

1. an application must be presented to the tribunal before the end of the period of seven days immediately following the effective date of termination;

2. (except in non-membership cases) an authorised official of an independent trade union to which the employee belonged or wished to belong must, within the same seven-day time limit, present a certificate in writing stating that there appear to be reasonable grounds for supposing that the reason for dismissal related to union membership or activity;

3. it must appear likely to the tribunal that at the final hearing, the employee will be found to have been dismissed for one of the unlawful reasons specified.

The tribunal should hear the application as soon as possible after receiving the application and certificate but must, at least seven days before the hearing, give the employer a copy of the application and certificate and notify him of the date, time and place of the hearing. When hearing an application for interim relief, the tribunal chairman may sit alone without lay members.

When interim relief is claimed in relation to a dismissal for non-membership and the employee has sought to join third parties who, he claims, have put pressure on the employer to dismiss him, and provided a request to join third parties has been made at least three days before the hearing date, the tribunal should give notice of that hearing to those third parties as soon as reasonably practicable. The third parties may then take part in the hearing.

The purpose of interim relief is to prevent a dismissal taking full effect before the tribunal has adjudicated on its fairness. If the claim succeeds, then the employer will be asked if he will be prepared to reinstate the employee pending the hearing, or if not, to re-engage him in another job on no less favourable terms, ensuring continuity of employment.

If the employer refuses to do either, or if he offers to re-engage the employee, but the latter refuses and his refusal is considered reasonable, the tribunal will in effect order the employee's suspension on pay.

In theory at least, the availability of interim relief may reduce the risk of strike or other action being taken in support of the dismissed employee.

19.7 Compensation

General

Special rules on compensation apply where an employee is dismissed for a trade union-related reason or where there is a redundancy and selection is for a trade union-related reason. Both of these types of dismissal are automatically unfair.

Basic award

The basic award is calculated in the normal way (see section 24.3 The basic award p237), subject to a minimum (before deductions, if any) which, as at 1 April 1990, was £2,000.

Compensatory award

The compensatory award is calculated in the normal way; see section 24.5 Quantifying the compensatory award p239.

Special award

A special award is calculated in accordance with section 75A of the 1978 Act. It applies only where the employee applies for re-engagement or reinstatement, but it is not necessary that any such order should be made before a special award can be made.

If the tribunal does not order re-engagement or reinstatement, the special award is 104 weeks' pay or £12,500, whichever is the greater, subject to a maximum of £25,000.

If the order is made but not complied with, and the employer fails to satisfy the tribunal that it was not practicable to comply, the special award is 156 weeks' pay, or £18,795, whichever is the greater. There is *no* statutory maximum in this case.

'A week's pay' for the purpose of a special award is not subject to a statutory limit. The financial maxima set out above are reviewable annually; the figures mentioned applied as at 1 April 1990.

The special award replaces the additional award (see Non-compliance with orders p236) which would normally be payable. It may be reduced by such extent as the tribunal considers just and equitable because of the conduct of the complainant – because he has unreasonably prevented an order of reinstatement or re-engagement being complied with, or because he has unreasonably refused an offer from the employer made other than in compliance with such an order, which would have had the effect of reinstating him.

The following will not justify a reduction in compensation:

1. the fact that membership or non-membership may involve the employee in breach of his contract of employment or any other arrangement or agreement;

2. where he is dismissed for non-membership, the fact that he refuses to pay a sum in lieu of membership, whether to the union or any other body, and whether his contract requires it or not;

3. where he is dismissed for non-membership, the fact that he objects, or proposes to object, to the employer making any deduction from his remuneration because of his non-membership, whether his contract permits the employer to do this or not.

19.8   Dismissal and the closed shop

Before 1988, closed-shop dismissals would have warranted a chapter of their own. However, this is one area where the law has become much simpler with the passage of time. The effect of the Employment Act 1988 is that, although a closed-shop agreement is not illegal, it is now unenforceable. All dismissals for non-membership of a trade union are unfair.

20
Business Transfers and Dismissals

20.1 Introduction

Dismissals often occur in the context of a business takeover. Special rules which apply when a business, or part of one, actually changes hands – as opposed to a mere change in shareholding control – mean that many of those dismissals are, or may be, unfair.

No better illustration of the impact of European Community law on UK industrial relations can be found than in these rules. Unfortunately, the importance of the rules is exceeded only by their complexity.

The key provisions are in the Transfer of Undertakings (Protection of Employment) Regulations 1981. The 1981 Regulations were intended to implement a 1977 Directive of the EC Council. This 'Acquired Rights' Directive seeks to 'provide for the protection of employees in the event of a change of employer, in particular to ensure their rights are safeguarded'. A cynic might add that they also have the effect of providing the legal profession with a great deal of work. This chapter outlines the main points but the potential pitfalls are such that, where business transfers are concerned, it is almost always sensible to seek specific expert advice.

In the leading case of *Litster v. Forth Dry Dock & Engineering Co Ltd* (1989), the House of Lords stressed that, when interpreting UK law in this area, courts should strive to give effect to the underlying purpose of the Directive. The trouble is that the Directive is couched in woolly 'Eurojargon' and there is scope for plenty of debate as to how to apply its stated objective in specific cases. Even worse, the drafting of the 1981 Regulations leaves much to be desired.

When the Regulations were originally introduced into the House of Commons, the Government spokesman responsible confessed to a marked lack of enthusiasm for them; many employers – and also insolvency practitioners – now feel much the same.

The 1981 Regulations add to the rules about continuity of employment on business transfers on the 1978 Act, which are outlined in Transfer of business p224. Those rules deal with the 'bridging' of continuity when an employer's identity changes. The 1981 Regulations apply much more widely.

Under common law, it was a basic principle that, when a business changed hands, the contracts of people working in the business did not pass to the new owner merely by virtue of the transfer. The 1981 Regulations reversed the common law position by providing for the automatic transfer of employees to the new owner.

No employer, whether a captain of industry contemplating a huge deal or a would-be purchaser of a corner shop, can afford to under-estimate the potential significance of this relatively unfamiliar regime. Courts and tribunals are becoming ever more willing to interpret the rules flexibly to the advantage of employees. Thus, in *Macer v. Abafast Ltd* (1990), the EAT said that, when interpreting the rules,

'a court should lean in favour of that interpretation which best gives effect to the preservation of continuity of service . . . and to obviate and discourage a tactical manoeuvre which seeks to avoid the clear intention of Parliament'.

20.2 Excluded categories

The main categories of employee excluded from the scope of the 1981 Regulations are:

• employees working in undertakings which are not commercial ventures (although an undertaking which is being run at a loss may still be a 'commercial venture');

• certain seamen;

• certain overseas employees.

In addition, the 1981 Regulations do not apply if there is no 'relevant transfer' (see section 20.3 Relevant transfers, below).

They do not come into play if a takeover involves, not a transfer of an undertaking, but simply a change in the ownership of shares in a company.

20.3   Relevant transfers

The 1981 Regulations only apply where there is a relevant transfer. This is defined in reg 3 as

> 'a transfer from one person to another of an undertaking or part of an undertaking situated immediately before the transfer in the United Kingdom or a part of one which is so situated'.

There has to be a transfer of an undertaking (or part of one) as 'a going concern'. Whether there is a transfer of a business as a going concern is a question of fact. A mere sale of assets by itself does not fall within the scope of the 1981 Regulations because it is not a transfer of business as a going concern. On the other hand, the mere fact that a business is unprofitable does not mean that it cannot be regarded as a going concern.

In considering whether there is a transfer of a business as opposed to a mere sale of assets, an industrial tribunal will look at the reality of the transaction. Typical factors which it may take into account include:

- whether items other than mere assets are sold;

- whether work in progress is sold;

- whether goodwill is sold;

- whether customers have been 'taken over';

- whether the former owner agrees not to compete with the new owner;

- whether the former owner's trading name has been assumed by the new owner;

- whether the same economic activities are carried on after the transfer.

As so often in employment law, however, a checklist of this kind must be treated with caution. The tribunal will look at the particular circumstances of each case.

Sometimes it is hard to tell whether there is a relevant transfer. Typical problem cases are those where a tenant, licensee or franchisee of a business gives up his interest in it. There have been cases when a change in identity of the following categories of employer has been ruled to constitute a relevant transfer:

- pub tenants;

- pub managers;

- petrol station tenants;

- franchisees.

Each situation must be considered on its own merits. A change of absolute ownership of the business is not always necessary for there to be a relevant transfer. This point was made by the European Court of Justice in a case concerning an enterprise which rejoiced in the name of Daddy's Dance Hall.

Reg 3 also contains provisions designed to defeat attempts to escape the legal net. The 1981 Regulations apply even if the transfer is not governed or affected by UK law and even if there is a series of linked transactions. It is not impossible that an ingenious corporate group structure could be devised that would fall outside the scope of the 1981 Regulations; to contrive this would, however, not only require sophisticated advance planning, but also perhaps a large measure of luck.

20.4   The effect of a relevant transfer

A relevant transfer does not terminate the contract of an employee working for the transferor in the undertaking or part transferred. Any contract which would have been terminated by the transfer at common law has effect after the transfer as if originally made between the employee and the transferee.

All the rights, powers, duties and liabilities of the original owner of the business under or in connection with an employment contract are transferred to the new owner. Anything done before the transfer is completed by or in relation to the original owner in respect of the employment contract is deemed to have been done by or in relation to the new owner. This is so, irrespective of the wishes of the employees or of the past or present owner of the business.

A person employed in the undertaking (or part transferred) is someone who is so employed 'immediately before' the transfer or someone who would have been so employed had he not been unfairly dismissed within the meaning of reg 8 (see below).

So, in addition to contractual liabilities, statutory rights such as continuity of employment and all rights flowing from continuity pass to the new owner.

Only a very limited number of matters do not pass to the new owner, including:

1. rights under or in connection with an occupational pension scheme;

2. liability in respect of a protective award;

3. criminal liability;

4. (subject to the wording of the scheme in question) stock option rights in certain cases.

In addition, the new owner may acquire liabilities under dismissal law in a variety of ways. Broadly speaking, there are three main risk areas.

Firstly, if the original owner has not terminated an employment contract before the transfer and the new owner refuses to take on the employee concerned, he is deemed to have dismissed that employee and will be liable for all potential claims arising out of that dismissal.

Secondly, even if the original owner dismissed an employee before the transfer, the new owner may become liable in respect of that dismissal if it is automatically unfair pursuant to reg 8; see section 20.5 Pre-transfer dismissals, below and section 20.8 Unfair dismissal and business transfers p204, and in particular the discussion of the *Litster* case below.

Otherwise, he will become liable for the original owner's dismissal if the employee was employed at the time of (or immediately before) the transfer; see section 20.5 Pre-transfer dismissals (below), and section 20.8 Unfair dismissal and business transfers p204, and the discussion of *Secretary of State for Employment v. Spence* (1986).

Thirdly, in the event of a substantial change in the transferred employee's working conditions to his detriment, the new owner risks a constructive dismissal claim: see section 4.6 Business transfers and section 20.8 Unfair dismissal and business transfers p204.

20.5 Pre-transfer dismissals

Buying a business may be much less attractive if it entails taking on everyone working in the business. The liabilities imposed upon new owners by the 1981 Regulations often carry a high price tag. This can have the effect of diminishing the amount that people are prepared to pay for a business. Prospective purchasers sometimes insist that the sale agreement should contain broadly-worded indemnities covering them against potential liabilities under the 1981 Regulations. They are also often keen to try to persuade would-be sellers of a business to dismiss some or all of the employees in the undertaking before the transfer takes place. The object may be to ensure that the unwanted employees are not employed 'immediately before' the transfer and are not therefore automatically passed to the purchaser. Is such a course legally viable?

This question was considered by the Court of Appeal in the *Spence* case. An employer went into receivership. One morning the workforce was sacked and three hours later the business was sold. The Court of Appeal ruled that, as the employees were no longer employed at the actual time of the transfer, they did not automatically join the purchaser by virtue of the 1981 Regulations.

There was a very different outcome in the *Litster* case. The workforce of a company in receivership was dismissed with immediate effect one hour before the company's business was transferred to a new company set up for that purpose. The new company started to recruit at lower wages. Eventually it acquired a workforce of similar size to the insolvent company, but it rejected several job applications from ex-employees of that company. The Law Lords decided that the 1981 Regulations applied to the transfer.

The decision in *Spence* was not actually overruled, because the facts of the two cases were slightly different. In *Spence*, the workforce was dismissed before any transfer had been agreed.

The decision in *Spence* will still apply if a pre-transfer dismissal is not connected with the transfer or (it seems) if it is connected, but nevertheless the dismissal is not automatically unfair because it was for an economic, technical or organisational reason entailing changes in the workforce; see section 20.8 Unfair dismissal and business transfers p204. In practice, if the buyer and seller of the business have colluded in a pre-transfer dismissal, *Spence* will seldom be relevant.

In summary, *Litster* means that, even if a dismissal takes place long before the transfer, the new owner will become liable in respect of that dismissal if it was connected with the transfer and was automatically unfair.

20.6 When does a transfer take place?

When a transfer of an undertaking (or part) occurs is a question of fact. The answer can be important in cases where the *Spence* principle continues to apply, or in connection with the pre-transfer duty to consult and inform discussed in section 20.9 The duty to inform and consult p205. There have been cases in which it has been said that a transfer occurs when contracts are exchanged between the seller and the purchaser. In other cases, it has been suggested that the transfer takes place over a period of time between exchange and completion.

The best view, however, is probably that, in a typical case, a transfer of an undertaking occurs at the time when the transaction is completed.

20.7 Hiving down

The 1981 Regulations contain special rules which deal with hiving down, a practice often adopted by receivers and administrators of insolvent companies, and a means of salvaging something from the wreckage of insolvency. Typically, a receiver or administrator sets up a wholly-owned subsidiary of the insolvent company and transfers the business to it. The employees needed to keep the business going are lent to the new company, which is in due course sold to a purchaser. The purchaser takes the new company free of the employees of the original insolvent company.

The 1981 Regulations were framed so as not to destroy the

commercial benefits of hiving down. They provide, in effect, for the postponement of a relevant transfer until the new company is sold on to the purchaser. However, if an administrator or receiver sacks the employees before the business is sold, simply in order to ensure that the sale goes ahead or to get a better price, *Litster* may now mean that liability for those dismissals will pass to the ultimate purchaser.

20.8   Unfair dismissal and business transfers

Any dismissal which is connected with a business transfer is, with one exception, automatically unfair: reg 8. This is so whether the original owner or the new owner dismisses and whether or not the dismissal occurs before or after the transfer (without any time limit).

This vital principle should never be forgotten by employers who become involved with a business transfer.

A dismissal connected with a business transfer is not *automatically* unfair where the reason for that dismissal is 'an economic, technical or organisational reason entailing changes in the workforce'. It remains possible, however, for such a dismissal to be unfair. It is deemed to be a dismissal for 'some other substantial reason' under section 57(1)(b) of the 1978 Act and is judged under the test of fairness set out in section 57(3) of that Act.

The rules apply equally to employees of a business purchaser as to those of a seller. So, if a purchaser dismisses his existing employees to make room for new employees acquired by virtue of the transfer, reg 8 will apply and he will be vulnerable to an unfair dismissal claim.

What will be considered to be an 'economic, technical or organisational' reason for dismissal? Not, it seems, a mere desire to obtain a better price for a business or to achieve its sale, according to the EAT in *Wheeler v. Patel* (1987). In that case, the original owner dismissed an employee at the purchaser's request prior to the transfer. The EAT held that for there to be an 'economic' reason for the dismissal within the meaning of the reg 8 defence, that reason must be related to the conduct of the business.

Very often, an employer who acquires new employees when buying a business will wish to harmonise their terms of employment with those of his existing employees. This can amount to an automatically unfair constructive dismissal. In *Berriman v. Delabole Slate Ltd* (1985), an employee was transferred pursuant to reg 5. He was offered new terms of employment which he did not wish to accept. When the new owner insisted on those terms, the employee claimed that he had been constructively dismissed. The Court of Appeal held that his dismissal was automatically unfair because it was not for an economic, technical or organisational reason entailing changes in the workforce. For there to be a change in the workforce within the meaning of reg 8, there had to be a change in the composition of the workforce. A mere change in the terms and conditions enjoyed by the workforce is not sufficient.

In *Crawford v. Swinton Insurance Brokers Ltd* (1990), the EAT said that, where a business transfer is followed by a constructive dismissal claim, an industrial tribunal must identify the principal reason for the employer's conduct entitling the employee to terminate the contract. It must then decide whether that reason was an economic, technical or organisational one entailing changes in the workforce. The workforce as a whole – separate from the individuals who make it up – must be looked at. The question then is whether the reason for the dismissal involved a change in that workforce. If, say, as a result of an organisational change resulting from a relevant transfer, the workforce becomes engaged in a different occupation, there is a change in the workforce. Dismissal is not then *automatically* unfair, although it may still be unfair if implemented unreasonably.

20.9   The duty to inform and consult

In sufficient time before a relevant transfer to enable consultation to take place between an employer of any 'affected employees' and representatives of a recognised trade union, reg 10 requires the employer to inform those representatives of:

1. the fact that the relevant transfer is to take place, when approximately it is to take place and the reasons for it;

2. the legal, economic and social implications of the transfer for the affected employees;

3. whether he envisages taking any measures connected with the transfer in relation to those employees, and if so what measures;

4. (if he is the transferor), whether the transferee envisages that he will take any such measures, and if so what measures.

An 'affected employee' means any employee of the transferor or transferee, whether or not employed in the business transferred, who may be affected by the transfer or by measures taken in relation to it. The wording of reg 10 suggests that the information must be given in writing, without specifically requiring it.

In contrast to the redundancy consultation provisions discussed in Chapter 9, there are no specific rules with regard to the timing of consultation. A trade union may complain to an industrial tribunal of a failure to inform and consult and if the complaint succeeds the tribunal:

1. must so declare; and

2. may order the employer to compensate affected employees subject to a maximum award of two weeks' pay for each employee in question.

So far, few cases have arisen in this area. The duty to consult is, arguably, neither burdensome nor particularly significant. However, the Acquired Rights Directive – unlike the 1981 Regulations – says that consultation must be 'with a view to seeking agreement'. A court or tribunal in touch with the contemporary Euro-ethos might regard this point as important, thus giving the law sharper teeth. As with so many aspects of the 1981 Regulations, employers should tread carefully.

21
Other Reasons for Dismissal

21.1 Introduction

The most usual reasons for dismissal are misconduct, incapability (whether arising through incompetence or sickness) and redundancy, but the law recognises that there may be other circumstances in which a dismissal is potentially fair. It is neither possible nor desirable to categorise those circumstances exhaustively.

Fortunately, tribunals have interpreted the residual category of 'some other substantial reason' justifying dismissal flexibly so as to cover a wide range of cases. This chapter outlines a number of specific problem areas.

21.2 Contravention of statute

It is potentially fair to dismiss for the reason that the employee could not continue to work in the position which he held without contravention (either on his part or on that of his employer) of a duty or restriction imposed by or under an enactment: section 57(2) of the 1978 Act.

By far the commonest example of this class of dismissal arises when an employee is disqualified from driving and therefore cannot continue to drive as part of his job. The employer in such a case should consider:

1. the terms of the contract (for example, was there a contractual requirement to drive?);

2. whether driving was the sole or main part of the job;

3. whether the job could be properly performed without the employee driving;

4. whether suitable alternative employment not involving driving was available.

If, having taken those steps, the employer reasonably concludes that it is impracticable to retain the employee, dismissal is very likely to be fair.

21.3   Changes in contract terms

It is a basic principle of law that a contract of employment, like any other contract, may not be varied unilaterally. Consent is required. Yet there may be circumstances in which it is fair to dismiss an employee who refuses to agree to a change in the terms and conditions of his employment. The factors which are relevant will vary from case to case, but typically will include:

1. the reason why the employer considers the change necessary in the interests of the business. A mere policy decision to aim for 'improved efficiency' may not be sufficient;

2. the reason why the employee objected to the change;

3. the procedure followed in implementing the change;

4. whether the vast majority of the workforce was agreeable to the change;

5. whether the sanction of dismissal was appropriate, or too severe.

It is also worth mentioning that, where a female employee resists a change to her working hours, say, because of problems with child-care arrangements, an employer needs to tread very warily, in case he is guilty of indirect sex discrimination.

Dismissal for refusal to agree to a change

In *RS Components Ltd v. Irwin* (1974), the employers had been suffering from competition from ex-employees. They were losing profits and salesmen were complaining of loss of commission. Management therefore tried to impose a restrictive covenant on their sales staff to prevent them from poaching customers for up to

12 months after leaving. An employee who refused to agree to the convenant was dismissed. The EAT held that, on the facts, there was an urgent need to protect the business and the employers had acted fairly.

Similar considerations might arise, for example, where there is a pressing need to require employees to work overtime and where overtime is not provided for in the contract. However, the general principles in this area are most often of relevance in the context of business reorganisation.

Dismissal coupled with offer of re-employment

Employers wishing to introduce changed working practices may need to contemplate dismissing the employees concerned, but offering them new employment subject to the desired terms and conditions.

This may not be necessary if the changes, properly understood, do not involve significant variations to the contract terms. A degree of flexibility may be inherent in those terms, especially as regards methods of working. For instance, a transition from manual systems in a job to utilising computer systems may not entail a change in the terms of the contract.

However, if a contract is to be changed, merely to give an employee advance notice of that change does not in itself validate it. The best solution may be to dismiss and re-employ on the new terms, but employers need to take care. The dismissals must be fairly handled, with prior consultation and discussion, even if they are being introduced in good faith and for sound business reasons. The risks are illustrated by *Kent County Council v. Gilham and others* (1985), in which a local authority wrote to school meals staff terminating their existing contracts, offering new contracts in accordance with proposed cost-cutting measures. The need to achieve economies forced upon the authority by a national policy to reduce public spending was a potentially fair reason for dismissal, but the handling of the dismissals was in this particular case considered unfair.

21.4 Business reorganisations

The reason for a dismissal in the context of business reorganisation may or may not fall within the technical definition of redundancy;

see section 7.2 The statutory definition p78. Where an employee is dislodged by reorganisation and cannot be fitted in elsewhere, it is open to the employer to dismiss. Whether the dismissal is fair will depend upon whether it is properly handled in the circumstances; fairness involves consultation and genuine consideration of proper alternatives to dismissal.

Sometimes an employer will require employees to accept changes to their contract terms as part of a reorganisation. It may be fair to dismiss an employee who refuses to accept such an amendment.

Thus, in *Hollister v. National Farmers' Union* (1979), the Court of Appeal held that it was fair to dismiss an employee who refused to accept proposed changes which, although they would improve his remuneration, would diminish his previous rights. Where there was some sound business reason for the reorganisation it might, depending on the facts, be 'the only sensible thing' to dismiss if the employee would not accept the change.

The decision in *Hollister* reflects the significance of managerial perogative in this area. Nevertheless, *Ladbroke Courage Holidays Ltd v. Asten* (1981), indicates that if an employer seeks to rely on business reorganisation or economic necessity as a reason for dismissal, he should have evidence available to show that there was a *bona fide* rationalisation and/or a genuine need for economy. Following a proper procedure is, again, extremely important.

It is sometimes argued that reorganisation can be used as a device to permit employers to circumvent contractual obligations. In *Evans v. Elemeta Holdings Ltd* (1982), the EAT suggested that if it was reasonable for an employee to decline new contractual terms, it would be unreasonable for the employer to dismiss him for such a refusal.

That conclusion was rejected by a different division of the EAT in *Chubb Fire Security Ltd v. Harper* (1983). In that case, the EAT took the view that the only relevant issue under section 57(3) of the 1978 Act was the reasonableness of the employer's conduct. It may be perfectly reasonable for an employee to decline to work extra overtime, yet from the employer's point of view, having regard to his business commitments, it may be perfectly reasonable to require the employee to work overtime.

The crucial question is whether the new terms offered to an employee are those which a reasonable employer could offer, according to the EAT in *Richmond Precision Engineering Ltd v. Pearce* (1985). Whether the advantages to the employer outweigh the disadvantages to the employee is not the only relevant issue. Certainly, the mere fact that the new terms involve disadvantages to the employee does not in itself render the dismissal unfair.

21.5   Disloyalty and trade espionage

The problem

Most employers have trade secrets of one kind or another. Leakage of confidential information, whether complex technical or economic data or mere customer lists, can do untold harm to any business. The greatest risk of trade espionage comes from those working within the enterprise itself.

Very often the risk of disloyalty becomes manifest when an employee is embroiled in a conflict of interests. Express contractual provision prohibiting spare-time work is the most effective safeguard. Even if there is no such contractual restriction, dismissal may be justifiable if the risk to the business is sufficiently great and the dismissal itself is properly handled.

It may be fair to dismiss an employee who sets up a competing company. When the employee's plans to indulge in competing activities of some kind have not matured at the time when his employer learns of those plans, dismissal may still be justified, even if the employer acts before positive steps have been taken.

Thus, the EAT in Scotland found little difficulty in holding that a hairdresser's firm had fairly dismissed two employees who planned to open a salon just 100 yards away: *Davidson and Maillou v. Comparisons* (1980). The employers had been prepared to retain the employees until they left, but at a different salon, subject to payment of travel expenses. When the employees refused to move, they were dismissed. The EAT said that an employer is entitled to defend himself against unfair competition and to take whatever reasonable steps are necessary to achieve that end. Even without making the offer of alternative employment, dismissal could have been justified.

Guilt by association?

An employee may sometimes find himself in a position of conflicting loyalties through no fault of his own. There may be no evidence that

211

he has done anything which may amount to trade espionage. How should an employer tackle such a case?

There seems to be little doubt that a properly handled dismissal may be fair in such circumstances, but the facts of *Coleman v. Skyrail Oceanic Ltd* (1980), provide an object lesson of how employers ought not to deal with cases of suspected conflicts of interest.

An employee in the employers' travel agency was dimissed because she was about to marry an employee in a rival firm. The two firms had consulted each other and agree on this action.

The EAT accepted that the reason for dismissal was 'some other substantial reason' and that the appropriate generalised test is whether,

> 'having regard to past conduct, the amount of access to confidential information, the importance of such information and the positions held by the two employees, it is fair and reasonable within section 57(3) to treat the risk as sufficiently great to justify dismissal'.

The dismissal was unfair on the facts because of the absence of consultation with the couple prior to the termination of the applicant's employment. She had not been given any warning that she would be dismissed when she married; nor was she advised to look for other work. Fairness required that she should be given prior warning of her employer's concern.

Although the EAT rejected the argument that Mrs Coleman had been unlawfully discriminated against, a majority of the Court of Appeal upheld her appeal. The dismissal of a woman based upon the assumption that husbands and not wives are breadwinners can amount to sex discrimination and on the evidence, the dismissal had been discriminatory.

Suspected disloyalty

Where disloyalty is suspected but not proved, the principles summarised in The legal test p153 relating to cases of suspected misconduct will again be relevant. Indeed, dismissal for disloyalty may be categorised as a 'conduct' dismissal, on the facts, as well as possibly a dismissal for 'some other substantial reason'.

21.6 Personality clashes

Occasionally, the working relationship between two employees breaks down to such a serious extent that it becomes necessary to contemplate the dismissal of one of those employees.

The EAT indicated in *Turner v. Vestric Ltd* (1981), that where there is such a breakdown, the employers must take reasonable steps to try to improve the relationship. Dismissal may, however, be justified where there is not only a breakdown, but that breakdown is irremediable. In such a case, every step short of dismissing an employee whose work, considered as work, is perfectly satisfactory should be taken.

In the *Turner* case, the employers had done very little to investigate the issue properly, sensibly and practically, to see whether an improvement could be effected in the relationship between the two employees. The dismissal was therefore unfair.

Where pressure from other employees takes the form of 'calling, organising, procuring or financing a strike or other industrial action, or threatening to do so' within the meaning of section 63 of the 1978 Act, the dismissal will be unfair if that pressure is the reason for the dismissal; see section 11.5 Industrial pressure p119.

21.7 Customer pressure

An employer may be placed in an invidious position when a customer or other influential third party applies pressure which, indirectly or directly, necessitates the dismissal of an employee. The problem sometimes arises with staff working in concession areas within large department stores or when, for some reason, the employee's behaviour upsets an important client.

Properly handled, a dismissal in such circumstances may be fair even if the employer is genuinely reluctant to dismiss and considers that the third party is behaving unreasonably. In *Dobie v. Burns International Security Services (UK) Ltd* (1983), the employers' services were governed by a contract with a metropolitan council which gave the council the right 'to approve or otherwise the employment or continued employment of any member of the company'. The employee was dismissed at the request of an agent of the council.

213

The EAT held that the dismissal was fair, but said that the question of potential injustice to the employee is relevant in determining whether or not the employer is acting reasonably and it is desirable for an employer who may be required to dismiss at the behest of a third party to make it plain in the contract of employment that this is the position. In any event, before dismissing an employee in such circumstances the employer should follow a proper procedure – for example, he should check whether or not he can provide alternative employment where there is no objection from the third party.

On appeal, the Court of Appeal confirmed that

'in deciding whether the employer acted reasonably or unreasonably, a very important factor which he has to take into account, on the facts known to him at the time, is whether there will or will not be injustice to the employee and the extent of that injustice'.

The Court of Appeal indicated that the matters which affect the justice or injustice to the employee of being dismissed would include:

- his length of service;
- the satisfactoriness or otherwise of that service;
- the difficulties he may face in obtaining other employment.

21.8 Dismissal of homosexual employees

It may, depending upon the circumstances, be fair to dismiss an employee because of his or her sexual orientation. In *Saunders v. Scottish National Camps Association Ltd* (1980), the employee was dismissed from his job as a maintenance handyman at a children's camp when it was discovered that he was homosexual and had been involved in a homosexual incident, although not one involving children. The EAT took the view that, even if it was scientifically untrue that homosexuals were more likely than heterosexuals to interfere with young children (the psychiatric evidence was uncertain on this point), nevertheless it was an opinion commonly held. On the facts, dismissal fell within the 'band of reasonableness'.

Where there is no express dismissal, an employer's harassment of a homosexual employee may amount to constructive dismissal, just as in the case of heterosexual harassment.

21.9 Husband and wife teams

It may be fair to dismiss an employee who works as part of a 'team' with his or her spouse when that spouse is dismissed. This point may arise, for example, in connection with public house managers or social club stewards or stewardesses and their spouses.

In *Kelman v. GJ Oram* (1983), the EAT rejected the argument that if the dismissal of one spouse was unfair, so was the dismissal of the other. So, where the husband's dismissal for misconduct was unfair, his wife's dismissal for 'some other substantial reason' because it was impracticable for her employment to continue once her husband had been dismissed, could still be upheld.

This is, perhaps, a surprising decision; its logic should not be pressed too far. The facts and outcome of *Wadley v. Eager Electrical Ltd* (1986), were different. A company summarily dismissed an employee after his wife, who also worked there but not as part of a 'team' with her husband, was arrested on charges of theft. Given Mr Woodley's length of service and good record, and the fact that he was dismissed without notice and without the case against him ever being put to him, the EAT ruled his dismissal to be unfair.

21.10 Discriminatory dismissals

The law on equal opportunities is growing steadily in importance, but discussion of the complicated structure of legislation on race and sex discrimination lies beyond the scope of this book. Suffice it to say here that a dismissal on racial grounds is unlawful under the Race Relations Act 1976 as well as almost certainly being unfair. Similarly, a dismissal on the grounds of an employee's sex or marital status is unlawful under the Sex Discrimination Act 1975 as well as being unfair.

An interesting example of the impact of anti-discriminatory law is provided by *Zarczynska v. Levy* (1978). The employee had been dismissed for refusing to obey an instruction not to serve black customers. The EAT held that she was entitled to bring a complaint under the Race Relations Act 1976 (for which no qualifying service is required), although she had insufficient continuous employment to claim unfair dismissal.

22
Continuous Employment and a Week's Pay

22.1 Introduction

The 1978 Act gives employees a number of individual rights, but many of those rights apply only to employees who have a minimum period of continuous employment. The rules governing continuous employment are quite technical. They are to be found in Schedule 13 to the 1978 Act as amended. To build up the minimum period of continuous employment and to qualify for rights, employees must work for a specified number of hours per week.

Many dismissal rights ultimately involve a payment to the dismissed employee which is linked to the legal concept of 'a week's pay'. This, in turn, depends upon the computation of the employee's 'normal working hours', if any. Both concepts, which are defined in Schedule 14 to the 1978 Act, are discussed below.

22.2 Calculating continuity

Start of period

Generally, the period of continuous employment begins on the employee's first day of work. In practice this means the date upon which the contract requires him to start work. Exceptionally, for the purposes of the redundancy payment scheme only, the employee's period of continuous employment begins no earlier than his eighteenth birthday.

In certain circumstances, the beginning of the period of continuous employment is subsequently deemed, in effect, to be postponed. Thus, where an employee is on strike, locked out or on

217

national service, his period of continuous employment is reduced by means of deducting a length of time equivalent to the length of the strike etc, from the start of the period of continuous employment. The number of days by which the start of the period of continuous employment is postponed is not necessarily the actual number of days for which the strike etc lasted. A similar principle applies in a redundancy payment case to weeks of overseas employment. The length of postponement is specified in section 151(6) of the Act and varies from case to case.

End of period

The period of continuous employment ends upon the relevant date for the dismissal right in question. In certain circumstances the relevant date is deemed to be artificially postponed; see Statutory postponement of the termination date p58. Thus, where an employee is wrongfully dismissed, the effective date of termination may be later than the date upon which the contract is terminated. The period of continuous employment will end on the effective date of termination rather than on the date when the employment actually ended.

The basis of calculation

The basis of calculation under the new scheme is either the calendar month or the calendar year, depending upon the right in question. For example, an employee who has worked for seven weeks has one month's continuous employment and an employee who works, say, for eighteen months has one year's continuous employment.

Presumption of continuity

A person's employment 'during any period' is presumed to be continuous until the contrary is shown. The effect of the presumption of continuity was considered by the EAT in *Nicoll v. Norrocode Ltd* (1981). The EAT held that:

1. it is for the employee to show that there was a contract of employment, and that he was dismissed;

2. it is for the employee to establish that there was a week or weeks which counted under Schedule 13; (see section 22.3 Weeks which count p219)

3. in respect of subsequent weeks, he may rely on the presumption and deem the weeks to count until the contrary is shown;

4. the contrary may be shown by his evidence or by that of the employer.

It can be argued, however, that the onus should not be placed on the employer under point (2). The statute does not seem to require that.

The presumption only applies where the employment is 'by the one employer', and complications may arise if a business changes hands. An employee may be able to establish continuity either by virtue of the 1981 Regulations discussed in Chapter 20 or on the basis set out in Calculating the amount p226. If he cannot do so, and no other evidence is available, a business transfer will not give rise to the presumption of continuity, according to the EAT in *Secretary of State for Employment v. Cohen and Beaupress Ltd* (1987).

22.3   Weeks which count

The weeks which may be counted towards the total period of employment are specified in Schedule 13. It is sometimes overlooked that an employee who once belonged to an excluded class of employment for any right under the 1978 Act but no longer does may count as part of his period of continuous employment the *whole* of his service, including the period when he was an excluded employee. *Weston v. Vega Space Systems Engineering Ltd* (1989), illustrates this point; see section 10.5 Work outside Great Britain p113.

Full-time work

If an employee actually works for 16 hours or more during a week, he may count that week towards his period of employment. Furthermore, a week counts if it is covered by a contract of employment under which the employee's normal working week is 16 hours or more. This applies, irrespective of the actual hours worked, if any.

The expression 'full-time work' does not appear in the statute, but it is often used as convenient shorthand to refer to an employee whose contract normally involves 16 hours' work or more a week. Holiday weeks will usually count and so may other temporary absences. As a result, an employee whose working hours are irregular may nevertheless be a 'full-time' employee.

An employee cannot bring himself within the rules merely by averaging the hours that he works and claiming that the average is more than 16 hours a week. The correct approach is to look at the contract and see how many hours it 'normally involves', in other words, exclusive of voluntary overtime: *Lake v. Essex County Council* (1979), in which the Court of Appeal refused to include a teacher's 'homework' for these purposes. Yet in *Society of Licensed Victuallers v. Chamberlain* (1989), the EAT decided that as a teacher's contract required him to do preparatory work but allocated no specific time for it, some of his free period time could be added to his contractual working hours of 15 hours 40 minutes per week so as to render him a 'full-time' employee.

In *Dean v. Eastbourne Fishermen's and Boatmen's Protection Society and Club Ltd* (1979), the hours of a barman were not set out in his contract and he worked the hours requested of him. The EAT looked at the hours actually worked in order to determine how many hours the contract 'normally involved'. Although a similar approach has been adopted by the EAT subsequently, it should be viewed with caution. Arguably, it is better to investigate what is contemplated by the contract as the normal working week.

What if an employee is on call but does not actually work for 16 hours a week? This question has arisen more than once in cases concerning 'retained firemen'. In *Suffolk County Council v. Secretary of State for the Environment and Alcock* (1985), the House of Lords ruled that there is a key distinction between a regular fireman who is on duty and a retained fireman who is merely on call. A retained fireman is not at the disposal of, or under the control or direction of, the fire authorities. His services cannot be sought until there is a fire, so he is not working until he is called.

Short time

If an employee's normal contractual working week changes from 16 hours or more to less than 16 hours for a period, a short-time week will only count if:

1. the normal working week is at least eight hours;

2. the week is one that would count if the normal hours were still 16 or more; and

3. the number of short-time weeks counted is within the specified maximum, ie 26 weeks.

Part-time employees

For these purposes, an employee works part-time when his normal working week is less than 16 hours. Schedule 13 provides in effect that, if an employee has been continuously employed for five years or more, he shall be treated as a 'full-time' employee, in other words, working more than 16 hours weekly, if throughout that period he has worked under a contract which normally involves employment for eight or more hours, but less than 16 hours, weekly.

Sickness or injury

Where there is no contract of employment during the employee's absence due to sickness or injury, he may still be able to count his period of sickness or injury towards his total period of continuous employment. Not more than 26 weeks may be counted under this head.

The House of Lords made it clear in *Ford v. Warwickshire County Council* (1983), that this rule does not become relevant until the contract ceases; it does not apply to an employee who is off sick but does not have his contract terminated.

Temporary cessation

An employee may count towards his total period of continuous employment any week during which, or during part of which, he was 'absent from work on account of a temporary cessation of work'.

Typically, a temporary cessation of work will be an unexpected crisis. Nevertheless, irregular cessation may be 'temporary' for these purposes. The *Ford* case concerned a teacher who was employed on eight successive contracts each lasting from September to July – an academic year. During the summer holidays she had no contract and the question was whether the vacation constituted a temporary cessation of work. The House of Lords held that it was.

Whether a cessation is 'temporary' will inevitably depend on the circumstances of the case. The EAT suggested in *Bentley Engineering Co Ltd v. Crown and Miller* (1976), that the following factors might be relevant:

- the nature of the employment;

- the length of prior and subsequent service;

- the duration of the break;

- what was said when the break occurred;

- what happened during the break;

- what was said on re-employment.

This broad approach was supported by the Court of Appeal in *Flack v. Kodak Ltd* (1986). A 'mathematical' approach that involves calculating the number of weeks at work in a particular year or years, and comparing this with the number of weeks out of work in the same period, is inappropriate. In *Sillars v. Charrington Fuels Ltd* (1989), however, the Court of Appeal said that it was open to a tribunal to take a mathematical approach where there has been regular, albeit intermittent, employment over several years; on the other hand, a broad approach is appropriate where the pattern of employment has been irregular.

The key point is whether the absence was on account of temporary cessation of work, not whether the employee was temporarily absent. It is the cessation which must be temporary, not the absence.

Custom or arrangement

An employee may count towards his period of continuous employment any week during which, or during part of which, he is absent from work, but by custom or arrangement he is still regarded as an employee of his employer, even though he has no contract of employment.

Such an arrangement may arise, for instance, where the employer allows unpaid leave of absence and actually terminates the contract at the beginning of the leave. Alternatively, an employer may loan an employee to another employer for a short period on the understanding that the employee will return to work with the original employer in due course.

An arrangement for these purposes cannot be made retrospectively. It must exist at the time when the absence commenced and, therefore, be in the mind of both the employer and the employee from the outset.

Pregnancy or confinement

A female employee may count towards her period of employment any week during which, or during part of which, she is absent because of pregnancy or confinement, whether that is the only cause of her absence or merely one of the causes.

There is a 26-week limit in this respect, but this is subject to the proviso that if an employee in fact comes back to work after pregnancy in compliance with her statutory right to return (see Chapter 17), then every week of that absence (which can be 40 weeks plus a possible four further weeks) will count in calculating her period of continuous employment.

Re-employment after an unfair dismissal claim

The Labour Relations (Continuity of Employment) Regulations 1976 provide that where an employee claims that he has been unfairly dismissed and is accordingly reinstated or re-engaged by his employer or by a successor or associated employer of the employer, then subject to certain conditions, his employment is deemed continuous throughout the interval and every week of the interval counts towards the period of continuous employment.

The employee must be re-employed in consequence of:

1. a complaint of unfair dismissal; or

2. a claim under a designated dismissal procedure agreement; or

3. the intervention of an ACAS Conciliation Officer called in to seek an agreed settlement of an alleged unfair dismissal.

Further modifications

Where the effective date of terminating is artificially postponed in any of the ways outlined in Statutory postponement of the termination date p58, every week of the period of postponement counts in computing the period of continuous employment.

The following modifications apply when computing a period of employment for redundancy purposes:

1. when an employee is reinstated or re-engaged after dismissal for redundancy in accordance with the 'alternative employment' provisions discussed in section 8.3 Offer of alternative employment p89 then every week of the interval counts;

2. where the employer dismisses in breach of the statutory minimum notice provisions (see section 5.3 Statutory minimum notice period p60), the period of continuous employment is computed to the date on which the statutory notice would have expired;

3. payment of a redundancy payment or an equivalent payment breaks continuity unless the employee alleges unfair dismissal, is re-employed under the 1976 Regulations (see Re-employment after an unfair dismissal claim p223) upon terms which require him to repay that payment and does repay it;

4. weeks before the employee is 18 years old do not count;

5. some overseas weeks are disallowed.

22.4   Change of employer

Generally, continuous employment means employment by a single employer, but there are a number of exceptional cases.

Transfer of business

Where one employer transfers to another the ownership of his 'trade, business or undertaking' then the continuity of employment of any employee therein at the time of the transfer will be preserved. Such an employee may treat his period of continuous employment with the first employer as part of his period with the second.

The phrase 'trade, business or undertaking' is not exhaustively defined. Whether there is such a transfer will depend upon the facts. A key element will usually be the transfer of goodwill, although that is not always conclusive. The acquisition of customer lists or customers of another employee may be evidence of the acquisition of goodwill. Lord Justice Buckley said, in *Woodhouse v. Peter Brotherhood* (1972), that the 'simple and accurate' test is 'whether B has become the proprietor of the trade, business or undertaking in succession to A'.

Associated employers

Where two employers are associated employers, as defined in section 153(4) of the 1978 Act, Schedule 13 provides that the transfer of an employee from one to the other does not break continuity, and employment with the first counts against the second.

Employers are associated where one of the employers involved is a company, controlled by the other employer (whether that employer is a company or an individual); or where both employers are companies, controlled by a third person (whether a company or an individual). 'Company' in this context means a limited company, but not necessarily one formed and registered under UK companies legislation: *Hancill v. Marcon Engineering Ltd* (1990).

'Control' may be direct or indirect, and may even be exercised by a group of persons, if that group in fact acts as one: *Zarb and Samuels v. British & Brazilian Produce Co (Sales) Ltd* (1978). In practice, evidence would be required showing that the group in fact controls both employers. 'Control' means voting control, rather than relying on the more nebulous concept of *de facto* control according to the Court of Appeal in *South West Laundrettes Ltd v. Laidler* (1986), although in *Payne v. Secretary of State for Employment* (1989), one member of the Court of Appeal suggested that there might be cases where *de facto* control could become relevant.

Miscellaneous cases

There are several exceptions to the general principle that continuous employment means employment with a single employer. For example:

1. the death of an individual employer will normally terminate the contract of employment automatically, but if the employee is thereupon employed by the deceased's personal representatives or his trustees, continuity is preserved;

2. if a statute substitutes one corporate employer for another in any contracts of employment, the change does not break continuity;

3. although in strict legal terms the identity of the employer changes every time a partner in a partnership leaves or joins, continuity is preserved and employment with previous partners may be counted as employment with the present partners. The same principles apply to employment by successive personal representatives or trustees.

22.5 A week's pay

Calculating the amount

The date at which a week's pay is calculated for the purposes of dismissal law rights is known as the calculation date. When assessing the amount of an unfair dismissal basic award or redundancy payment, the calculation date is the effective date of termination or the relevant date. If the statutory minimum notice period should have been given but was not, the calculation date is the date when notice would have expired.

The amount of a week's pay for certain calculations is subject to statutory maxima. From 1 April 1990, the limit for the purpose of calculating a basic award or a redundancy payment is £184, and this limit is reviewed from time to time. The figure currently applicable should therefore be checked with the Department of Employment.

An employee's 'remuneration' determines the amount of his week's pay. Bonus or commission payments, for example, will be taken into account if they are contractual in nature, but not if they are *ex gratia*.

Normal working hours

If the contract fixes the number, or minimum number, of hours that the employee is required to work, those will be his normal working hours. Overtime hours will only be regarded as part of

226

normal working hours if they are compulsory for the employee and guaranteed by the employer.

If the employee's pay for work done in normal working hours does not vary, a week's pay will be the pay due for the contracted hours. However, if the employee's pay varies with the amount of work done, such as under a piece-work system or where pay comprises a variable performance bonus or commission, a week's pay must be calculated in accordance with a special rate. This is the average hourly rate over a 12-week period, ending on the calculation date, if that date is the last day of the pay week or, if it is not, on the last day of the previous pay week. Only hours when the employee was working (including overtime hours) can be taken into account.

Slightly different rules apply to employees who are contractually required to work on a shift or rota basis, where pay varies, for example, because normal hours worked at night or at the weekend attract a higher rate of pay. To allow for variation of hours, the average number of normal weekly working hours is found by dividing by 12 the total number of normal working hours during a period of 12 weeks, ending on the calculation date if that date is the last day of the pay week, or, if it is not, on the last day of the previous pay week. For the method of working out the average hourly rate, see above.

No normal working hours

For an employee with no normal working hours, such as a sales representative paid wholly by commission, the amount of a week's pay is the average weekly pay over a 12-week period ending on the calculation date if that date is the last day of the pay week or, if it is not, on the last day of the previous week. Any week for which no pay was due should be replaced by the last previous week for which pay was due, so as to bring up to 12 the number of weeks to be averaged.

23
Contracting Out and Conciliation

23.1 Introduction

Modern employment legislation prevents employees from being able to 'sign away' their statutory rights, except in certain narrowly defined circumstances. Thus, section 140(1) of the 1978 Act renders void any provision in an agreement in so far as it purports:

1. to exclude or limit the question of any provision of the 1978 Act; or

2. to preclude any person from presenting a complaint to, or bringing any proceedings under the Act, before an industrial tribunal.

The practical effect of this bar on contracting out of statutory rights is illustrated by *Council of Engineering Institutions v. Maddison* (1976). An employee was made redundant and handed a letter saying that the cheque for £1,000 which accompanied it constituted a 'lump sum payment for severance (including redundancy payment), the acceptance of which is final settlement leaving you with no outstanding claim against the Council'.

The EAT was not satisfied that this amounted to a binding agreement, but held that, even if it did, it would have been void, because it would have been an agreement purporting to preclude the employee from presenting a complaint to a tribunal.

So, employers who make *ex gratia* settlements which they consider to be generous may, if they do not take care, suffer the galling experience of seeing an ex-employee pocket the money and then still make a complaint to an industrial tribunal.

228

It is therefore vital to know when it is possible for employees effectively to contract out of their statutory rights. The rules on contracting out described in this chapter do not apply to the common law action for wrongful dismissal, discussed in Chapter 6.

23.2   Fixed-term contracts

It is possible for employees to negotiate the exclusion of statutory rights with employees through the medium of a fixed-term contract of employment. For such an exclusion to be effective, a number of stringent restrictions must be met.

The main provisions are as follows:

1. a fixed-term contract for one year or more entered into from 1 October 1980 can include a provision whereby the employee agrees in writing to exclude any claim that he may have for unfair dismissal, where the dismissal consists only of the expiry of that term without its being renewed;

2. a fixed-term contract for two years or more entered into from 6 December 1965 can include a provision whereby the employee agrees in writing to exclude any claim that he may have for a redundancy payment, where the dismissal consists only of the expiry of that term without its being renewed.

Such an exclusion need not be contained in the original contract document, but the employee must agree to the exclusion in writing before the term expires. In practice, it is usual to seek agreement at the outset of the term.

The fact that a fixed-term contract can be terminated by either party giving notice during the term does not prevent it from being a fixed-term contract. If, however, there is a series of fixed-term contracts, the final contract in that series must be for the relevant period. It is not possible to aggregate the cumulative total of all the contracts and regard them as constituting a single fixed term. Finally, because the exclusions only relate to non-renewal of the contract upon expiry, they do not apply where the employee is dismissed during the term or is constructively dismissed.

23.3 Dismissal procedure agreements

A collective agreement made between an employer and a trade union may exclude statutory rights if the parties to the agreement apply to the Secretary of State and he makes an order to that effect. Before making an order, he must be satisfied as to various matters but, once made, the order may only be revoked in a limited number of circumstances.

At the time of writing, only the electrical contracting industry has gained exemption under this head.

23.4 Conciliation

The significance of conciliation

Settlements of claims where a conciliation officer from ACAS has 'taken action' are binding. This is so even where it is agreed as one of the settlement terms that the employee will refrain from presenting or continuing with an application to a tribunal.

The immense importance of this exception is underlined by the statistics disclosed by ACAS in its annual reports. Roughly two-thirds of all unfair complaints each year are resolved without reference to a tribunal, and most of these are conciliated through the medium of ACAS. Naturally, the conciliation process is not coercive. It is designed to supplement, rather than to supplant, direct negotiations between the parties.

The conciliation officer's duties

The conciliation officer's statutory responsibilities in relation to dismissals are set out in section 134 of the 1978 Act. He is enjoined to promote a settlement of an employee's complaint without the dispute having to go to a tribunal. He may be requested to act by the parties or may, on his own initiative, intervene if he thinks he has reasonable prospects of success.

Although the conciliation officer usually becomes involved after the filing of an originating application, from which time he will receive copies of correspondence passing between the tribunal and the parties, conciliation is also sometimes initiated before a dismissal takes place, if one of the parties so requests. Recently, however, conciliation officers have tended to respond to such requests with caution. They are, in particular, keen neither to exceed their statutory powers nor to act merely as 'rubber stamps'.

The legislation provides that the conciliation officer should give priority to the settlement of unfair dismissal claims on the basis of re-employment rather than compensation. Nevertheless, re-employment is achieved through conciliation only in a small percentage of cases. Indeed, there has been a tendency over the years for the success rate to decline.

It is unnecessary, however, for an employee specifically to argue that he could complain of unfair dismissal before a conciliation officer can act. In *Hennessy v. Craigmyle & Co Ltd* (1986), the Court of Appeal said that all that is needed is for the potential claimant to be alleging action which would enable him to present a complaint – whether successfully, or otherwise.

The conciliation process

Impartiality is a crucial feature of the conciliation officer's role. He is an independent party through whom employer and employee may communicate, rather than a negotiator or someone playing devil's advocate. Consequently, he will not advise on the merits of a settlement offer, although, with a view to increasing the likelihood of agreement, he may point out the strengths and weaknesses of the parties' respective cases. He is not obliged to promote a settlement which is 'fair' to both sides. An argument to that effect was expressly abandoned when the leading case of *Moore v. Duport Furniture Products Ltd* (1982), reached the House of Lords. In that case, the conciliation officer ascertained that the parties had already reached agreement which he then recorded on a form specially designed for the purpose, known as form COT3. He was held to have 'taken action' under his statutory powers and the House of Lords declined to overturn the settlement.

To facilitate the process of conciliation, anything communicated to a conciliation officer orally or in writing in connection with that process cannot be disclosed in evidence at a tribunal hearing, unless the person who communicated it gives consent. This does not, however, mean that the parties can make evidence inadmissible at a hearing simply by communicating it to a conciliation officer. The test is whether the evidence exists in an admissible form apart from evidence based upon such communication to the conciliation officer.

If agreement is finally reached on a monetary settlement, form COT3 (which is only available from ACAS) will generally be used to record the agreed terms. Occasionally, when it is desired not to disclose to the world the agreed terms, a complaint to a tribunal may be withdrawn on form COT4 simultaneously with payment of the agreed sum.

There is no standard wording which must of necessity be used to record the terms, but employers will usually be wise to insist that the agreement covers all claims which the employee may have. To do so will, for example, preclude a possible claim in respect of wrongful dismissal.

Sometimes the employer undertakes to supply the employee with a reference, and such an offer may induce an otherwise intransigent employee to surrender his right to a day in court. In this event, form COT3 should either refer to the principal terms of the reference or at least to the fact that its terms have been expressly agreed between the parties. Similarly, if one of the parties agrees to give the other a written apology, it is wise to agree the precise terms of that apology before form COT3 is signed.

The courts have taken a realistic view of the mechanics of achieving a conciliated settlement in unfair dismissal claims. In *Moore*, the House of Lords was willing to give a liberal interpretation to the statutory basis upon which conciliation is founded. Subsequently, the EAT confirmed in *Slack v. Greenham Plant Hire Ltd* (1983), that a conciliation officer is not obliged to follow any specific formula and that, provided he acts within his statutory powers, how he performs his function is up to him, depending on the circumstances of a particular case. In particular, he is not obliged to explain the framework of the unfair dismissal legislation in detail to the parties.

A settlement duly recorded will therefore be very difficult to challenge, although the EAT did accept in *Slack* that a settlement would be a nullity if the conciliation officer acted in bad faith or if he adopted unfair methods when promoting a settlement.

In *Gilbert v. Kembridge Fibres Ltd* (1984), a settlement was reached between the parties through a conciliation officer. The employee later changed his mind and crossed out his signature on form COT3, but the EAT held that there were, on the facts, all the constituent elements of a binding agreement. Since the conciliation officer had undertaken his duties under section 134 of the 1978 Act, there was no question of that agreement being rendered void by the bar on contracting out.

A conciliation officer may still act even if a tribunal has already reached a decision on the question of whether or not a dismissal was unfair: *Courage Take Home Trade Ltd v. Keys* (1986). If an employer settles a case after that time, therefore – for example, to save the need for a further hearing to decide the employee's remedy for unfair dismissal – it will be prudent for him to have that agreement recorded on form COT3, in case the employee later changes his mind.

The value of conciliation

Sometimes employers and employees, and (less frequently, but less pardonably) their advisers, express scepticism about the value of the conciliation process or simply ignore the services that are offered.

The simple fact that conciliation resolves so many complaints illustrates its value. The uncertainties of unfair dismissal law and the cost of proceeding to a hearing obviously explain the figures to some extent, but it would be churlish not to acknowledge the level of success which conciliation officers achieve.

Employers will find noteworthy the fact that the median level of payment in conciliated settlements has consistently been lower than the median award made by tribunals on a finding of unfair dismissal. Given the uncertainties of unfair dismissal law in particular, seeking a compromise in preference to litigation often makes very good sense. It is also more likely to reflect a constructive approach to industrial relations.

From an employee's point of view, the possibility of negotiating a reference and the marginally greater likelihood of achieving re-employment are among the attractions of using the conciliation service. Furthermore, even if the settlement sum on offer is much less than the theoretical maximum compensation for unfair dismissal, there is often truth in the cliché that a bird in the hand is worth two in the bush.

24
Remedies for Unfair Dismissal

24.1 Introduction

If a tribunal holds a dismissal to be unfair, it must consider which remedy to grant. The possibilities are:

- reinstatement;

- re-engagement;

- compensation (usually comprising a basic award and a compensatory award).

The tribunal must consider the remedies in that order, but in practice reinstatement or re-engagement are seldom ordered. This is presumably because industrial realities often militate against re-employment. Even so, it is surprising that re-employment is not more frequently ordered, given high levels of unemployment and the problems that even an employee who has succeeded in an unfair dismissal claim may face in finding another job. Even if re-employment is ordered, an employer cannot at the end of the day be forced to take the employee back on. The ultimate sanction is compensation; see Non-compliance with orders p236.

Tribunals adopt a broad approach when quantifying compensation. Just as it is sometimes hard to predict in advance whether a dismissal will be held to be unfair, so is predicting the likely level of compensation difficult. Small wonder, given the uncertainty, that so many unfair dismissal claims are settled before the hearing.

24.2 Re-employment

Reinstatement

An order for reinstatement is as an order that the employer shall treat the employee in all respects as if he had not been dismissed. All contractual rights as at the dismissal date must therefore be restored. Furthermore, any improvement in terms (such as a pay rise) occurring since the dismissal date will also apply retrospectively.

In making a reinstatement order, the tribunal must specify the relevant terms of employment, including any improvements, and the date by which the employer must comply with the order.

Re-engagement

Re-engagement means, in effect, re-employment on terms which are not identical to those enjoyed at the date of dismissal. The employment may be with the original employer, his successor, or an associated employer and may involve a different job, provided that the new job is comparable to the old job, or other suitable employment.

The tribunal therefore has some discretion. However, if the employee did not partly contribute to his dismissal, re-engagement must, so far as reasonably practicable, be on terms as favourable as an order for reinstatement. In this context the employee is, exceptionally, not under any duty to mitigate his loss by bringing an unfair dismissal complaint at the earliest opportunity. Thus, an employee awarded re-engagement in *City and Hackney Health Authority v. Crisp* (1990), was also entitled to full back pay, despite having been slow to present her complaint.

Ordering re-employment

In deciding whether to grant an order for reinstatement or re-engagement, the tribunal must consider:

1. whether the employee wishes an order to be made (and, if not, no such order can be made);

2. whether the employee caused or contributed to his dismissal;

3. whether it is practicable for the employer to comply with such an order. For example, a tribunal is unlikely to grant an order if it would promote serious industrial strife or cause profound disruption within a very small family business.

An order for re-employment may be less likely in the case of a senior employee than, say, a worker on the shop floor. Having said that, however, the proper test is whether re-employment is practicable, not just whether it is expedient.

The mere fact that the dismissed employee has been replaced should not be taken into account by the tribunal, unless the employer shows:

1. that it was not practicable for the dismissed employee's work to be done without engaging a permanent replacement; or

2. that the replacement was reasonably engaged to do the work after the lapse of a reasonable period without the dismissed employee having told the employer that he desired re-employment.

Non-compliance with orders

An employer cannot be forced to comply with a re-employment order, and the ultimate sanction upon him is financial. If an employer fails to comply, then unless he shows that it was not practicable to comply with the order, the tribunal must make an additional award of compensation (unless the 'special award' provisions discussed in Special award p195 apply instead).

The additional award will be not less than 13 nor more than 26 weeks' pay, subject to two exceptions. First, if the dismissal was unfair for a reason relating to trade union involvement (see Chapter 19), or because it was sexually or racially discriminatory, the award will be not less than 26 nor more than 52 weeks' pay. Secondly, if the failure to comply is only partial, the additional award is discretionary.

The additional award serves not only to compensate an employee for at least some of the loss he may suffer by reason of a refusal to comply, but also to indicate the tribunal's disapproval of the employer's behaviour. The tribunal has a wide discretion in fixing an additional award. In *Motherwell Railway Club v. McQueen* (1989), the EAT accepted that a deliberate refusal to comply justified an additional award of 20 weeks' pay, even though the employee turned out to have been ill, so the order could not have been complied with anyway.

A notable example of refusal to comply occurred in *O'Laoire v. Jackel International Ltd* (1990). Most unusually, a tribunal ordered the reinstatement of a joint managing director. The company disobeyed. Even though Mr O'Laoire's total losses were in excess of £100,000, he received a mere £12,185 in total compensation for his unfair dismissal, plus another £9,495 as a result of bringing an action for wrongful dismissal.

24.3 The basic award

The concept of the basic award is akin to that of the redundancy payment – it reflects loss of job security. It is calculated in almost exactly the same way (see section 8.6 Calculating redundancy payments p95) and the limit on the amount of 'a week's pay' which can be taken into account is the same – £184 per week as at 1 April 1990. However, deductions may be made from the basic award in the following cases:

1. where the conduct of the employee was such that it would be just and equitable to make a deduction;

2. where it is just and equitable to make a deduction because the employee unreasonably refused an offer of reinstatement;

3. where the effective date of termination falls after the employee's 64th birthday, in which case the award is reduced on a sliding scale.

Furthermore, a statutory redundancy payment will be offset against the basic award. If a payment in excess of the statutory maximum was made, the excess will be set off against the compensatory award.

24.4 The compensatory award

An employee entitled to compensation for unfair dismissal usually receives a compensatory award as well as a basic award. The compensatory award compensates an employee for financial loss resulting from unfair dismissal. The award will be the amount that the tribunal considers just and equitable in all the circumstances.

It will cover any expenses reasonably incurred (but not legal costs for assistance with an unfair dismissal claim), and any lost benefit which the employee might reasonably be expected to have had but for the dismissal.

It is for the employee to show that he has suffered loss and, if he has suffered no loss because the employment would have ended at the same time in any event, there will be a nil award.

Compensation may be limited where dismissal would (or might) have occurred shortly, in other words, where the unfairness lay primarily in accelerating the dismissal.

In *Winterhalter Gastronom Ltd v. Webb* (1973), an employee was dismissed unfairly for lack of competence, not having been allowed a fair period to improve, but he nevertheless saw his compensation halved by the EAT. They concluded that 'his chances of improving sufficiently to hold down his job were poor and . . . only a modest sum can be fairly attributed to the loss of this chance'.

This does not only apply in cases of misconduct or lack of capability. For example, where an employee is unfairly made redundant because consideration was not given to offering him another job, compensation may be discounted to take account of the fact that, had proper consideration been given, he still might not have been offered that job.

This principle has become even more important following the House of Lords' decision in the *Polkey* case (see section 12.11 When do procedural errors affect fairness? p129), which increased the likelihood of findings of technical unfairness. Thus, in *Mining Supplies (Longwall) Ltd v. Baker* (1988), a redundancy was held unfair though lack of consultation, although the tribunal thought that the employee would still have been dismissed after a reasonable period of consultation. The EAT agreed with this basic approach, but said that consultation for two weeks – not six weeks, as the tribunal thought – would have been reasonable.

Sometimes the dividing line between acting fairly and unfairly is very fine, even where there is no contributory fault on the employee's part. Should the compensation be discounted to take account of the marginal nature of the unfairness? In *Townson v. Northgate Group Ltd* (1981), the EAT indicated that, in deciding what is just and equitable, the tribunal should look at all the relevant factors and decide 'how unfair was the unfair dismissal?'. This suggestion has, however, been strongly criticised as amounting to an unjustified gloss upon the statute, and it would be unwise to assume that a similar line will be taken in future cases.

In assessing compensation, a tribunal has wide discretion. The EAT is very reluctant to interfere with the exercise of that discretion unless a serious error is made. In *Fougere v. Phoenix Motor Co Ltd* (1976), the EAT accepted this approach 'may mean that sometimes an employee will get a bit less than he might have expected; it may mean that sometimes an employer will have to pay a little more than he had expected'. Any other view would tend to defeat the system's objectives of speed, informality and accessibility.

24.5   Quantifying the compensatory award

Basic principles

Unfortunately, but perhaps inevitably, there are few hard and fast rules for calculating the compensatory award. Making advance estimates of its amount in particular cases usually involves guesswork.

A number of principles for determining the overall loss of an employee who has been unfairly dismissed have been evolved. The EAT stressed in *Norton Tool Co Ltd v. Tewson* (1972), that tribunals should set out details of the heads under which compensation is awarded and how the figures have been reached. Nevertheless, tribunals retain much discretion in quantifying the award.

Section 74(1) of the 1978 Act imposes an extremely important ceiling on the compensatory award, which is reviewed from time to time. As at 1 April 1990 it stood at £8,925. The effect of this wholly arbitrary restriction is that, for a senior employee, an unfair dismissal claim may provide only limited redress for the losses stemming from the unjust termination of his employment. From an employer's point of view, to dismiss a shop-floor worker may prove in some cases even more costly than unfairly dismissing the managing director.

Payment for the notice period

If an employee is dismissed with pay in lieu of notice, he is bound to bring into account those earnings, ruled the Court of Appeal in

239

Babcock FATA Ltd v. Addison (1987). If he is dismissed without proper notice and then obtains a new job, wages earned during the notice period will be disregarded for the purposes of any claim against his original employer, although the Court of Appeal said there might be cases where full notice pay would exceed what an employer ought to pay in line with good industrial relations practice, eg if the notice period is lengthy. Thus, in *Isleworth Studios Ltd v. Rickard* (1988), an employee with 29 weeks to run of his fixed-term contract was summarily dismissed but found another job which actually paid him £10,000 more in the relevant period. The EAT did not compensate him for the 29-week period, saying that to do so would not have been 'just and equitable' in accordance with the statute.

Manner of dismissal

Where the manner of an unfair dismissal causes an employee financial loss, he will be compensated for that loss: the *Norton Tool* case. In practice, an employee will usually find it difficult to show that he has suffered such loss.

An employee is not in any event entitled to compensation for emotional distress sustained because of the unfair handling of his dismissal.

Loss to date of hearing

The employee will be entitled to the net amount that he would have earned between the date of the dismissal and the date of the hearing. From this will be deducted the amount that he has earned in a new job. If the employee begins new employment before the hearing, that will not operate as a 'cut-off date'. The earnings in the new job will be set off against what he has lost.

In an appropriate case, an employee may be compensated for the loss of a tax rebate that is due to the timing of the dismissal.

Sickness benefits received prior to the hearing need only be brought into account where the employee's wages would have been reduced on account of sickness.

Social security benefits will not be set off against the employee's loss. The relevant rules are contained in the Employment Protection (Recoupment of Unemployment Benefit and Supplementary Benefit) Regulations 1977. A tribunal must specify various elements in its award to an unfairly dismissed employee who has received certain state benefits.

First, the total monetary award will be calculated. Second, the amount of the compensation, and the period covered by it, from date of dismissal to date of hearing, will be identified. This amount is called 'the prescribed element'. Finally, the amount by which the total award exceeds the prescribed element must also be specified.

The prescribed element is, in effect, frozen for the time being and should not be paid by the employer. The Department of Employment may serve a recoupment notice on the employer within 21 days of the end of the hearing, or within 9 days after the decision is sent to the parties (21 days in the case of a reserved judgment). The employer should pay the amount so claimed by the Department in respect of social security benefits paid to the employee. Any part of the prescribed element remaining should then be paid to the employee.

The 1977 Regulations do not bite where a claim is settled; thus an additional incentive is provided to parties to reach a private agreement.

Future loss

The onus is on the employee to show that he will suffer loss after the hearing date as a result of being unfairly dismissed. Where the employee has found a job at a lower rate of pay before the hearing, the tribunal will have to project his loss forward for a period which it considers appropriate. Oddly, perhaps, no discount will be allowed to reflect the fact that the employee is being awarded compensation in a lump sum, rather than having to earn it over a period of time: *Les Ambassadeurs Club v. Bainda* (1982).

If the employee is still out of work, the tribunal has to look into the future. It will in effect, have to guess how long the employee will be out of work. The employee's age and skills, as well as the local employment situation, will usually be relevant factors, but the tribunal's discretion is very wide indeed. The EAT has made it clear that tribunals should not attempt to fix an unduly precise sum under this heading.

Fringe benefits

Account will generally be taken of lost fringe benefits, such as a

241

company car, tips, rights under share option schemes, and so on. Quantifying the value of those benefits is often, however, another exercise in 'guesstimation'.

Loss of employment protection rights

A sum will generally be awarded in respect of lost industrial rights, for example, because the employee has to requalify for the right not to be unfairly dismissed. Traditionally this has been a relatively nominal sum but, again, the discretion of the tribunal is virtually unrestricted. At the time of writing, a typical award under this head is £100, but higher figures are not unknown.

Expenses

Certain expenses can be taken into account, including those incurred in seeking new employment. Those expenses will not necessarily be nominal. Conceivably, they might include removal expenses or, as in *Gardiner-Hill v. Roland Berger Technics Ltd* (1982), costs incurred by an employee in setting himself up in business.

Pensions

Quantifying the value of pension rights which the employee may have lost is an important but complex task. A committee of industrial tribunal chairmen has prepared a useful document which sets out a basis for making the calculation (available from HMSO). First published in 1990, it expands upon the guidance issued by the Government Actuary's Department ten years earlier.

In *Manpower Ltd v. Hearne* (1983), the EAT held that a tribunal had erred by misinterpreting the Government Actuary's 1980 guidelines, while at the same time stressing that, for all the complexity, the assessment of compensation is inevitably a rough and ready exercise.

24.6   Deductions from compensation

Contributory fault

If a tribunal decides that an unfairly dismissed employee has, by any action, caused or contributed to his dismissal, it should reduce the amount of compensation by the amount it considers just and equitable. This may apply even if the employer has acted in breach of natural justice or in a case of constructive dismissal. The tribunal's discretion here is very wide indeed. It is even possible, in appropriate cases, for the employee's contributory conduct to be assessed at 100 per cent, thus in effect disentitling him to compensation.

Findings as to contribution are seldom overturned on appeal. An exception to this general 'rule' occurred in *Nairne v. Highland & Islands Fire Brigade* (1989), when the Court of Appeal said that, where the unfairness was procedural in nature, a finding of 100 per cent contributory fault might well be logical; on the facts, a tribunal's finding of only 25 per cent contributory fault was perverse and therefore overturned.

The EAT said in *Robert Whiting Design Ltd v. Lamb* (1978), that 'the weight to be given to the employee's conduct ought to be decided in a broad common sense manner'. Bloody-mindedness may in certain circumstances amount to contributory fault, as may any especially unreasonable behaviour.

Assessments of contributory fault can sometimes be very wide of the mark, as the unsatisfactory case of *Ladup Ltd v. Barnes* (1982) shows. An employee charged with possessing cannabis was held to have been unfairly dismissed and not guilty of any contributory fault. After the hearing, he was tried and convicted. With the benefit of hindsight, the EAT accepted that the question of contribution should be reviewed and made an order for contribution of 100 per cent. However, the decision leads to all sorts of unsatisfactory possibilities – what would happen, for example, if the employee appealed successfully against conviction?

Surprisingly, it has been suggested that there should be no finding of contributory fault if an employee is dismissed for incompetence arising from lack of ability rather than laziness or unwillingness to improve. This view has been criticised and, in any event, in such a case compensation would probably be limited on the basis that a fair dismissal would sooner or later have become possible.

Where industrial pressure was the reason for dismissal (see section 11.5 Industrial pressure p119), it is still possible for an employee to have been guilty of contributory fault. This would be the case if, for example, he had antagonised his workmates or unreasonably refused to co-operate with the employer's attempts to resolve the conflict.

Mitigation of loss

The compensatory award may be reduced if the employee has failed to mitigate his loss. The rules here are similar (but not identical) to those that apply at common law (see Mitigation of loss p71), according to the EAT in *Fyfe v. Scientific Furnishings Ltd* (1989). Thus, the onus is on the employer to allege and prove a failure to mitigate.

In fixing the amount to be deducted for a failure to mitigate, the tribunal has to identify what step should have been taken and the date on which that step would have produced an alternative income. Thereafter, it should reduce compensation by the alternative income which would have been earned: *Gardiner-Hill v. Roland Berger Technics Ltd* (1982).

Ex gratia *payments*

Quantifying compensation may be complicated if an *ex gratia* payment has been made to the employee. In *Chelsea FC Ltd v. Heath* (1981), the EAT indicated that an *ex gratia* payment will not automatically be treated as meeting any liability stemming from the basic award. There can be a set-off where it was clearly intended that the *ex gratia* sum should include an element for that head of liability, but not otherwise. If a general payment is made, it is a question of interpretation in each case as to whether it covers both basic and compensatory awards, although that will normally be presumed.

If an *ex gratia* payment would have been made in any event, a tribunal may not give any credit for it in calculating unfair dismissal compensation, as in *Roadchef Ltd v. Hastings* (1988), where the payment would have been made to the employee if and when he had later been made redundant after proper consultation.

An interesting and important question arises if the *ex gratia* payment exceeds the current maximum compensatory award. Does this mean that even an unfairly dismissed employee cannot be entitled to the award of any additional monies? The answer is no. The *ex gratia* payment should be deducted from the total gross award, which may far exceed the statutory limit, before applying that limit: *McCarthy v. BICC Metals Ltd* (1985). Thus, if the total gross award is large enough, an *ex gratia* payment will not reduce the employer's legal liability at all.

Furthermore, any reduction in respect of contributory fault should only be made *after* the *ex gratia* payment has been subtracted from the total gross award. Again, this may have the effect of 'penalising' an employer who has made an *ex gratia* payment, but failed to take the precaution of insisting that the employee signs form COT3. This underlines the desirability of making settlements under the auspices of ACAS so that no claim to a tribunal can be made; see section 23.4 Conciliation p230.

24.7   Enforcement of awards

An industrial tribunal has no power to enforce any award of compensation that it makes. If the employer declines to pay up, the employee must bring enforcement proceedings in the ordinary civil courts.

As from 1 April 1990, a tribunal may levy interest on overdue awards, at the 'Judgements Act rate', which at the time of writing was 15 per cent.

25
Industrial Tribunals

25.1 Introduction

The vast majority of claims arising from dismissal law rights are made to an industrial tribunal. Tribunals are intended to be speedy, informal and easily accessible. In England and Wales, their procedure is governed by the Industrial Tribunals (Rules of Procedure) Regulations 1985, and similar rules apply in Scotland.

The 1985 Regulations confer a wide discretion upon tribunals in the exercise of their powers, and there are sometimes regional variations in the way those powers tend to be exercised. The individual approach of different tribunals may differ from case to case. Inevitably, a difficult balance has to be struck between flexibility and simplicity on the one hand and consistency and fairness on the other. Tribunals are composed of human beings and as such are not perfect; an eccentric decision will occur now and then. However, considering the strains that a heavy caseload places upon it, the system works reasonably well.

There is no magic formula for success in handling industrial tribunal cases, and even the most experienced advocate will sometimes receive an unwelcome surprise. But there is no reason why handling even a complex tribunal case should prove traumatic. The best approach will combine thorough preparation with an adaptable attitude and, although this is sometimes overlooked, courtesy.

25.2 The originating application

Tribunal proceedings are started by the applicant presenting an 'originating application', usually on form IT1, stating:

1. his name and address;

246

2. the name(s) and address(es) of the person(s) against whom the complaint is made;

3. the grounds, with particulars, on which relief is sought.

If the application contains an error, the tribunal may in its discretion amend it either prior to or at the hearing. The applicant will not be restricted to the grounds he has set out in the application, although any contradictory evidence which he gives may be challenged and damage his credibility.

The Secretary of the Tribunals will register the application and send a copy to the other parties and the conciliation officer assigned to the case. Exceptionally, if it appears that the tribunal does not have jurisdiction to hear the complaint, the Secretary may raise the matter with the applicant before registering the application. The mere fact of registration does not mean that the tribunal accepts jurisdiction. An employer who believes that the claim cannot be brought – for example, because the applicant lacks the necessary qualifying service – may ask for a preliminary hearing to be held to determine the point.

25.3   Presenting a claim in time

Basic principles

There is a time limit for making all complaints to an industrial tribunal, and whether or not an application has been presented in time is a question of jurisdiction. The tribunal must consider the point even if the respondent fails to, or does not wish to, take advantage of the point.

The precise rules vary depending upon the nature of the complaint, as do the terms of the 'escape clauses' which allow the extension of time in certain circumstances. In unfair dismissal cases, there is a three-month time limit beginning with the effective date of termination, but a claim can be presented before that date, provided that notice has been given. On the other hand, a claim for a redundancy payment must be made within a period of six months beginning with the relevant date, and there is no provision allowing premature claims.

A claim is presented to a tribunal when it is received by the tribunal and not when it is posted. If the application arrives at the tribunal office before midnight on the last day of the limitation period, it is presented on time. An application is presented if placed through a letter-box or otherwise received by the tribunal. Thus, the general rule is that, even if the last day of the limitation period is, say, a Saturday, Sunday or public holiday, that will still be the last day; the limitation period will not automatically be extended to include the next working day. However, in *Ford v. Stakis Hotels and Inns Ltd* (1988), an application was held to have been presented on time when it was pushed under the office door (there being no letter-box) on the day after the bank holiday which had been the last day for presentation of a claim.

Postal delays

Sometimes an application may be delayed in the post. If the application would, in the normal course of post, have arrived in time, the tribunal will ask whether in the circumstances it could reasonably have been expected that the application would arrive in time. It may not, for example, always be reasonable to rely on an application being delivered the following day if sent by first class post. If it was reasonable, the tribunal will usually invoke the 'escape clause' and extend the time. This happened in *Beanstalk Shelving Ltd v. Horn* (1980), where evidence was given that the application should have arrived in time, but the EAT pointed out that it was 'an extremely dangerous practice' to leave posting an application to the last minute.

The escape clause

The burden of showing that it was not reasonably practicable to present a claim in time rests on the applicant. It is a question of fact for the tribunal, whose decision on the point will seldom be appealable.

The test, according to Lord Denning in *Wall's Meat Co Ltd v. Khan* (1978), is whether the applicant had just cause or excuse for not presenting his complaint within the prescribed time. Ignorance of his rights, or ignorance of the time limit, are not just causes or excuses unless it appears that the applicant or his advisers could not reasonably have been expected to have been aware of them.

It is not, however, reasonably practicable for an employee to complain of unfair dismissal until he learns a fundamental fact which may render an apparently fair dismissal unfair. This was the situation in *Machine Tool Industry Research Association v. Simpson* (1988), where a redundant employee only learned after the expiry of the time limit that a colleague had been re-engaged. This led him to suspect that redundancy was not the real reason for his dismissal.

If the tribunal accepts that it was not reasonably practicable for the application to be presented in time, it must then consider whether it was presented within a reasonable time thereafter. Again, the tribunal has considerable discretion.

Where an applicant's advisers are at fault, and the application is presented out of time as a result, their fault will be attributed to the applicant himself and he will not be allowed to rely upon the escape clause: *Riley v. Tesco Stores* (1980). Any remedy that he may have will be against his advisers.

The mere fact that criminal or other proceedings, or an internal appeal against dismissal, are pending, will not necessarily – or usually – justify a failure to present a claim in time, although it may do so in exceptional cases.

25.4   The notice of appearance

A party who wishes to resist a claim must complete and return, within 14 days of receiving the application, a written notice of appearance, usually on form IT3,stating:

1. his name and address;

2. whether or not he intends to resist the application;

3. if so, on what grounds.

It is vital to set out the grounds of resistance accurately and carefully. An employer who intends to engage a representative will be wise to discuss the matter with him before entering the defence. If necessary, an extension of the 14-day time limit may be sought. If the notice of appearance is not entered in time, the respondent cannot participate in the proceedings, but an application for an extension of time for entering a late defence may still be made. Unlike the time limit for presentation of an application, the time limit for entering the notice of appearance does not raise a question of the tribunal's jurisdiction.

The notice of appearance may be amended subsequently, but only with the leave of the tribunal. Leave will not be granted automatically. If an application for leave to amend is made at the hearing for the first time, it should be made at the outset, as the tribunal will usually be reluctant to permit a major amendment once the hearing has begun. In any event, if an employer shifts ground significantly at a late stage, this may cast serious doubt on his credibility.

25.5   Preparing the case

Further particulars

Sometimes an application or notice of appearance is so brief or unclear that the other part is unable to identify why a particular allegation has been made. Either party may seek clarification of the other's case by asking for further particulars to be supplied. Usually it is sensible to stipulate a time limit of, say, seven or 14 days.

If the particulars are not supplied, the tribunal can be asked to grant an order that they be supplied. The tribunal will not accede to such a request automatically. A party is not, for example, entitled to a full account of the evidence that will be given against him. The important point is that he should not be taken by surprise at the hearing by the raising of a completely fresh issue.

The tribunal may also make an order of its own volition, without a request, if it thinks it necessary to do so. If a party fails to comply with an order, he may be debarred from proceeding further.

Discovery of documents

If a party considers that the other party, or any other person, possesses a document relevant to the case, he should first write requesting to see the document or to be sent a copy, again within a specified time limit.

If the request is not complied with, the tribunal can be asked to grant an order for discovery, ie disclosure, of the document. As ever, the tribunal has considerable discretion in deciding whether or not to compel production. The test is whether disclosure is necessary for disposing fairly of the proceedings. Where an employer has obtained medical reports on an employee to help in deciding whether or not to dismiss, disclosure of those reports will usually be ordered, even if the employer only relies on the reports' conclusions: *Ford Motor Co Ltd v. Nawaz* (1987).

A party against whom an order for discovery is made may apply for it to be varied or set aside. If he fails to comply with an order without reasonable excuse, he may be fined on conviction and debarred from taking further part in the proceedings.

If no formal order for discovery is made, there is no duty on a party to disclose documents to his opponent. However, if he does disclose documents – as will usually be the case – he must not conceal the existence of any relevant documents, whether or not they support his case: *Birds Eye Walls Ltd v. Harrison* (1985).

Witnesses

If a witness is thought necessary to the case, he should be asked to attend voluntarily. If he refuses, the tribunal can be asked to order his attendance. It will grant an order if it thinks that he can give relevant evidence and that an order is necessary, but the witness may apply to have the order set aside. Breach of an order without reasonable excuse is a criminal offence.

Witness orders should only be sought as a last resort. A hostile – or unpredictable – witness can often do more harm than good. In any event, there is a widespread tendency for parties to call more witnesses to hearings than are strictly necessary. Doing this may blur the important issues and test the tribunal's patience.

The tribunal may admit an affidavit from a witness who is unable to give oral evidence for some good reason. Occasionally, the tribunal may admit an unsworn statement, but it will usually attach only a limited amount of weight to a statement which cannot be cross-examined.

Joining parties

A tribunal may, either upon request or of its own volition, add parties to proceedings where it appears that they may be affected by the outcome, or dismiss them from the proceedings where it appears that they have ceased to be so affected.

Consolidating proceedings

A tribunal may consolidate two or more applications in which the same question of law or fact arises or where for some other reason it is desirable. This is a useful power, which permits the saving of time and costs. It may therefore be worth asking the tribunal to consolidate in appropriate cases.

Organising the case

Advance preparation is the key to success in tribunal cases. All the necessary witness statements, documents and other evidence must be organised in a coherent manner. Documents should be exchanged well before the hearing and it will be helpful if a single paginated bundle of documents can be agreed. There should be copies for each party, each member of the tribunal and the witnesses.

Fixing a date

There are regional variations in the procedure for listing an application for hearing, but at least 14 days' notice must be given. It is sensible to assess at an early stage how long the hearing may last and inform the tribunal accordingly, so that there is no need for any adjournment. Belated requests for postponement once a hearing date has been arranged are apt to be frowned upon and are often refused. Applications are intended to be dealt with expeditiously.

Tribunals may be more sympathetic to a request for a postponement if there is a pending action in the High Court involving similar issues. In *First Castle Electronics Ltd v. West* (1989), the EAT said the factors weighing in favour of postponement in that case included:

1. the fact that the issues in the wrongful dismissal claim in the High Court were much the same as those in the unfair dismissal case;

2. the extremely complicated nature of those issues;

3. the fact that clear findings of fact from a High Court judge might later prove helpful to the tribunal;

4. the desirability of applying the High Court's strict rule of evidence to the particular case in question.

In *Warnock v. Scarborough FC* (1989), where (unusually) postponement was sought by the employee, it was also relevant that:

1. much more money was at stake in the High Court case;

2. costs were more likely to be awarded in the High Court;

3. the High Court decision would probably determine the outcome of the tribunal case.

25.6 Pre-hearing assessments

The tribunal may at any time before the hearing arrange a pre-hearing assessment, either on the application of one of the parties or on its own initiative. A request for a pre-hearing assessment must be made in writing to the Secretary of the Tribunals and such a request will not be granted automatically. If it is granted, the parties will be notified and allowed to submit written representations and to attend.

The purpose of a pre-hearing assessment is to consider, in effect, the merits of the case and to weed out hopeless arguments. No oral evidence will be heard, but documents are frequently produced and oral argument will be considered.

Sometimes the tribunal will conclude that the applicant's claim is unlikely to succeed or that a contention of a party has no reasonable prospect of success. If so, it may indicate its opinion that, if the claim or contention is persisted with, costs may be ordered against the party in question at the hearing if the claim or contention fails.

The tribunal's opinion will be recorded in writing and sent to the parties. It will also be available at the hearing, if the case proceeds. However, no member of the tribunal giving the opinion may sit at the hearing and in practice the opinion will only be considered once the case has been concluded and an application for costs made.

Pre-hearing assessments have a useful but limited role. Employers request pre-hearing assessments far more frequently than do applicants, and this is not surprising. Even a successful defence of a claim at a full hearing can sometimes prove to be a pyrrhic victory given the cost of management time and, perhaps, legal representation.

The system is not universally popular or effective and the number of assessments held in recent years has shown a marked decline. Regional variations in the approach of tribunals are noticeable. Tribunals may be reluctant to deter a party from taking a point further when they have not had the opportunity to consider sworn evidence. If no opinion is granted, the party whom it is sought to deter may actually be encouraged to proceed, and even if an opinion is given, there is no guarantee that costs will be awarded. Indeed, there is a significant minority of cases in which a party warned against proceeding in fact succeeds at the full hearing. In so far as it is possible to generalise at all about something so unpredictable, it will be more appropriate to seek a pre-hearing assessment where the strength of the case can be demonstrated on paper, without relying on oral testimony.

25.7 Deposits

The pre-hearing assessment system seems, for the reasons just mentioned, to be withering on the vine. A new concept designed to discourage hopeless claims was therefore introduced by the Conservative Government in the Employment Act 1989.

Prior to a hearing, a tribunal may, either at the request of one of the parties or on its own initiative, at a 'pre-hearing review', require a deposit of up to £150 from a party as a condition of proceeding further with the case if it considers that party's arguments to have no reasonable prospect of success.

Time will tell whether the deposit scheme is effective – undoubtedly, there are a minority of cases in which 'time-wasters' ought to be discouraged – but much depends on whether individual tribunals are willing to make use of their new power. It would be unwise to expect deposits to have a major impact on the conduct of tribunal cases.

25.8 Striking out

A tribunal may strike out an originating application or notice of appearance if it is scandalous, frivolous or vexatious. It may also strike out an application 'for want of prosecution'. On the latter point, the EAT emphasised in *O'Shea v. Immediate Sound Services Ltd* (1986), that tribunal proceedings should be swift and that

> 'if applicants or their advisers think that the leisurely approach to litigation which obtains in the High Court can happily go on before industrial tribunals, they should be disabused now'.

However, before a party's claim (or defence) can be struck out, he must be given an opportunity to explain why such an order should not be made.

25.9 The hearing

Tribunal hearings are held in public, with a few narrowly defined exceptions, for example, if the evidence relates to national security. If a party does not attend, the tribunal may treat his originating application or notice of appearance as a written representation and may deal with the case in his absence.

The tribunal comprises a legally qualified chairman, an employer representative and an employee representative. A clerk will be present and a list of any cases upon which it is proposed to rely should be given to him before proceedings start.

The case will be opened by the party upon whom the initial burden of proof rests. Thus, in an unfair dismissal case where dismissal is admitted, the employer has to show the reason for the dismissal and so he will begin. Conversely, in a constructive dismissal claim the employee, who has to prove dismissal, will be asked to start the case.

The tribunal may conduct the hearing in the way it considers appropriate to the particular case. There are no rigid rules, but a typical sequence of events in a simple unfair dismissal case where dismissal is admitted is as follows:

1. opening speech by respondent;

2. evidence of respondent's witness;

3. cross-examination by applicant;

4. questions of witness from tribunal members;

5. re-examination of witness dealing with any matters arising out of cross-examination or questions;

6. applicant's evidence;

7. cross-examination and questions;

8. closing speech by applicant;

9. closing speech by respondent.

The chairman will make notes of what is said and evidence should be given clearly and slowly. The notes need not be verbatim, but may have to be produced if there is an appeal.

The strict rules of evidence which apply in ordinary courts do not apply and the tribunal may, for example, decide to admit hearsay evidence. Occasionally, where the party on whom the burden of proof rests concludes his case, the other party may submit that he has not discharged that burden and that there is no case to answer. This will only be appropriate in the clearest of cases.

Often, the tribunal announces its decision (which need not be, but usually is, unanimous) on the day of the hearing, but in difficult cases or if time has run out it may reserve its decision. The reasons for the decision will be confirmed subsequently to the parties in writing, either in full or summary form.

25.10 Costs

Costs are not normally awarded to a successful party. This accords with the original philosophy of tribunal proceedings that legal representation is not a necessity; indeed, legal aid is not available for representation before a tribunal. Whether the basic principle is still realistic is debatable.

Costs may be awarded against a party who, in the tribunal's opinion, has acted frivolously, vexatiously or otherwise unreasonably in bringing or conducting a case, for example, by ignoring a warning given at a pre-hearing assessment. Costs may also be awarded if, for example, a party's default has caused the adjournment or postponement of the hearing. If an order is made, it will usually be in a specified sum.

It is best to apply for costs at the end of the hearing – if at all – although this may be premature or even tempting fate in cases where the tribunal reserves its decision. In any event, an application must be made within a reasonable time.

25.11 Review of decisions

An application for a review can be made either at the hearing or within 14 days from the date on which the written decision was entered on the register and sent to the parties. The possible grounds for review are where:

1. the decision was wrongly made as a result of an error on the part of the tribunal staff;

2. a party did not receive notice of the proceedings;

3. the decision was made in the absence of a party entitled to be heard;

4. new evidence has become available since the decision, provided its existence could not reasonably have been known of or foreseen;

5. the interests of justice require a review.

An application for a review will not be granted automatically. If it is granted, it will usually be heard by the tribunal which decided the case. If the application succeeds, the tribunal may either vary its decision or revoke it and order a re-hearing – usually before a different tribunal.

A review is not an appeal by the back door. It is a useful means of correcting obvious and readily apparent error, but the catch-all 'interests of justice' category, while conferring a wide discretion, tends to be interpreted stringently. Tribunals take heed of the need for finality in litigation and will not allow a party to exploit the review procedure to keep alive an unsuccessful argument that has already been rejected once.

A party dissatisfied with the tribunal's decision on the application may appeal on a question of law within the 42-day time limit referred to below. Applying for a review of a decision does not stop time running for the making of an appeal against that decision.

25.12 Appeals

An appeal against an industrial tribunal's decision may be made to the EAT. An appeal must be made within 42 days of the date on which the written decision was sent to the parties, and although there is power to extend this time limit, it is usually enforced strictly. The relevant practice and procedure is set out in the Employment Appeal Tribunal Rules 1980 as amended and the Practice Directions made from time to time by the President of the EAT.

An appeal can only be made on the grounds that the tribunal has erred in law, ie if:

1. it misdirected itself in law, or misunderstood or misapplied the law;

2. it misunderstood or misapplied the facts;

3. its decision was one which no reasonable tribunal could have reached, in that either it was perverse on the evidence or there was no evidence on which the decision could have been reached.

Few tribunal decisions are successfully appealed. Tribunals have a considerable discretion in reaching their conclusions and have the inestimable advantage of observing the witnesses at first hand. This underlines the importance of preparing and handling a case competently from the outset, to minimise the risk of an unsatisfactory result.

26
Summing Up

26.1   Introduction

Dismissal law problems come in an endless variety of forms. Most commonly, however, employers and employees are concerned with the fairness or unfairness of dismissal for misconduct, redundancy, incompetence or absence from work.

Mr Justice Waite, a former President of the EAT, once said that it is simply necessary to 'see how the circumstances of each case are to be dealt with in the light of the guidance afforded by the section', ie section 57(3) of the 1978 Act. Employers and employees might be entitled to wonder whether the statutory criterion of 'reasonableness', by itself, offers much helpful guidance. One man's fairness is another man's injustice.

More specific guidelines must inevitably be accompanied by warnings. There is no particular magic in the brief checklists set out in the following four sections; they should be read in conjunction with the contents of relevant earlier chapters and, in particular, with recommendations made in the ACAS handbook *Discipline At Work*. It is hoped, however, that they will at least help employers to avoid some of the more usual pitfalls.

26.2   Handling disciplinary hearings – checklist

1. The manager responsible for conducting the hearing should prepare carefully and make sure he knows the relevant facts;

2. the employee should be made aware when called to the hearing that the hearing is to be of a disciplinary nature;

3. the employee should specifically be offered the right to be accompanied by a trade union representative or fellow employee of

his own choice. He will not necessarily be entitled to be accompanied by a person who is not a trade union representative or fellow employee, even if that person is his legal adviser, but any such request should be considered on its merits and not automatically refused;

4. disciplinary proceedings should not be initiated in the case of a trade union official until a senior trade union representative or full-time official has become involved;

5. if an employee declines to attend a disciplinary hearing without good reason, it will usually be reasonable to proceed in his absence. In some cases, the cautious employer will wish to satisfy himself that there is no good reason (such as illness) for non-attendance and may wish to take the precaution of offering the recalcitrant employee a further opportunity to attend at an alternative time and date, while making clear the consequences of non-attendance;

6. more than one representative of management should usually be present. This will help to provide corroboration of what was said in the event of subsequent dispute;

7. the complaint (and its seriousness) should be explained fully to the employee, as should the allegations made by any relevant witnesses;

8. the employee will not necessarily be entitled to insist upon the right to question witnesses, but any such request should be treated on its merits in the light of the particular facts of the case;

9. the employee and his representative should be given every opportunity to state his case;

10. it is desirable for the employee to be present throughout the proceedings, but it may be fair, as sometimes happens, for his representative to conduct the case in part in the employee's absence, provided that he safeguards the employee's interests;

11. careful consideration should be given to the employee's representations;

12. if the matter is complex, or if further investigation is necessary, it may be appropriate to adjourn the interview and/or suspend the employee (on pay, unless his contract permits suspension for a short period without pay) pending further consideration;

13. once a decision has been taken, it should be communicated to the employee without delay and in most cases it will be sensible to confirm the position in writing;

14. it is usually helpful for a clear note to be kept of the salient points made during the interview. A verbatim transcript is seldom necessary, but the note should be made without delay and it will be especially helpful if the employee and his representatives are willing to acknowledge in writing that the note is a true and accurate summary of the interview;

15. an employee who is informed of disciplinary action taken against him should also be made aware of his right to appeal against the decision and the procedure to be followed.

26.3 Handling redundancy dismissals – checklist

1. An assessment should be made of the facts which are believed to give rise to the need for staff cuts and possible alternatives should be considered;

2. if redundancies appear at first sight to be necessary, the position should be fully discussed with the employees' representatives and the consultation/notification provisions discussed in Chapter 9 should be complied with. If there is no recognised trade union, it will be appropriate to consult with the Works Council or any other suitable authorised representatives;

3. if redundancies are necessary, the appropriate selection group should be identified and objective criteria for selection agreed with the employee representatives;

4. the selection criteria should be applied objectively;

5. the employees affected should be informed at the earliest opportunity;

6. the employees' views should be sought and any possible alternatives to redundancy again investigated;

7. if redundancy becomes inevitable, the employees concerned should be given time off to seek new work;

8. all monies due should be paid and a statement of redundancy pay entitlement provided.

26.4   Handling dismissals for incompetence – checklist

1. The evidence for the belief that the employee fails to meet requirements should be assessed carefully;

2. if it seems that the employee is at fault, the employer should discuss the problem with the employee at a meeting. The procedure suggested in section 26.2 Handling disciplinary hearings p259 may to some extent be capable of adaptation to the context of incompetence. In particular:

    a) the employee should be advised prior to the meeting of its purpose and should be allowed to be accompanied by a colleague or employee representative;

    b) at the meeting, the employer should itemise the precise complaints;

    c) the reasons for the shortcomings should be investigated;

    d) means of improving performance should be considered;

    e) the time within which a sustained improvement is required should be specified;

    f) the consequences of failure to improve, eg a final warning, should be made clear;

    g) the position should be confirmed in writing, eg by way of first written warning.

3. in the event of continued poor performance, the employer should repeat the procedure of investigation, consultation and warning;

4. in the event of it becoming clear that the employee is not able to meet the required standards, the process of investigation and consultation should again be followed before any decision to dismiss is taken.

26.5   Handling sickness dismissals – checklist

1. Management should keep in touch with the employee who is absent through sickness and keep him informed if his job is at risk;

2. the medical position should be investigated and the employer should comply with the Access to Medical Reports Act;

3. where there is reasonable doubt about the nature or effect of the illness or injury, the employer should ask the employee to attend an examination conducted by a doctor approved by the employer;

4. if the employee fails to co-operate, he should be warned that a decision will be taken in the light of the available facts and that it could result in his dismissal;

5. generally, the employer should consider possible alternatives to dismissal, such as a transfer to lighter duties;

6. an employee dismissed because of lack of capability due to sickness should be given the appropriate period of notice and told of any right to appeal.

Appendix A

Abbreviations

Statutes

'the 1944 Act	Disabled Persons (Employment) Act 1944
'the 1974 Act'	Trade Union and Labour Relations Act 1974
'the 1975 Act'	Employment Protection Act 1975
'the 1978 Act'	Employment Protection (Consolidation) Act 1978

Statutory Instruments

'the 1976 Regulations'	Labour Relations (Continuity of Employment) Regulations 1976 (SI 1976 No 660)
'the 1981 Regulations'	Transfer of Undertakings (Protection of Employment) Regulations 1981 (SI 1981 No 1794)
'the 1985 Regulations'	Industrial Tribunals (Rules of Procedure) Regulations 1985 (SI 1985 No 16)

General

ACAS	Advisory, Conciliation and Arbitration Service
EAT	Employment Appeal Tribunal
LIFO	Last in, first out

Law Reports (Appendix B)

AC	Appeal Court Cases

ATC	Annotated Tax Cases
ICR	Industrial Cases Reports
IRLR	Industrial Relations Law Reports
IRLIB	Industrial Relations Legal Information Bulletin
ITR	Industrial Tribunals Reports
WLR	Weekly Law Reports

Appendix B

Table of cases

Appendix C

ACAS code on disciplinary practice and procedures

This Code is Crown Copyright and is reproduced by kind permission of the Controller of Her Majesty's Stationery Office. The Code, which came into effect on 20 June 1977, is reproduced as issued and readers should note that some of the statutory references have subsequently been amended or repealed.

A failure on the part of any person to observe any provision of a Code of Practice shall not of itself render him liable to any proceedings; but in any proceedings before an industrial tribunal or the Central Arbitration Committee any Code of Practice issued under this section shall be admissible in evidence, and if any provision of such a Code appears to the tribunal or Committee to be relevant to any question arising in the proceedings it shall be taken into account in determining that question. (Employment Protection Act 1975 section 6(11).)

1. Introduction

This Code supersedes paragraphs 130 to 133 (inclusive) of the Code of Practice in effect under Part I of Schedule I to the Trade Union and Labour Relations Act 1974, which paragraphs shall cease to have effect on the date on which this Code comes into effect.

This document gives practical guidance on how to draw up disciplinary rules and procedures and how to operate them effectively. Its aim is to help employers and trade unions as well as individual employees – both men and women – wherever they are employed regardless of the size of the organisation in which they work. In the smaller establishments it may not be practicable to adopt all the detailed provisions, but most of the features listed in paragraph 10 could be adopted and incorporated into a simple procedure.

2. Why have disciplinary rules and procedures?

Disciplinary rules and procedures are necessary for promoting fairness and order in the treatment of individuals and in the conduct of industrial relations. They also assist an organisation to operate effectively. Rules set standards of conduct at work; procedure helps to ensure that the standards are adhered to and also provides a fair method of dealing with alleged failures to observe them.

3.   It is important that employees know what standards of conduct are expected of them and the Contracts of Employment Act 1972 (as amended by the Employment Protection Act 1975) requires employers to provide written information for their employees about certain aspects of their disciplinary rules and procedures.*

4.   The importance of disciplinary rules and procedures has also been recognised by the law relating to dismissals, since the grounds for dismissal and the way in which the dismissal has been handled can be challenged before an industrial tribunal.† Where either of these is found by a tribunal to have been unfair the employer may be ordered to reinstate or re-engage the employees concerned and may be liable to pay compensation to them.

5. Formulating policy

Management is responsible for maintaining discipline within the

---

* Contracts of Employment Act 1972 S.4(2) as amended by Employment Protection Act Schedule 16 Part II requires employers to provide employees with a written statement of the main terms and conditions of their employment. Such statements must also specify any disciplinary rules applicable to them and indicate the person to whom they should apply if they are dissatisfied with any disciplinary decision. The statement should explain any further steps which exist in any procedure for dealing with disciplinary decisions or grievances. The employer may satisfy these requirements by referring the employees to a reasonably accessible document which provides the necessary information.

† The Trade Union and Labour Relations Act 1974 Schedule I para 21(4), as amended by the Employment Protection Act 1975 Schedule 16 Part III, specifies that a complaint of unfair dismissal has to be presented to an Industrial Tribunal before the end of the 3-month period beginning with the effective date of termination.

organisation and for ensuring that there are adequate disciplinary rules and procedures. The initiative for establishing these will normally lie with management. However, if they are to be fully effective the rules and procedures need to be accepted as reasonable both by those who are to be covered by them and by those who operate them. Management should therefore aim to secure the involvement of employees and all levels of management when formulating new or revising existing rules and procedures. In the light of particular circumstances in different companies and industries trade union officials‡ may or may not wish to participate in the formation of the rules but they should participate fully with management in agreeing the procedural arrangements which will apply to their members and in seeing that these arrangements are used consistently and fairly.

6. Rules

It is unlikely that any set of disciplinary rules can cover all circumstances that may arise: moreover the rules required will vary according to particular circumstances such as the type of work, working conditions and size of establishment. When drawing up rules the aim should be to specify clearly and concisely those necessary for the efficient and safe performance of work and for the maintenance of satisfactory relations within the workforce and between employees and management. Rules should not be so general as to be meaningless.

7. Rules should be readily available and management should make every effort to ensure that employees know and understand them. This may be best achieved by giving every employee a copy of the rules and by explaining them orally. In the case of new employees this should form part of an induction programme.

8. Employees should be made aware of the likely consequences of breaking rules and in particular they should be given a clear indication of the type of conduct which may warrant summary dismissal.

---

‡ Throughout this Code, trade union official has the meaning assigned to it by S.30(1) of the Trade Union and Labour Relations Act 1974 and means broadly, officers of the union, in branches and sections, and anyone else, including fellow employees, appointed or elected under the union's rules to represent members.

9. Essential features of disciplinary procedures

Disciplinary procedures should not be viewed primarily as a means of imposing sanctions. They should also be designed to emphasise and encourage improvements in individual conduct.

10. Disciplinary procedures should:

(a) be in writing;

(b) specify to whom they apply;

(c) provide for matters to be dealt with quickly;

(d) indicate the disciplinary actions which may be taken;

(e) specify the levels of management which have the authority to take the various forms of disciplinary action, ensuring that immediate superiors do not normally have the power to dismiss without reference to senior management;

(f) provide for individuals to be informed of the complaints against them and to be given an opportunity to state their case before decisions are reached;

(g) give individuals the right to be accompanied by a trade union representative or by a fellow employee of their choice;

(h) ensure that, except for gross misconduct, no employees are dismissed for a first breach of discipline;

(i) ensure that disciplinary action is not taken until the case has been carefully investigated;

(j) ensure that individuals are given an explanation for any penalty imposed;

(k) provide a right of appeal and specify the procedure to be followed.

11. The procedure in operation

When a disciplinary matter arises, the supervisor or manager should first establish the facts promptly before recollections fade, taking into account the statements of any available witnesses. In serious cases consideration should be given to a brief period of suspension while the case is investigated and this suspension should be with pay. Before a decision is made or penalty imposed the individual should be interviewed and given the opportunity to state his or her case and should be advised of any rights under the procedure, including the right to be accompanied.

12. Often supervisors will give informal oral warnings for the purpose of improving conduct when employees commit minor infringements of the established standards of conduct. However, where the facts of a case appear to call for disciplinary action, other than summary dismissal, the following procedure should normally be observed:

(a) In the case of minor offences the individual should be given a formal oral warning or if the issue is more serious, there should be a written warning setting out the nature of the offence and the likely consequences of further offences. In either case the individual should be advised that the warning constitutes the first formal stage of the procedure;

(b) Further misconduct might warrant a final written warning which should contain a statement that any recurrence would lead to suspension or dismissal or some other penalty, as the case may be.

(c) The final step might be disciplinary transfer, or disciplinary suspension without pay (but only if these are allowed for by an express or implied condition of the contract of employment), or dismissal, according to the nature of the misconduct. Special consideration should be given before imposing disciplinary suspension without pay and it should not normally be for a prolonged period.

13. Except in the event of an oral warning, details of any disciplinary action should be given in writing to the employee and if desired, to his or her representative. At the same time the employee should be told of any right of appeal, how to make it and to whom.

14. When determining the disciplinary action to be taken the supervisor or manager should bear in mind the need to satisfy the test of reasonableness in all the circumstances. So far as possible, account should be taken of the employee's record and any other relevant factors.

15. Special consideration should be given to the way in which disciplinary procedures are to operate in exceptional cases. For example:

(a) *Employees to whom the full procedure is not immediately available*. Special provisions may have to be made for the handling of disciplinary matters among nightshift workers, workers in isolated locations or depots or others who may pose particular problems for example because no one is present with the necessary authority to take disciplinary action or no trade union representative is immediately available.

(b) *Trade union officials*. Disciplinary action against a trade union official can lead to a serious dispute if it is seen as an attack on the union's functions. Although normal disciplinary standards should apply to their conduct as employees, no disciplinary action beyond an oral warning should be taken until the circumstances of the case have been discussed with a senior trade union representative or full-time official.

(c) *Criminal offences outside employment*. These should not be treated as automatic reasons for dismissal regardless of whether the offence has any relevance to the duties of the individual as an employee. The main considerations should be whether the offence is one that makes the individual unsuitable for his or her type of work or unacceptable to other employees. Employees should not be dismissed solely because a charge against them is pending or because they are absent through having been remanded in custody.

16. Appeals

Grievance procedures are sometimes used for dealing with disciplinary appeals though it is normally more appropriate to keep the two kinds of procedure separate since the disciplinary issues are in general best resolved within the organisation and need to be dealt with more speedily than others. The external stages of a grievance procedure may however, be the appropriate machinery for dealing with appeals against disciplinary action where a final decision within the organisation is contested or where the matter becomes a collective issue between management and a trade union.

17. Independent arbitration is sometimes an appropriate means of resolving disciplinary issues. Where the parties concerned agree, it may constitute the final stage of procedure.

18. *Records*

Records should be kept, detailing the nature of any breach of disciplinary rules, the action taken and the reasons for it, whether an appeal was lodged, its outcome and any subsequent developments. These records should be carefully safeguarded and kept confidential.

19.   Except in agreed special circumstances breaches of disciplinary rules should be disregarded after a specified period of satisfactory conduct.

20. *Further action*

Rules and procedures should be reviewed periodically in the light of any developments in employment legislation or industrial relations practice and, if necessary, revised in order to ensure their continuing relevance and effectiveness. Any amendments and additional rules imposing new obligations should be introduced only after reasonable notice has been given to all employees and, where appropriate, their representatives have been informed.

Appendix D

Ready reckoner for calculating redundancy payments

To use the table:

• Read off employee's age and number of complete years' service. The table will then show how many weeks' pay the employee is entitled to. For the definition of a week's pay, see section 22.5 A week's pay p226. (The table starts at 20 because no one below this age can qualify for a redundancy payment – service before the employee reached the age of 18 does not count.)

• For employees aged between 64 and 65, the cash amount due is to be reduced by one-twelfth for every complete month by which the age exceeds 64.

The basis of calculation is explained at 8.6.

Service (years)

Age (years)	2	3	4	5	6	7	8	9	10	11	12	13	14	15	16	17	18	19	20
20	1	1	1	1	—														
21	1	1½	1½	1½	1½	—													
22	1	1½	2	2	2	2	—												
23	1½	2	2½	3	3	3	3	—											
24	2	2½	3	3½	4	4	4	4	—										
25	2	3	3½	4	4½	5	5	5	5	—									
26	2	3	4	4½	5	5½	6	6	6	6	—								
27	2	3	4	5	5½	6	6½	7	7	7	7	—							
28	2	3	4	5	6	6½	7	7½	8	8	8	8	—						
29	2	3	4	5	6	7	7½	8	8½	9	9	9	9	—					
30	2	3	4	5	6	7	8	8½	9	9½	10	10	10	10	—				
31	2	3	4	5	6	7	8	9	9½	10	10½	11	11	11	11	—			
32	2	3	4	5	6	7	8	9	10	10½	11	11½	12	12	12	12	—		
33	2	3	4	5	6	7	8	9	10	11	11½	12	12½	13	13	13	13	—	
34	2	3	4	5	6	7	8	9	10	11	12	12½	13	13½	14	14	14	14	—

Service (years)

Age (years)	2	3	4	5	6	7	8	9	10	11	12	13	14	15	16	17	18	19	20
35	2	3	4	5	6	7	8	9	10	11	12	13	13½	14	14½	15	15	15	15
36	2	3	4	5	6	7	8	9	10	11	12	13	14	14½	15	15½	16	16	16
37	2	3	4	5	6	7	8	9	10	11	12	13	14	15	15½	16	16½	17	17
38	2	3	4	5	6	7	8	9	10	11	12	13	14	15	16	16½	17	17½	18
39	2	3	4	5	6	7	8	9	10	11	12	13	14	15	16	17	17½	18	18½
40	2	3	4	5	6	7	8	9	10	11	12	13	14	15	16	17	18	18½	19
41	2	3	4	5	6	7	8	9	10	11	12	13	14	15	16	17	18	19	19½
42	2½	3½	4½	5½	6½	7½	8½	9½	10½	11½	12½	13½	14½	15½	16½	17½	18½	19½	20½
43	3	4	5	6	7	8	9	10	11	12	13	14	15	16	17	18	19	20	21
44	3	4½	5½	6½	7½	8½	9½	10½	11½	12½	13½	14½	15½	16½	17½	18½	19½	20½	21½
45	3	4½	6	7	8	9	10	11	12	13	14	15	16	17	18	19	20	21	22
46	3	4½	6	7½	8½	9½	10½	11½	12½	13½	14½	15½	16½	17½	18½	19½	20½	21½	22½
47	3	4½	6	7½	9	10	11	12	13	14	15	16	17	18	19	20	21	22	23
48	3	4½	6	7½	9	10½	11½	12½	13½	14½	15½	16½	17½	18½	19½	20½	21½	22½	23½
49	3	4½	6	7½	9	10½	12	13	14	15	16	17	18	19	20	21	22	23	24
50	3	4½	6	7½	9	10½	12	13½	14½	15½	16½	17½	18½	19½	20½	21½	22½	23½	24½
51	3	4½	6	7½	9	10½	12	13½	15	16	17	18	19	20	21	22	23	24	25
52	3	4½	6	7½	9	10½	12	13½	15	16½	18	19	20	21	22	23	24	25	26
53	3	4½	6	7½	9	10½	12	13½	15	16½	18	19	20	21	22	23	24	25	26
54	3	4½	6	7½	9	10½	12	13½	15	16½	18	19½	20½	21½	22½	23½	24½	25½	26½
55	3	4½	6	7½	9	10½	12	13½	15	16½	18	19½	21	22	23	24	25	26	27
56	3	4½	6	7½	9	10½	12	13½	15	16½	18	19½	21	22½	23½	24½	25½	26½	27½
57	3	4½	6	7½	9	10½	12	13½	15	16½	18	19½	21	22½	24	25	26	27	28
58	3	4½	6	7½	9	10½	12	13½	15	16½	18	19½	21	22½	24	25½	26½	27½	28½
59	3	4½	6	7½	9	10½	12	13½	15	16½	18	19½	21	22½	24	25½	27	28	29
60	3	4½	6	7½	9	10½	12	13½	15	16½	18	19½	21	22½	24	25½	27	28½	29½
61	3	4½	6	7½	9	10½	12	13½	15	16½	18	19½	21	22½	24	25½	27	28½	30
62	3	4½	6	7½	9	10½	12	13½	15	16½	18	19½	21	22½	24	25½	27	28½	30
63	3	4½	6	7½	9	10½	12	13½	15	16½	18	19½	21	22½	24	25½	27	28½	30
64	3	4½	6	7½	9	10½	12	13½	15	16½	18	19½	21	22½	24	25½	27	28½	30

men only { (rows 60–64)

Index